"Today, when every company has to be a tech company, developing a strong digital mindset may be the single most important step toward achieving your future success. *The Digital Mindset* is an invaluable resource for anyone looking to become a better leader, future-proof their career, or simply gain a better understanding of the present and future of business."

—MICKEY (HIROSHI) MIKITANI, founder, Chairman, and CEO,
Rakuten Group

"If you're worried that algorithms will replace our judgment, big data will make our little knowledge obsolete, or robots will steal our jobs, this book is for you. Paul Leonardi and Tsedal Neeley are leading experts on how technology is transforming work, and they offer the practical insights you need to understand the next wave of digital change—and ride it smoothly."

—ADAM GRANT, *New York Times* bestselling author, *Think Again*;
host, TED podcast *WorkLife*

"We've all heard it a million times: You need to be more digital. Finally, here's a book that explains what that really means, a book that ascribes real meaning to the buzzword. With clarity and a surprising level of detail, Paul Leonardi and Tsedal Neeley prepare you for the digital future by developing your digital mindset."

—SHELLYE ARCHAMBEAU, former CEO, MetricStream; author,
Unapologetically Ambitious

"Digital transformation doesn't stop with good strategy. It starts there. *The Digital Mindset* provides critical and actionable insights that make it possible for everyone—from the executive team to individual contributors—to help their company succeed in the digital era. Today's CEOs must make sure their entire workforce has a digital mindset. This book is the place to start."

—JEFF HENLEY, Executive Vice Chairman, Oracle

"If we continue to consider the digital age as a purely technological revolution, we will miss the most significant economic, political, and behavioral disruption of our societies since the Industrial Revolution. This is exactly what *The Digital Mindset* offers: the 360-degree understanding necessary to seize this moment."

—ELIE GIRARD, former CEO, Atos

"This breakthrough book is the ideal guide to enable you to operate or lead with a digital mindset. Down-to-earth and practical, it makes digital transformation achievable for anyone committed to learning new ways of thinking about the three *c*'s of collaboration, computation, and change in order to solve complex systems problems. Most importantly, you don't need to be a computer guru to transform your organization using these principles."

—BILL GEORGE, Senior Fellow, Harvard Business School;
   former Chairman and CEO, Medtronic;
   and bestselling author, *Discover Your True North*

"Leonardi and Neeley have produced the indispensable, foundational playbook for leaders looking to thrive in the digital age. In *The Digital Mindset* they have managed to effectively combine a crisp review of key concepts and practical advice on how to put them to work."

—HUBERT JOLY, former Chairman and CEO, Best Buy;
   Senior Lecturer, Harvard Business School;
   and author, *The Heart of Business*

THE
DIGITAL MINDSET

THE
DIGITAL MINDSET

What It Really Takes to Thrive in the Age of Data, Algorithms, and AI

PAUL LEONARDI & TSEDAL NEELEY

HARVARD BUSINESS REVIEW PRESS · BOSTON, MASSACHUSETTS

Copyright 2022 Harvard Business School Publishing Corporation

Library of Congress Cataloging-in-Publication Data

Names: Leonardi, Paul M., 1979– author. | Neeley, Tsedal, author.
Title: The digital mindset : what it really takes to thrive in the age of data,
    algorithms, and AI / Paul Leonardi and Tsedal Neeley.
Description: Boston, Massachusetts : Harvard Business School Publishing
    Corporation, [2022] | Includes index.
Identifiers: LCCN 2021047511 (print) | LCCN 2021047512 (ebook) |
    ISBN 9781647820107 (hardback) | ISBN 9781647820114 (epub)
Subjects: LCSH: Technological innovations. | Computer literacy. |
    Numeracy. | Artificial intelligence. | Success in business.
Classification: LCC HD45 .L434 2022 (print) | LCC HD45 (ebook) |
    DDC 658.5/14—dc23/eng/20211202
LC record available at https://lccn.loc.gov/2021047511
LC ebook record available at https://lccn.loc.gov/2021047512

ISBN: 978-1-64782-010-7
eISBN: 978-1-64782-011-4

The paper used in this publication meets the requirements of the American National Standard for Permanence of Paper for Publications and Documents in Libraries and Archives Z39.48-1992.

For Rodda, Amelia, Norah, and Eliza, who all have brilliant minds and, most impressively, the courage to change them.
—Paul Leonardi

For my mother, the wisest person I know, who embodies curiosity, courage, and lifelong learning.
—Tsedal Neeley

CONTENTS

PART THREE

CHANGE

Introduction

The 30 Percent Rule

The world as we have created it is a process of our thinking.
It cannot be changed without changing our thinking.

—Albert Einstein

Sara Menker sat at her desk in Manhattan staring at her computer screen. It was the summer of 2008 and she was watching the financial markets collapse before her eyes. As an energy commodities trader at Morgan Stanley, she knew the numbers running across her screen were catastrophic. A loud gasp from her colleague at the next desk made her turn. He had his face in his hands, as if to hide from the horror. "The world's coming to an end," he said. "This is Armageddon. We better start buying up gold."

"What are you going to do with all that gold if the world's economies collapse?" Sara blurted out. "Forget gold. Buy a sack of potatoes! You need potatoes. We'll all need potatoes."

Her colleague laughed. Then Sara laughed too, uneasily.

Later that evening, Sara was still thinking about potatoes. Born and raised in Ethiopia, a country with a history of catastrophic famine, she understood the value of food security in ways that many of her peers on Wall Street did not.[1] She found herself researching farmland prices in her home country. Thinking like a trader, she saw an investment opportunity. The land was cheap. It was selling for $1.50 an acre in some areas. It also seemed relatively easy to purchase tens of thousands of acres.

Intrigued, Sara decided to take a trip home to learn more. She didn't know anything about agriculture, but she had confidence that she could learn about a new industry quickly. After a few days of firsthand exposure, she was amazed at what she saw. To successfully grow crops, an Ethiopian landowner would have to buy crop insurance. But there was no crop insurance market. If no bank would lend money without the security of crop insurance, then the cost of capital would be much higher. The land was also remote, which meant leveling and road building. To grow potatoes, a farmer would have to essentially build out an entire agricultural infrastructure. That was much too costly and too risky for most people—including Sara. She quickly abandoned her idea of becoming a potato farmer.

But what she saw on her trip continued to gnaw at her. If farmers were unable to do their work, people wouldn't have enough food. The agricultural system's structural capacity to produce food would soon be surpassed by future demand. "The next time markets crumble," Sara told us, "people won't just lose money. They won't be able to eat. People could starve and governments may fall." Sara was so alarmed by the possibility of a global food shortage that she felt compelled to do something to help. So she quit her job at Morgan Stanley.

Five months later, Sara was leaning over her kitchen table and peering into her glowing computer screen. It was almost midnight on a Friday evening. She had planned to be in bed hours ago but needed one last look at the dense chunk of Python code she had been trying to understand since before sunset. If it weren't dark outside her window she would barely have sensed that any time had passed at all. She read the code from top to bottom once again, her nose inches from the screen. She needed to understand how the program was working and from where it was pulling the data that fed a core algorithm. "OK, progress," she said to herself as she closed her laptop. "Back at it tomorrow." Outside, only a sprinkle of light decorated the small Kenyan farm town she had just moved to from New York City. As a Black woman who had forged a successful career on Wall Street, she was no stranger to adversity. She knew there were no shortcuts. She had to understand the data for herself.

• • •

Why would a successful energy commodities trader quit her job, move halfway around the world, and then wind up reviewing code in the middle of the night? Sara's aha moment came when she discovered that even an industry as seemingly earthbound and analog as agriculture was in the throes of a massive digital transformation. A global ecosystem of digital technologies including sensors, forecasting tools, and databases were allowing farmers, researchers, and industry analysts to collect and store data about crops, weather conditions, and soil and erosion patterns at tremendous speed and scale. Digital tools had been turning agriculture into a data-intensive operation, but she was one of the few people outside the industry who knew it. How? By having the courage to ask questions about what she didn't know. Sara's quest to contend with the destructive force of the global financial meltdown led her to discover what we know to be an important fact about life in the twenty-first century: There is no area of the economy and no type of work that will remain disconnected from digital technology and the data it produces, captures, and stores.

As Sara learned, the agricultural industry collected mountains of data at every stage of its process. But the data were scattered. There was no unified system connecting the troves of information, especially given the global scope of the industry. Agriculture was a labyrinthine ecosystem spread across multiple continents. Take, for example, the Ethiopian coffee market. Although it was obviously dependent on what happened in neighboring countries like Uganda and Kenya, it was even more crucially dependent on what happened in distant places like Vietnam and Brazil because they were the largest coffee producers. A coffee grower in Ethiopia needed to understand how each of those regions produced, which meant understanding their individual climates and markets. Also, understanding European consumption trends was necessary because Germany was the world's largest importer and re-exporter of coffee and a huge driver of prices. Other crops were relevant as well. Because coffee competes with tea, it was important to know tea markets. Sara concluded that the complexity was just too difficult and expensive to unravel in the way that agricultural businesses would traditionally manage it. If the various aspects of the global agricultural markets were interdependent, their corresponding data also needed to be connected to be useful.

Sara thought back to her shock upon calculating that the real cost of a $1.50-per-acre land deal in Ethiopia was $12,000 an acre when you factored in all the other requirements to put that land to work—insurance, infrastructure, and so forth. The reason it cost significantly less to invest in US agriculture than Ethiopian agriculture had to do with access to data and analysis. The United States has troves of data on which to base risk-taking decisions. In some African countries, banks didn't lend, insurance companies didn't insure, and logistics operators didn't exist, because none of those industries had the data required to provide the services. How could any of those entities price the risk of a farmer if they couldn't understand in numerical terms what a production cycle looks like in a particular location in Africa?

Sara had found her mission: translate and connect the data to allow better predictions about the dynamics of a global ecosystem. As a commodities trader she had developed a set of analytic skills that enabled her to recognize what opportunities might lie in connecting disparate data. But it wasn't until she developed a *digital mindset* that it was possible for her to understand how a powerful digital platform, purpose-built to help connect fragmented data sets, could help to revolutionize agriculture. Her digital approach enabled her to launch Gro Intelligence, a data and analytics company focused on all things agricultural.

With employees in New York and Kenya, Gro Intelligence developed a platform that can ingest over 40 million unique agricultural data sets that amass to more than 500 trillion data points. Using data inputs from multiple countries, along with real-time information from satellite imagery, Sara's company built a prediction engine that uses machine learning algorithms to provide sophisticated daily forecasts. Their forecasts have the power to move agricultural markets, and their predictive models are routinely more accurate than those generated by the United States Department of Agriculture (USDA). In 2019, Gro Intelligence stepped in to provide real-time estimates for commodities production, which are normally produced by the USDA but were not available due to the US government shutdown that year.

Sara Menker, who had nervously joked about potatoes a few years earlier, was now leading an industry as essential as food production into the digital age. Sure, learning the technical skills—like how to understand code well enough to know what data sources it was pulling—was a key part of the process. But the foundation of her success was not just a matter of aptitude or ability. It was a *mindset*—defined above all by the courage to be humble, admit that you don't know what you don't know, and set out on the path to learning it. When she began to investigate farming in Ethiopia, she didn't know how to access the agricultural data or why it was categorized the way it was. So Sara started asking questions. Lots of questions. When she wanted to figure out how to build dynamic maps that visualize massive amounts of agricultural data in real time, she tracked down her old classmate, a software engineer who then taught her about the processing power of cloud computing platforms. When she wanted to learn how to build environmental models with the data, she tracked down the foremost expert on the subject—an agricultural professor based in South Dakota. As she learned how to do experiments that would help her identify the right digital products to help farmers, she also began to think about ways to keep the data in those products secure. By then, it's safe to say that she'd learned about "this whole digital thing." Digital learning had provided answers to her questions about agricultural development in the United States, Ethiopia, and the rest of the world. But it always began with a question. Whatever the topic was, she would find the person who could teach her. This is a humility that is historically rare among executives, and it is crucial to a digital mindset.

From her perch above Wall Street all those years before, Sara never could have imagined that she would be running a highly successful AI firm that would be selected as one of *Time* magazine's one hundred most influential companies in 2021.[2] At the time, she didn't understand what it meant to "be digital" nor did she have the know-how to do it. But she could see the world changing around her and she recognized that to make a difference, to find personal and professional fulfillment, and to be successful in an era of rapid change, she had to become digitally literate. In the process, she learned the basics of computing, how to aggregate data, how to build relationships with employees across two continents, and how to structure a company in which people could make decisions based on rapidly changing data. But the most crucial step in this journey for Sara—a self-avowed "nontechnical" person—came before any of the technical skills she acquired along the way. From the very start, she committed to a digital mindset. The rest followed.

Sara's powerful journey is proof: operating successfully in the digital world is not only essential for thriving; it's within your grasp. It takes a digital mindset.

The goal of this book is to help you take that crucial first step on your own path into digital literacy. We're not here to teach you the specific technical skills you will need to thrive in a digital world; that will come later. This book is about putting you in the position to get there. It's for those of us who understand that competition has intensified in all industries, further pushing for participation in more digital ecosystems and making digital transformation a key priority for company boards across all industries.[3] Most people hear their customers' demands for digital solutions loud and clear. They also hear the requests of their managers to develop digital competencies in roles that they don't traditionally think of as technologically focused.[4] And they hear what the world's most prescient leaders have been saying for years: the digital age is ushering in fundamental changes to how work gets done, how industries are structured, and how people collaborate. As legendary Cisco CEO John Chambers remarked in his final public address before stepping down to become the company's executive chairman, "This digital era will dwarf what's occurred in the information era and the value of the Internet today. As leaders, if you don't transform and use this technology differently—if you don't reinvent yourself, change your organization structure; if you don't talk about speed of innovation—you're going to get disrupted. And it'll be a brutal disruption, where the majority of companies will not exist in a meaningful way 10 to 15 years from now."[5] Chambers was not known for hyperbole.

Nevertheless, many people still can't shake the notion that they're just "not technical" enough to think digitally.[6] It's understandable. We've been conditioned to see ourselves within an either/or dichotomy of technical and nontechnical workers. But that paradigm is outdated. We are all digital workers, whether we are a software engineer in Silicon Valley, a marketer at a Hollywood ad agency, an entrepreneur in the food production industry, or an instructor of any academic subject whatsoever. Training ourselves out of the old paradigm isn't easy. In many ways, a mindset shift can be even more challenging than developing the practical tech skills that follow. That's why we wrote this book.

In these pages, you will have the opportunity to address the following questions, which will be familiar to anyone who has observed the tidal shifts in the way we work:

- How much technical capability do I need?

- Do I need to learn how to code?

- What do I need to know about algorithms?

- What do I need to understand about big data?

- How do I use digital tools effectively?

- What exactly is AI?

- Do I need to prepare to have a bot or robot on my team?

- How do I collaborate successfully when people are working remotely?

- What are the best ways to make sure my data and systems are secure?

- How do I develop skills to compete in a digital economy?

- Is digital transformation different than other transformations?

- How do I build a digital-first culture?

- Where do I start?

Our message in this book is simple: If you develop a digital mindset, you'll be able to answer these questions and many more. You'll be poised to thrive in the digital age. *Anyone can build a digital mindset.* That's what Sara Menker did. She didn't become a tech whiz or a computer programmer. She developed a digital mindset that allowed her to see the world in new ways and to ask new, big, important questions. Developing a digital mindset will require you to develop new insights and to be open to change. But getting to the minimum threshold of technical acumen necessary to achieve a digital mindset is absolutely doable for anyone reading this book. And, dare we say, it's even fun.

Over the past decade, we have researched, consulted for, served on advisory boards of, taught managers from, and written case studies about hundreds of technology-enabled organizations around the world. We have explored how these organizations and the people working in them have developed a digital mindset. We developed the idea of the digital mindset through our discussions with thousands of professionals, managers, and executives who provided us with insights into the ways of thinking that create opportunities in the digital workplace. They all shared a common belief that to "be digital" required first developing a new mindset that allowed them to acquire and apply technology-based competencies, ranging from data acquisition and computing fundamentals to large-scale organizational change. In addition to our own research, we drew from a war chest of research articles, stories, and cases produced by leading experts in the field to develop the concept of the digital mindset and to identify the approaches that it encompasses.

We've seen that people who develop a digital mindset are more successful in their jobs, have higher satisfaction at work, and are more likely to get promoted at their company. They also have more portable skills they can take with them if they decide to move jobs. Leaders who have a digital mindset are better able to set up their organizations for success and build a broad employee workforce that can adapt quickly to change. When companies have people with digital mindsets, they react faster to shifts in the market and find themselves better positioned to take advantage of new business opportunities. Thriving in the digital age requires more than simply acquiring skills to work with digital technologies. To be successful it is necessary to *think* differently. This book will show you how to get there.

Definitions

Before we get too far, we should set out some definitions. Terms like digital mindset can be interpreted in many ways. These are our working definitions for this book.

We like to think about *digital* as the interaction between data and technology.

Data refers to any information that can be used for reference, analysis, or computation. Your grocery shopping list is data, and so is the weather forecast. Today, most people think of data as specifically numbers, but other things like images and text are data, too, because they are turned into numbers that can be processed, stored, and transformed through computing.

Technology creates, captures, transforms, transmits, or stores data. For most of human history the technologies that performed these tasks were simple—stone tablets, papyrus, and paper. Today, data are transformed at exponentially higher volumes and speed through myriad devices. In fact, we experience most data through multiple interconnected devices— sensors, computers, software programs, cloud-based storage. Your phone, for example, is many, many technologies working together to mediate data. The combination of sensors, hardware, and software that make up the phone convert analog inputs like sounds and images into binary code that is processed, stored, and rendered for you as music, pictures, and words. Your phone doesn't just store data; it produces and reproduces data in novel ways.[7]

A *mindset* is the set of approaches we use to make sense out of the world. How you approach something shapes the way you think about it, its importance to you, and how you act.[8]

A *digital mindset*, then, is the set of approaches we use to make sense of, and make use of, data and technology. This set of attitudes and behaviors enable people and organizations to see new possibilities and chart a path for the future. Big data, algorithms, AI, robotic teammates, internal social media, blockchain, experimentation, statistics, security, and rapid change are some of the major digital forces that are reshaping how we live and work. These forces are disrupting how we interact with our colleagues and creating new demands to restructure organizations to become more competitive.

With this working definition we can dive one level deeper. Developing a digital mindset means we are redefining fundamental ways of approaching three key processes:

- Collaboration

- Computation

- Change

Redefining approaches to these processes means, of course, learning some new concrete skills. But it's not enough just to build skills. Skills give you the vocabulary, knowledge, and intuition to see the bigger picture—to ask the important questions.[9] Developing a new mindset means that you build *from* your new skills to *see* the world in a new way and to change your behavior.

In this book we've developed a framework that outlines the skills you must learn to develop your approaches to collaboration, computation, and change so that, from there, you can build a digital mindset. We don't just tell you what those technical skills are; we actually help you to learn them.

Rest assured that you won't need to master the intricacies of programming, how to build your own algorithms, or how to run advanced multinomial logit models. You may end up doing those things someday, but our focus is only on what you need to be digitally proficient. And here's the good news: you only need about 30 percent fluency in a handful of technical topics to develop your digital mindset. We call this the 30 percent rule.

The 30 Percent Rule

To understand the 30 percent rule, think about learning a foreign language. To demonstrate *mastery* of the English language, a nonnative speaker must acquire roughly 12,000 vocabulary words. But to be able to communicate and interact effectively with other people in the workplace, all they need is about 3,500 to 4,000 words—about 30 percent of what it takes to achieve mastery.[10] In practical terms, a nonnative speaker does not need to master the English language to work effectively with others. Similarly, to work effectively with a digital mindset, you don't need to master coding or become a data scientist. But you do need to understand what computer programmers and data scientists do, and to have proficient understanding of how machine learning works, how to make use of A/B tests, how to interpret statistical models, and how to get an AI-based chatbot to do what you need it to do. We will define all these terms and techniques in the chapters that follow.

We've devoted the past decade to figuring out exactly what that 30 percent looks like and we've taught many learners how to develop a digital mindset.[11] We want to share the lessons we've learned so you too can begin to approach collaboration, computation, and change in ways that introduce you to some of the exciting new possibilities that digital transformation can offer.

Over the course of this book, we specify the categories of skills that you'll need and what 30 percent competence looks like in each of those categories. Once you have achieved that 30 percent (or more than 30 percent if you are interested to do more), you will have created the platforms from which you'll start to think differently—to think digitally. While you might already be familiar with *some* of the content we present, it is likely that you will find insights that are new or about which you need to learn more. And even for concepts you're familiar with, you likely will find new ways to think about them and connect them to your job, your organizational strategy, and other aspects of being digital.

The goal of this book is to get you to the 30 percent in each of the areas in which you need to have a digital mindset. For each of the three approaches we have distilled, synthesized, and curated the key insights that you need to know to achieve the minimal threshold across various digital domains.

How We'll Proceed

We'll start in part one with a deep dive into new approaches to *collaboration* in the digital era. The first element of this approach is to learn how to collaborate with machines, which with AI and machine learning are quickly becoming our teammates and colleagues, not just tools we use. To learn how to collaborate with a machine, we show the 30 percent you need to know about how AI operates. We describe how teams in the military are learning psychological as well as technical methods to work side by side with AI-powered robots. We clue you into why it's unwise to interact with AI devices as if they are human and provide tips on how to avoid the common traps that people fall into when they do so. Next, we examine new imperatives for collaborating successfully with your human colleagues in the digital age. We take you to a bank where employees have been able to successfully innovate by using internal social media to expand whom they pay attention to and whom they learn from. We explore how one of the world's largest e-commerce companies is able to connect people from around the globe by encouraging them to share nonwork information at work. And we discuss how the new imperative for successful collaboration in the digital world is about making yourself present to others when you're working remotely. Becoming proficient in at least 30 percent of these new collaboration behaviors will improve work for you, your team, and your coworkers.

Part two of the book takes you through what you need to know to approach *computation*. We start by focusing on data. We believe that if you understand even 30 percent of how various technologies collect, categorize, and store data, you will be able to make decisions through data. You will also learn how to present data persuasively—a key translation skill. To do this, we will look at how professional basketball teams collect and analyze data on player performance. We tell you the story of how one Indiana county's folly with data cost them millions of dollars in tax revenue and stalled city improvement projects for years. And we explore how companies like Netflix as well as city governments across the United States use their data to build models that shape the environments you live in. Perhaps as importantly, we discuss how bias can creep into representations of data and how you can learn what data models are and are not telling you. We also take a deep dive into the fundamental statistical reasoning strategies you need to use in a digital environment. To be able to think with data and to evaluate the predictions and prescriptions that other people make, you simply can't avoid statistics. Don't worry: we won't put you through Stats 101. But we do provide the requisite material that will foster your intuition to accurately interpret the vital stories statistical tests tell and ask the right questions about recommendations that cite statistical data. To illustrate how this can be done we look at small companies (a startup that makes wearables that detect body temperature) and large organizations (a major video game developer) to demonstrate how statistical analyses can inform product decisions and how statistical skills allow confidence in those decisions. Learning 30 percent of statistical analysis and reasoning skills will help you make smarter and better decisions.

In part three of the book we support you in developing a new approach to *change*. We start by showing you how to rethink what security looks like in the digital era. Unfortunately, there is no such thing as a perfectly secure database or organization. There are going to be security failures at some point, and what matters is how you are set up to deal with them. We don't belabor the obvious by telling you to get a stronger password and to set up multifactor authentication. Instead, we look at breaches—about a major oil producer and social media platforms—so you can learn to approach change that will equip you to respond and adapt when security problems arise. We also take a relatively deep dive into blockchain—and how companies like diamond importers are using it—to introduce you to the essential 30 percent of conceptual vocabulary that will expose you to this emerging technology that can reshape the security around your data assets. Next, we'll tackle experimentation. Change happens so rapidly now that the best technique to determine what works is to test, fail, learn, and try again. We walk you through a step-by-step process for how to use experiments by taking advantage of *digital exhaust*—a vast subject from which we've distilled the 30 percent you need to know. We also provide you with guidelines for how to build the right structure and culture for experimentation. We recast change from a set of periodic activities to a continuous process we call *transitioning*. Because digital transformation is central to transitioning, we illustrate its essential features, from the underpinning mindset shift to concrete activities that require it. We cover how Moderna, the pioneering vaccine developer, innovated an integrated organization to use data and technology most efficiently, and we outline the (re)design and alignment of cultural change undertaken at Unilever. We also address the pivotal question of how to upskill and implement continuous learning for individuals and an entire workforce. We provide an appendix with several case examples of continuous learning that range from Spotify, Yelp, AT&T, and Booking.com to Capital One. These case examples provide insights into what is most effective to motivate employees' voluntary ongoing learning and demonstrate the need to maintain a digital mindset over time.

Throughout this book we draw on a mix of content that includes case examples, published studies, and interviews. Sometimes we're able to mention the people and companies by name because information about them was already public or because they've given us permission to discuss them in this book. In other cases, we describe companies without naming them. We also give people pseudonyms when they've asked not to be identified.[12] We hope that as you consider our evidence-based suggestions for how to begin thinking and acting digitally and read the stories and examples woven throughout, you'll begin to see that developing a digital mindset is something that is well within your grasp.

The Big Question

One of the most common questions we're asked—and for those asking it's a big one—is this: *Do I need to learn how to code or how to read a programing language to build a digital mindset?*

The short answer is probably not. For most people, it's sufficient to understand what operations are occurring behind the digital technologies that you use. For others, learning basic aspects of coding might be the mechanism by which you will gain the requisite baseline to feel comfortable. It all depends on how technical your background and job role have been and how close you are to the core technologies your company uses. Ironically, we have found that those with some technical experience believe that it isn't necessary to learn how to code because they have already met the 30 percent threshold. Less experienced people find that learning how to code gives them the confidence and the lens to understand programming and data work.

What is important to know is that all digital technologies are developed through the use of specific programming languages that make data work by implementing algorithms.

If that sentence makes sense to you and you feel comfortable with what an algorithm is, how programming languages work, and how computing commands make a computer do things, you can probably treat the next section as a quick review. But if these concepts are unfamiliar or you need a refresher—they're terms you've heard but you don't really get how they all fit together—we encourage you to read the next section before going on. We are not going to bombard you with technical specs; we will simply explain how computer programs work so that you understand what the digital technologies that are reshaping our work and our world actually do behind the slick facades presented by their user interfaces.

We're diving into this here because it's a set of ideas that will affect almost everything that follows. The basics of algorithms will come up again and again whether we're talking about collaboration, computation, or change. Knowing this material will help contextualize the insights and skills that we introduce in later chapters.

Behind the Digital Facade: An Abbreviated Guide to Algorithms, Scripts, and Code

All digital operations are built on the back of a relationship among three entities: computers, software, and data. Computers do things. Algorithms are implemented in software to tell the computer what to do and how to do it. Data are what software programs use to decide what to tell the computer to do. Algorithms live at the intersection of computers, software, and data, so let's start there.

What is an algorithm?

Although you may believe that algorithms belong only to the realm of advanced mathematics, in reality and at its most basic an algorithm is a set of instructions for how to do a series of steps to accomplish a specific goal. The idea behind developing an algorithm is that it will follow the same steps every time, even if the data it uses change. We all follow algorithms all the time. A recipe is an algorithm because it's a finite list of instructions used to perform a series of tasks in a specific order. Typically, it's the order that matters most for algorithms. Think about baking chocolate chip cookies. The recipe tells you to first cream the butter, sugars, and vanilla extract. Next you add the dry ingredients—flour, baking powder, and chocolate chips. Then you put the batter in the oven to bake. If you tried to change the order by, for example, putting the batter in the oven before adding the dry ingredients, your cookies wouldn't turn out right. That's true of pretty much any kind of cookies you make. Although the ingredients and their proportions might change,

FIGURE I-1

What is an algorithm?

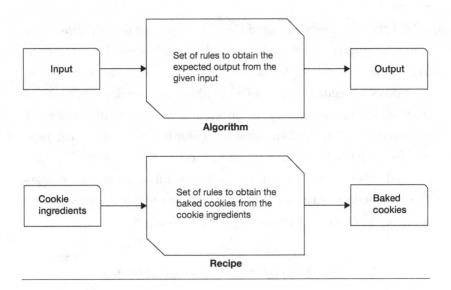

Algorithm

Recipe

the basic steps—first, combine wet and dry ingredients, then bake—are virtually the same for every kind of cookie. In figure I-1 the cookie ingredients are the input, the recipe is the set of rules, and the delicious cookies are the output.

Where the cookie-making analogy begins to break down is that baking relies to a certain degree on tacit knowledge, which a computer does not have.[13] For example, your cookie recipe might tell you to cream the wet ingredients until they are "fluffy" and bake until "slightly golden." There are no explicit instructions for helping you to definitively determine "fluffy" or "slightly golden." People learn how to be good bakers through experience, observation, and learning from others who transfer knowledge about, say, determining what "fluffy" means to them. This lack of specificity poses problems for computers because they cannot deal in the tacit realm. If you want your computer to do something once your data are "fluffy" you have to tell that computer specifically, numerically, what fluffy equals. Computer-programmed algorithms need to be unambiguous.

That should give you a good basic understanding of what an algorithm is. (For a deeper, more technical explanation, please consult the glossary.)

To perform, computers need algorithms or a set of instructions that follow the criteria described above. While a simple algorithm can instruct a computer to, for example, add 1 to a number, in order to perform complex tasks it needs a group of algorithms that work in concert. To continue the recipe analogy, if you wanted to prepare an entire meal, you would need more than just a recipe for baking cookies. You need one for preparing spaghetti, a third for cooking a sauce, and another for a side dish, a beverage, and so on. You might need yet another algorithm for making sure everything was ready at the same time. The point is that a computer runs on countless algorithms.

How do we tell a computer what to do?

A recipe tells the baker what to do through verbs the baker understands. Mix. Sift. Bake. Cool. To tell the computer how to follow the instructions in an algorithm, we have what's called source code, or just *code*. Coding is a process of using a programing language to tell a computer how to behave. Each line of code tells the computer to do something specific. Think of each as a verb. Add. Compare. Reorder. Wait. Delete.

A document full of many lines of code is called a script. Scripts are combined to build algorithms. Below is an example of a script coded in the programming language Python. This is a very basic script called *hello_name*.[14] On line 1, the code is instructing the computer to put on the screen the phrase "What is your name?" Line 2 tells the computer to wait for the user to input his or her name and, then, when they do enter their name, to save that name as an object. Line 3 puts the word "Hello" on the screen along with the name that the user entered.

```
1 print("What is your name?")
2 name = input()
3 print("Hello" + name)
```

```
python hello_name.py
What is your name?
Joe
Hello Joe
c:\Users\Joecomputer\Desktop\temp
```

But how does this program know what *print* means and why *input* is what the user types in and how to preserve that input in such a way that it can make it appear on the screen? It knows because this language, Python, is actually a way for humans to interact with a more fundamental language, called *machine language.* Machine language is binary numbers, long strings of 0s and 1s that combine in complex patterns that the computer can use. It takes millions or billions of these 1s and 0s to run computer programs. It would be impossible for humans to interact with computers, or for them to get computers to do anything useful, if we had to code with what the machine understands—0s and 1s.

To get from what you see on the screen to 0s and 1s, scripts go through a *compiler.* The compiler does the tedious work of turning each command into the 0s and 1s that a computer can understand. Once the code is compiled (translated into machine language) it is stored in a program that can be used over and over again. Every piece of consumer software you use, every app, every game, every website is a program that started out as someone coding within a programming language to create a script that was compiled into millions or billions of 0s and 1s so it could be read and executed by a computer.

Computers don't do anything on their own. They need someone or something to tell them what to do. We can't stress this enough. They have no tacit knowledge. A good illustration of this point is an old joke about a computer programmer who was unable to get out of the shower after washing their hair because the instructions on the shampoo bottle read "Wash, Rinse, Repeat" but did not say "Stop." That's how computers operate: if instructions aren't explicit they won't follow them.

Understanding the limits of what a computer can do is an important foundation to developing a digital mindset because it underlines both how a machine "thinks" and why a computer is different than a human being. Unless we include the command "Stop" at the end of a line of code, the computer will not stop, no matter how obvious it seems to you that the computer *should* stop.

Python is currently one of the more widely used programming languages. However, know that up to 250 programming languages are in active use today, and more than 700 have been developed.[15] Other widely used programming languages include Java, C++, and Ruby. Just as human languages—English, Spanish, Mandarin, Farsi, and on and on—have different syntaxes and grammatical structures, so do computer programming languages. Also, programming languages, like our spoken languages, have evolved in a specific time and place to serve a particular set of needs.

Overall, your digital mindset journey will include understanding the basic tenets of coding, programming languages, scripts, algorithms, compiling, and machine language. This knowledge is crucial for understanding how digital applications are programmed and how computers are made to execute. Coding and programming activities are part of a complex relationship between hardware and software that undergirds digital tools.

Let's review some of the basics we've covered here:

- Digital is about the interplay of data and technology that runs much of modern life, such as smartphones, apps, and streaming services, as well as the major forces that are reshaping how we work that include big data, AI, robotics, machine learning, and blockchain.

- Digital technologies can transform and handle data at exponentially higher volumes and speed.

- All digital operations require computers, software, and data to work together. Analog technologies, such as windup clocks, rely on physical signals.

- An algorithm is a set of instructions that tells a computer how to perform a certain task. Algorithms are made up of scripts, which are lines of code put together.

- Coding is a process of using a programing language to tell a computer how to behave. Each line of code tells the computer to do something specific.

Now you're armed with what you need to get started. Congratulations! You've already begun embracing the 30 percent rule and building your digital mindset. With this foundation we can get into the three core areas that will set you on a path to success. Let's start with collaboration.

PART ONE

COLLABORATION

1

Working with Machines

When Human Intelligence Meets Artificial Intelligence

Late one afternoon, UCLA professor Burt Swanson was about to leave his office for home when an email caught his attention. Subject: "Interested in Meeting You." It was from a professor named Todd who worked at a university across the country. Todd worked in a similar area to Swanson and wanted to meet up while he was visiting Los Angeles. He closed: "I copied my assistant, Amy, who can help with scheduling. Please reply all with time(s) and location(s) that are convenient for you if you are interested."

Swanson provided Todd's assistant with several dates and times as options. By the time he arrived home, Amy had written back. Todd was not available for any of the times Swanson had indicated. She asked that he propose new times. Swanson did. By early the next morning, Amy had confirmed a meeting. Several hours later, though, Amy wrote again, saying that Todd was no longer available at that time, and she suggested several other times. Swanson felt annoyed that Todd was making so many changes, especially since it was Swanson who was going out of his way to fulfill Todd's request. Still, he picked a time. At the end of his email, he politely wrote that he would appreciate if they could stick to this newly agreed upon time. Much to his surprise, Amy responded immediately that the time Swanson selected was no longer available. She suggested more proposed times. Thoroughly frustrated, Swanson typed out a lengthy response to Amy expressing how unpleasant the experience of trying to accommodate Todd had been and that he was not available at other times. Amy never wrote back.

A few weeks later, Swanson was surprised to learn that Amy was not a person. She was an AI scheduling agent created by a company called x.ai. The product is used by companies around the world including Disney, Coca-Cola, and Nike. The easy conclusion to draw from this is that Swanson's scheduling fiasco was caused by a poorly functioning AI. But it's the wrong conclusion. Scenarios like the one described above are common when people begin to enter into relationships, however brief, with AI, bots, and machine learning algorithms. The problem isn't the AI's capability; it's the lack of experience we have interacting with such machines. Because they mimic the functionality of humans, people tend to treat them like humans. Developing a digital mindset means overcoming that understandable error and knowing how to treat AI agents on their own terms as computers, even if they are programmed to present human-like characteristics.

New Rules of Interaction

Computational and machine learning algorithms perform an ever-increasing number of activities within organizations. Among them: They have fundamentally shifted the nature of Wall Street trading.[1] They determine credit scores for existing and potential customers. They are used to screen applicants and assist in hiring. They enable chatbots to respond in real time to queries and suggest new courses of action for people with computer trouble, for those looking for new loans, and for workers who hope to find new information in their jobs.

The rapid scaling of computational power means that digital technologies have migrated from tools that people use to platforms upon which they interact.[2] Now they're beginning to migrate again, to agents with which people actively collaborate—like Amy the scheduler. If this change conjures images of working side by side with a robot on your team, you're actually not far off. We already have integrated robots into many aspects of our lives. Think of the robot you interact with when you call for an airline reservation, the chatbot that helps you open a new bank account, the physical robots (controlled by digital automation tools) that workers on a high-tech product assembly line interact with by giving commands and receiving feedback. Each of these digitally controlled bots uses AI and machine learning techniques to evaluate data inputs, make suggestions for behaviors and actions, and learn from your responses in order to improve its performance in the next interaction.[3]

One important feature of a digital mindset is to understand that the keys to working successfully with machines are not the same as the skills needed to work successfully with humans. You might think that's an obvious point. But in countless experiments, subjects who know that they're interacting with machines instead of people overwhelmingly tend to treat the machines as if they are people.[4] As we'll elaborate shortly, that behavior causes problems for how we approach individual tasks and get work done. Developing a digital mindset means recognizing that the rules of interaction are not the same when you're working with machines and that when you deploy machines to work for you and interact with friends, family, or customers on your behalf, all of those people are likely to treat the machines as people too.

In this chapter, we draw on our work with more than eight hundred people across multiple companies who have begun to interact regularly with robots, chatbots, and other AI-powered autonomous agents. We discuss how to effectively build relations with these digital technologies when they interact with us verbally and when they become members of our teams. The chapter is designed to help you build the skills to work effectively with machines by treating them as machines.

But before we can get there, you need to understand what artificial intelligence actually is and how AI agents "think." You don't need to know how to build your own AI, but you do need to know:

- What machine learning is

- How AI train on certain data sets

- How models are built from those data, and how the machine uses prediction techniques to determine how best to interact with you

Along the way we'll define machine learning, neural networks, natural language processing, and computer vision. These are all building blocks for developing a digital mindset that can interact with machines as machines. You may be surprised at how simple some of this technology is on its surface, even if how it goes about doing that work is marvelously complex.

How artificial intelligence works

If you're like most people, you used to think that artificial intelligence was far-fetched science fiction—maybe you think of movies like *Star Wars*, *The Terminator*, *Minority Report*, or *Interstellar* that depict autonomous computers or robots doing things that humans can't totally explain or control. John McCarthy, who coined the term *artificial intelligence* in 1956, lamented that "as soon as it works, no one calls it AI anymore."[5] In other words, we tend to think of AI as something futuristic that hasn't quite happened yet. But that's not true. If you speak to Siri or are driving a car that lets you know when you are drifting out of lane, you are using AI. AI is found in many applications. We use AI in our daily lives, even if we don't realize it.

The type of AI we use today focuses on one specific task. Think of the AI applications that routinely beat human chess champions. That specific AI is very good at playing chess and nothing else. Alibaba, one of the world's largest e-commerce platforms, like Amazon uses AI to predict what customers might want to buy. We don't yet have AI that can, for example, like Rosey in *The Jetsons*, discuss detailed decisions about housecleaning. There's no AI to help solve a murder mystery the way

Sonny does in the movie *iRobot*. In other words, for all its dazzle, AI has not yet achieved high enough levels of intelligence to converse and solve problems across a range of topics or issues. We also don't have the type of AI in which computer-programmed robots take over the world and rule human beings. AI thinker Nick Bostrom defines this superintelligence as "an intellect that is much smarter than the best human brains in practically every field, including scientific creativity, general wisdom and social skills."[6] Not only would AI in this capacity need to surpass humans in every way, but it would likely also be capable of having emotions and relationships.

Don't worry about any of that. Our focus is on single-task AI—what's real now—and learning how to treat machines like machines. That requires a mindset shift. One of the reasons we may have difficulty treating machines as machines is that AI is defined as a machine displaying a kind of intelligence akin to that of humans. Machines mimic the "cognitive" functions of people by executing algorithms.[7] Therefore, AI is a machine that perceives its environment and takes actions that maximize its chance of successfully achieving its goals. Today, those goals are programmed by humans.

It's also important to remember that robots are not AI, though we often hear these two conflated. Robots are simply containers for AI: the AI is what is inside the robot making it run. For example, the software, data, and algorithms running behind Alexa make up the AI while the voice that speaks to us is just the personification of that AI. Similarly, the figures of steel that perform many industrial tasks, from building cars to packing boxes, are the robots—collections of metal and actuators and electrical circuits. AI is the software programmed to make that pile of stuff act like an arm and tighten a screw or pick up a box.

The AI ecosystem broadly encompasses data, tools, and statistical models.

The statistical models process large-volume data sets. Before processing, the data must be "cleaned" and converted into formats the algorithms understand. Cleaning involves fixing or removing incorrect, incomplete, or duplicate data. Data aren't always collected in perfectly consistent pristine ways, and combining multiple data sources often results in duplications, incongruencies, and mislabeling. Say you're combining different sources of demographic data and one includes "Population Data" and the other includes "PopDat." They're the same, but the computer doesn't know it. You have to clean it to make it so the computer knows to treat them as the same group.

Today we see AI all around us. Here are a few examples of AI doing very specific activities that equal or exceed a human's ability to do them, though the AI can do them more quickly and efficiently:[8]

- Cars are full of AI systems, from the computer that figures out when the anti-lock brakes should kick in to the computer that tunes the parameters of the fuel injection systems. Self-driving cars will contain robust AI systems that allow them to perceive and react to the world around them.

- Smartphones are practically an AI factory. When you navigate using your map application, receive customized music recommendations, check tomorrow's weather, ask your phone a question, or perform dozens of other everyday activities, you're using AI.

- Your email spam filter is a classic AI. It starts off loaded with intelligence about how to figure out what's spam ("Congratulations, you've won $1,000,000") and what's not ("update on Thanksgiving plans"), and then it learns and tailors its intelligence to you as it gets experience with your particular preferences.

- Controllers like thermostats can use AI. For example, the Nest Thermostat adapts as it starts to figure out your typical routine and adjusts your house's climate accordingly.

- Google Translate is impressively good at one narrow AI task. Voice recognition is another. Some apps mash those together, allowing you to speak a sentence in one language and have the phone spit out the same sentence in another.

- When your plane lands, it's not a human that decides which gate it should go to. Just like it's not a human that determined the price of your ticket.

- Google Search is one large AI brain with incredibly sophisticated methods for ranking pages and figuring out what to show you in particular. Same goes for Facebook's Newsfeed.

And those are just consumer-facing examples. Sophisticated AI systems are more widely used in sectors and industries like military, manufacturing, and finance (algorithmic high-frequency AI traders account for more than half of equity shares traded on US markets), and in expert systems that, for example, help doctors make diagnoses.[9]

How Do Machines Learn?

Let's start by understanding how AI really works. Key building blocks of AI are machine learning techniques, which are algorithms that derive predictions from data using statistics. While humans use complex natural languages and visual cues, computers work with numbers to generalize from examples and gain the ability to "learn" without being explicitly programmed.

Machine learning expert Marily Nika loves to explain machine learning by showing how it learns the difference between cats and dogs.[10] First we label pictures "cat" or "dog." Then we feed the algorithm the labeled pictures. (See figure 1-1.)

The machine reads the patterns of pixels in each labeled picture and stores it as an example of the label: this pattern equals cat, and that pattern equals dog. Of course, not all patterns of pixels that make up a cat in a picture are going to be the same. Maybe the cat is head-on in one picture and side-viewed in another. So the computer needs *a lot* of pictures of cats and dogs to store many patterns and get good at identifying a cat versus a dog.

Nika adds that we can correct the computer when it incorrectly says, "This is a cat." The computer makes a note of its mistake. It has learned

FIGURE 1-1

Teaching a model how to identify dogs and cats

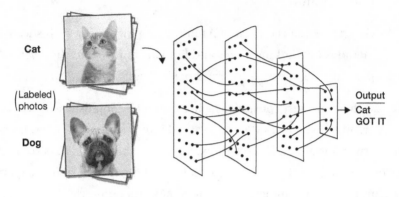

Source: Marily Nika, "An Intro to AI/ML and Deep Learning," https://marilynika.medium.com/an-intro-to-ai-ml-and-deep-learning-ffd2f2fbf1e.

not to include that pattern as a "cat." That ability to adapt is why we use the term "intelligence" to describe this learning process.

The mathematics to do this have been around for a long time, but it took the availability of vast amounts of data and much higher computer processing power to make the math useful in the real world.[11]

Let's look at how machine learning works through an example provided by Mark Robins, head of corporate AI strategy at Intel, whose face you can see depicted in figure 1-2.[12] In a typical machine learning approach, some person identifies a set of features that uniquely represent one person's face, like Mark's. The distance between the eyes, the nose width, and eye socket depth are common examples. A machine learning algorithm takes these features and builds classification systems of them using various algorithms based on different kinds of statistical models. By repeating this process multiple times and being corrected (at least at first) by humans who know the face, the machine learning algorithm learns to associate a given pattern of features with a particular person.

As Robins observes, and many other experts have also noted, the difficulty with this approach is that it is not always obvious what features are most useful for determining one particular face.[13] And even if we

FIGURE 1-2

Classic machine learning vs. deep learning

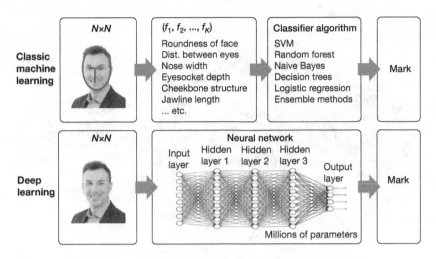

Source: "The Difference Between Artificial Intelligence, Machine Learning, and Deep Learning," Intel, https://www.intel.com/content/www/us/en/artificial-intelligence/posts/difference-between-ai-machine -learning-deep-learning.html.

know that a feature is important, it may be hard to compute it. For example, in order to compute the distance between the eyes, you need to first be able to find the eyes in the image and calculate the distance based on how far the face is from the camera, which in and of itself can be complicated. Enter deep learning.

Deep learning is a type of machine learning in which the algorithm doesn't need to be told about the important features by a person. Instead, it is able to discover features on its own by using a *neural network* to examine the data themselves. The term comes from a mathematical object called an artificial neuron that "fires" if inputs exceed some threshold, just like a neuron in the brain fires. Artificial neurons can be arranged in layers, and deep learning has many layers of artificial neurons. Deep learning requires millions of parameters, which is why it has only become powerful recently, now that we have enough data for it to learn from and the processing power to do the very complex math it has to do in a reasonable amount of time.

FIGURE 1-3

Machine learning vs. deep learning

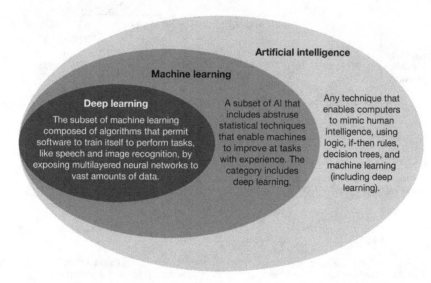

Artificial intelligence

Machine learning

Deep learning

The subset of machine learning composed of algorithms that permit software to train itself to perform tasks, like speech and image recognition, by exposing multilayered neural networks to vast amounts of data.

A subset of AI that includes abstruse statistical techniques that enable machines to improve at tasks with experience. The category includes deep learning.

Any technique that enables computers to mimic human intelligence, using logic, if-then rules, decision trees, and machine learning (including deep learning).

Source: "The Difference Between Artificial Intelligence, Machine Learning, and Deep Learning," Intel, https://www.intel.com/content/www/us/en/artificial-intelligence/posts/difference-between-ai-machine-learning-deep-learning.html.

In the context of facial recognition, deep learning avoids having to try to relate various shapes in an image to prespecified features. Feed it enough "labeled data" (that is, images of known faces) and give it the right training, and a deep learning model will decide what the most relevant features are from the data on its own. This process dramatically improves the accuracy of the algorithm.[14] When used with images deep learning is called *computer vision*.[15] (See figure 1-3.)

Machine learning algorithms can also be applied to written text or spoken word to identify patterns and make correlations in much the same way. Natural language processing (NLP) is to spoken text what computer vision is to images.[16] NLP works by following a script that classifies certain language into categories. It's a similar winnowing through statistics. First, phrases are labeled based on some classification scheme. Then, the computer cleans the phrases, getting rid of stop words ("a," "and," "the," "but," "or," and so forth) and punctuation.

Then words are "lemmatized" (a technical way of saying that they are sorted by grouping variants of the same word together, such as "stopping," "stopped," and "stopper"). They are then stemmed, which simply means that the words are reduced to their word stem ("stop"). Finally, the cleaned data are "vectorized," or turned into numbers that can be analyzed statistically.

Yelp combines such techniques and uses machine learning to help its staff compile, label, and categorize images and descriptions of restaurants more efficiently.[17] Labels in broad categories like "menu," "food," "tacos," and "sushi" are attached to images based on comments supplied by the users who uploaded the images. Additional validation of these extracted labels is done through crowdsourcing. Then the images and labels are used to train a type of deep learning neural network that does computer vision. Once it has learned what makes a menu, or food, or tacos, or sushi, the neural network will itself classify and label previously unlabeled images in a fraction of the time it would take an army of humans to do the same task. With an increase in the number of labeled images, Yelp can offer additional features, like tabbed photo browsing based on categories like "food," "menus," and "drink."

As we discussed in the introduction, algorithms are sequences of instructions that can be used to solve a problem. Algorithms developed by programmers to instruct computers to do certain tasks are building blocks for our digital world. But developing these algorithms takes time. The advantage of using neural networks and similar techniques is that they can create new algorithms themselves. They recognize the rules guiding the patterns and are then programmed to generate new rules based on what they learn, and again, in a fraction of the time it would take humans to do the same.

So, for a machine learning algorithm to generate new rules, it needs to first be trained (usually by a human) to identify patterns and extract rules from those patterns. Applying labels to phrases is a good example of the way that a programmer would train a machine learning algorithm. This kind of training is often referred to as *supervised learning*. A phrase is labeled, say, positive, negative, or neutral. The algorithm can now identify the rules to classify a phrase as good or bad. It might decide a rule is that phrases with "worst" in them are negative, for example (though it's more complicated than this; we are keeping this simple for explanation's sake).

Once an algorithm has been trained through supervised learning it is ready for a more advanced phase, called *unsupervised learning*. This is where the algorithm automatically sorts through the Yelp pictures and reviews and classifies certain restaurants as good or bad on its own. Unsupervised learning is how Alibaba and Amazon figure out that two items are often bought together.

A third and even more advanced phase of learning is called *reinforcement learning*, when the machine learning algorithm is constantly corrected based on feedback. For an example of reinforcement learning, consider a few everyday examples that you've likely experienced. If a machine learning algorithm infers that sweatshirts and socks are frequently bought together, it serves an advertisement for socks to the buyer of a sweatshirt. But if that buyer doesn't buy the socks, the algorithm takes that feedback and uses it to refine its model about who is likely to buy what. Similarly, if the driver of a self-driving car takes the wheel to make a correction, the algorithm learns that its model of the vehicle's trajectory was off and takes this correction data into account in reconstituting the model.[18]

Developing a digital mindset also means accepting that, in many cases, machines are better than humans at making certain predictions and doing specific tasks. Advances in computational power paired with massive amounts of data generated in health-care systems make many clinical problems perfect candidates for AI applications. Researchers at Seoul National University Hospital and College of Medicine developed an AI algorithm called DLAD (Deep Learning–based Automatic Detection) to analyze chest radiographs and detect abnormal cell growth, such as potential cancers.[19] In a four-year study, the hospital found that the AI was able to dramatically reduce the number of overlooked lung cancers on chest radiographs without a proportional increase in the number of follow-up chest CT examinations. For physicians and their patients, this technological breakthrough means adjusting expectations for diagnosis and practice. In another example, Google Health created a machine learning algorithm, LYNA (LYmph Node Assistant), to identify metastatic breast cancer tumors from lymph node biopsies.[20] What was unique about this AI was that the algorithm could identify suspicious regions undistinguishable to the human eye. LYNA was tested on two data sets and was shown to classify a sample as cancerous or noncancerous correctly 99 percent of the time. When given to doctors to use in conjunction with their typical manual analysis of stained tissue samples, LYNA halved the average slide review time. Again, doctors had to integrate this new level into their practice. Although ultimately an advance to be celebrated—more accurate diagnostics in less time—workflows and human roles then need to be adjusted, and that's not always easy. In health care, for example, it can feel threatening to have a machine contradict your diagnosis.[21] That's where the idea that machines aren't human is important. It feels threatening, but code doesn't make threats. It's just a tool for us to harness.

What it really means when you hear that AI is getting more powerful (and when movies caution us that machines are about to take over our lives) is that more and more data are becoming available and we are acquiring more and more computer processing power. This also means that computer scientists are able to take advantage of more powerful processing to design better algorithms to train AI. Think of all the digital transactions conducted online daily, or the number of sensors being deployed into all the devices you own (today's cars have more than one hundred sensors that monitor functions such as fuel level and tire pressure). Although those numbers have grown rapidly in the past decade, the march to even more powerful processing and more data is continuing unabated. Every year we produce more data than all the previous years combined.[22] What's state of the art today will soon be considered slow. Companies like IBM are working to develop quantum computing systems to power their Watson AI.[23] If nothing else, you need to know that the future progress of AI will depend on a combination of data, computing power, and more advanced algorithms.

Get to Know Your Technology Stack

Have you played the game Jenga? Rectangular blocks are cross-stacked in a number of consecutive layers to create a tower of interdependent layers. You can extract some pieces at each layer without knocking over the tower, but if you weaken those lower layers too much the whole structure will come crumbling down.

AI is a lot like a Jenga tower. AI systems are built out of an increasingly complex and interdependent web of software, hardware, and databases. For example, to do something as seemingly simple as showing a webpage about your favorite musical artist when you ask Alexa to do it requires a mix of technologies that do everything from storing, accessing, and securing those data, to computing them and displaying them to the page's viewer. All this requires a Jenga-type level of interdependence and cross-stacking with multiple layers.

In the world of IT, these layers are called a *technology stack*, which is simply all the hardware and software systems needed to develop and run a single application. Software developers can use a preconfigured technology stack (think of a Jenga set with all the pieces already included and set up for you) to develop a new application, or they can build their own technology stack (by finding and assembling their own blocks for the game).

Typically, a technology stack is built as two subsystems. The first is the "front-end" system or the "client side," and comprises all of the technologies and data sources that users (you, your employees, your customers) will interact with. This might include the buttons you click or the forms you fill on a computer survey. The second system is the "back-end" system or the "server side," which is the underlying infrastructure that powers the client experience. Technicians and engineers are concerned with the back end.

Linking these layers of the stack together are software applications known as middleware. Middleware operates as a hidden translation layer, almost like a house's plumbing connecting the sink and the tub and other

FIGURE 1-4

Generic technology stack

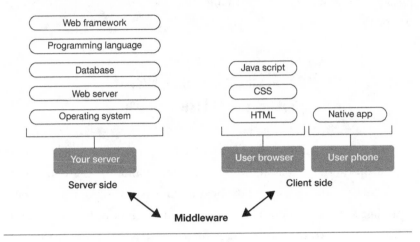

appliances into the same system; middleware enables communication between database and data. For example, when you submit a form on a web browser, the middleware retrieves content for the web page you'll see based on the information you submitted. Many software developers describe middleware as "the software glue" that holds the various layers of the stack together—so that the Jenga structure won't easily topple over. Figure 1-4 provides a visualization of a generic technology stack.

It's important to know about a technology stack so that you have an appreciation for the many, many technologies required to make even simple things happen with digital data. Also, it should make you realize that if you decide you need new data, or a new kind of analysis, you're going to have to do much more than simply ask a software developer to write a script for you. What might seem like a simple change can have dramatic implications for the lowest levels of the technology stack, like trying to swap out one of those blocks at the bottom of the Jenga tower. Certain applications in the stack favor certain programming languages and certain servers are optimized for particular kinds of data categorization, storage, and retrieval activities (which we'll discuss in chapter 3). If you want to change anything high up in your technology stack, you may be limited by the arrangement of applications lower down. These layers are interdependent. Knowing that can help you to ask the right questions to assess whether a change that seems small is actually small or not.

Treat AI Like a Machine, Even If It Seems to Act Like a Human

We are accustomed to interacting with a computer in a visual way: buttons, drop-down lists, sliders, and other features allow us to give the computer commands. However, advances in AI are moving our interaction with digital tools to more natural-feeling and human-like interactions. What's called a conversational user interface (UI) gives people the ability to act with digital tools through writing or talking that's much more the way we interact with other people, like Burt Swanson's "conversation" with Amy the assistant.[24] When you say, "Hey Siri," "Hello Alexa," and "OK Google," that's a conversational UI.

The growth of tools controlled by conversational UIs is staggering. Every time you call an 800 number and are asked to spell your name, answer "Yes," or say the last four numbers of your social security number you are interacting with an AI that uses conversational UI. Conversational bots have become ubiquitous in part because they make good business sense, and in part because they allow us to access services more efficiently and more conveniently.

For example, if you've booked a train trip through Amtrak, you've probably interacted with an AI chatbot. Its name is Julie, and it answers more than 5 million questions annually from more than 30 million passengers. You can book rail travel with Julie just by saying where you're going and when. Julie can pre-fill forms on Amtrak's scheduling tool and provide guidance through the rest of the booking process. Amtrak has seen an 800 percent return on their investment in Julie. Amtrak saves more than $1 million in customer service expenses each year by using Julie to field low-level, predictable questions.[25] Bookings have increased by 25 percent, and bookings done through Julie generate 30 percent more revenue than bookings made through the website, because Julie is good at upselling customers!

One reason for Julie's success is that Amtrak makes it clear to users that Julie is an AI agent, and they tell you why they've decided to use AI rather than connect you directly with a human. That means that people orient to it as a machine, not mistakenly as a human. They don't expect too much from it, and they tend to ask questions in ways that elicit helpful answers. Amtrak's decision may sound counterintuitive, since many companies try to pass off their chatbots as real people and it would seem that interacting with a machine as though it were a human should be precisely how to get the best results. A digital mindset requires a shift in how we think about our relationship to machines. Even as they become more human-ish, we need to think about them as machines— requiring explicit instructions and focused on narrow tasks.

x.ai, the company that made meeting scheduler Amy, enables you to schedule a meeting at work, or invite a friend to your kids' basketball game by simply emailing Amy (or her counterpart, Andrew) with your request as though they were a live personal assistant. Yet Dennis Mortensen, the company's CEO, observes that more than 90 percent of the inquiries that the company's help desk receives are related to the fact that people are trying to use natural language with the bots and struggling to get good results. Perhaps that was why scheduling a simple meeting with a new acquaintance became so annoying to Professor Swanson, who kept trying to use colloquialisms and conventions from informal conversation. In addition to the way he talked, he made many perfectly valid assumptions about his interaction with Amy. He assumed Amy could understand his scheduling constraints and that "she" would be able to discern what his preferences were from the context of the conversation. Swanson was informal and casual—the bot doesn't get that. It doesn't understand that when asking for another person's time, especially if they are doing you a favor, it's not effective to frequently or suddenly change the meeting logistics. It turns out it's harder than we think to interact casually with an intelligent robot.

Researchers have validated the idea that treating machines like machines works better than trying to be human with them. Stanford professor Clifford Nass and Harvard Business School professor Youngme Moon conducted a series of studies in which people interacted with anthropomorphic computer interfaces.[26] (Anthropomorphism, or assigning human attributes to inanimate objects, is a major issue in AI research.) They found that individuals tend to overuse human social categories, applying gender stereotypes to computers and ethnically identifying with computer agents. Their findings also showed that people exhibit over-learned social behaviors such as politeness and reciprocity toward computers. Importantly, people tend to engage in these behaviors—treating robots and other intelligent agents as though they were people—even when they know they are interacting with computers, rather than humans. It seems that our collective impulse to relate with people often creeps into our interaction with machines.[27]

This problem of mistaking computers for humans is compounded when interacting with artificial agents via conversational UIs. Take for example a study we conducted with two companies who used AI assistants that provided answers to routine business queries. One used an anthropomorphized AI that was human-like. The other wasn't.

Workers at the company who used the anthropomorphic agent routinely got mad at the agent when the agent did not return useful answers. They routinely said things like, "He sucks!" or "I would expect him to do better" when referring to the results given by the machine. Most importantly, their strategies to improve relations with the machine mirrored strategies they would use with other people in the office. They would ask their question more politely, they would rephrase into different words, or they would try to strategically time their questions for when they thought the agent would be, in one person's terms, "not so busy." None of these strategies was particularly successful.

In contrast, workers at the other company reported much greater satisfaction with their experience. They typed in search terms as though it were a computer and spelled things out in great detail to make sure that an AI, who could not "read between the lines" and pick up on nuance, would heed their preferences. The second group routinely remarked at how surprised they were when their queries were returned with useful or even surprising information and they chalked up any problems that arose to typical bugs with a computer.

For the foreseeable future, the data are clear: treating technologies— no matter how human-like or intelligent they appear—like technologies is key to success when interacting with machines. A big part of the problem is they set the expectations for users that they will respond in human-like ways, and they make us assume that they can infer our intentions, when they can do neither. Interacting successfully with a conversational UI requires a digital mindset that understands we are still some ways away from effective human-like interaction with the technology. Recognizing that an AI agent cannot accurately infer your intentions means that it's important to spell out each step of the process and be clear about what you want to accomplish.

Build Trust to Team with Machines: Human-Agent Teaming

We typically think of technology as something that enables teams of people to interact with each other—think of a team working together via Skype, sharing an Excel spreadsheet, or accessing the same Oracle database. But with advances in machine learning, NLP, and AI, technologies are becoming more like "real" team members themselves that can interact with you, make suggestions, and act on decisions.

The US military is one of the most advanced users of human-agent teaming. They use it to help determine, for example, a convoy's route through a battle zone, or to make tactical battle plans. Companies are also increasingly putting AI team members into their operations. Google is incorporating smart digital technologies into executive decision-making teams. Foxconn is using smart digital tools on shop-floor manufacturing teams, and banks are using smart digital technologies on underwriting teams.

Our ability to trust the machines in this "human-agent teaming" is a key factor for success working with machine team members, and it's not always there.[28] As much as we tend to humanize machines, we can also be wary of trusting them.

Think of the battlefield: How do you know if you can trust a digital technology to give you the best coordinates for an attack, or the safest route through an enemy encampment?

To answer this question, and to learn to trust AI team members, we have to return to some of the machine learning lessons we discussed earlier. Machine learning is the ability of computers to adjust their behavior based on the data to which they are exposed. In a battle zone, this could mean having a specific goal—such as minimizing the number of misses, as well as a set of rules that define a miss or a hit—to enable computers to adjust their decisions based on their experiences. This learning process requires a large amount of data that can be used for training. The important thing for you to remember is that when properly trained, AI is able to make accurate decisions with newly presented similar data and adjust its behavior when necessary.

Developing the digital mindset to work with an AI machine as a teammate means you trust that's true even though the specific calculations that lead computers to make the decision, and which are based on the data, are mostly unknown. Also, you trust that the computers are able to use data to a greater extent than humans and may therefore achieve better results than humans.

For example, consider Arthur Samuel, one of the pioneers of machine learning, who taught a computer program to play checkers. His goal was to teach it to play better than he could, which was not something he could program it to do himself. As data, Samuel provided a large number of annotated games, with the "good moves" distinguished from the "bad moves" and a copy of the book *Lees' Guide to the Game of Draughts or Checkers* to adjust the criteria for choosing moves. This data programmed the computer to choose moves checkers experts rated as "good" as often as possible.

In 1962, Samuel's program beat the Connecticut checkers champion, who was the fourth top player in the nation. The key takeaway is that even though the computer program was applying preprogrammed rules, it could make decisions in a better way than the programmer could.

The stakes don't seem so high when you're playing checkers against a machine. Thus, people who use AI for gaming and other simple purposes don't worry much about whether they can trust that the machine's moves are accurate. In fact, most studies show that people just assume that AI-powered machines can crunch numbers and follow simple rules better than people can. Research by Jennifer Logg at Georgetown University bears this out.[29] In her work, participants received advice about simple predictions about business success, song popularity, or romantic attraction. Some were told the advice came from a person, others that it came from an algorithm. In either case the advice was identical. Overwhelmingly people relied more on advice when they believed it came from an algorithm rather than from other people. They even showed a willingness to choose algorithmic advice over their own judgment.

Interestingly, willingness to defer to AI in decision-making was lower among participants with a less developed digital mindset and among experts who were simply less open to taking any advice. The accuracy of their judgments suffered as a result.

The trust in machines here was in low-stakes, fairly straightforward and numeric (based on accurate counting) tasks. And that typically results in better outcomes.

But the stakes are a lot higher when you're collaborating with a machine on more complicated and less numerical predictions about, say, consumer behavior or to determine the best tactical plan for a military strike or to diagnose a disease. Trust in machines is still needed but harder to come by.

David Newman and colleagues from the University of Southern California conducted a series of experiments in which students and employees were told that they were receiving feedback on their performance from either a manager or an AI tool.[30] The results showed that when people were being evaluated on what they perceived as "objective" criteria, like how many sales calls they closed in a certain amount of time, the AI did a better job at recognizing their performance than human managers—a similar outcome to Logg's. But when they were being evaluated on what they perceived as "subjective" criteria, like how hard they worked to close the deal or whether or not they built a relationship with the potential customer, they felt that human managers were more accurate than the AI. Clearly, our trust in the accuracy of AI depends a great deal on the kinds of tasks the technology performs.[31]

Given these characteristics of AI, it is important to recognize that there are differences between trusting humans and trusting technology. AI's complexity suggests a need for a leap of faith to trust in processes that cannot be directly observed or cognitively understood. Ella Glikson of Bar-Ilan University and Anita Woolley of Carnegie Mellon University have argued that learning to trust AI requires that at least two conditions are met:[32]

1. *AI must be transparent.* This means that people have to be able to understand how a set of algorithms works, or at least recognize the assumptions through which the algorithms are operating.

2. *AI must be reliable.* Low reliability significantly decreases trust and the way to restore trust is difficult and takes time.

Glikson and Woolley also argue that although anthropomorphic AI can increase trust to a point by making people liken the technology to a human counterpart, it also creates high levels of expectation that can be violated when the AI does not perform as expected.

To build on these assumptions about trust, a team of researchers at the US Army Research Laboratory led by D. Jessie Chen built a small ground robot (they called it the "Autonomous Squad Member") that interacted directly with members of an infantry squad to make tactical battlefield decisions.[33] Few situations require more trust in team members (people or machines) than combat—where the situation is changing rapidly, highly uncertain, and people's lives are on the line. Because AI-powered robots can process incoming data more quickly than people can and calculate probabilities in real time, they have the potential to be key team members in such high-stakes situations, but only if the rest of the team feels comfortable trusting their recommendations.

To ensure transparency, the robot showed visual information at three levels. At the first level, the robot provided the team members the basic information about its current state and goals, intentions, and plans. At the second level, it described its reasoning process and the various contextual factors that it was considering when planning its actions. At the third level, the robot provided the team members with information regarding its projection of future states, predicted consequences, and the likelihood of success or failure of its recommendation.

When the robot made this kind of information transparent, team members reported higher levels of trust and a higher likelihood to take its recommendations than if the robot made a bunch of decisions and the team members didn't know how or why. They also found that when team members took care to explain to the robot the reasoning behind their actions, the robot learned better. It turns out that being explicit and purposeful in how we communicate is key to a successful human-machine interaction whether you're a human or a machine.

What does it mean for people interacting with machines to do their work? For engineers designing AI-powered machines that will be used as teammates, it means making their decision processes transparent.[34] For the rest of us, developing a digital mindset that helps us to work alongside intelligent machines means understanding that trusting an AI-based agent is important and can be safe, but also understanding that doing so is different than trusting a person. When we interact with human colleagues we don't know well, we use many proxies to determine if they're trustworthy—for example, their level of education, where they work, what role they have, whether people we know trust them, whether they sound intelligent, and so forth. If we trust them and good things happen, we build a tendency to trust them again in the future. If bad things happen, we don't.

Those same cues aren't available to us when working with AI-powered machines. Instead, to determine if we can trust their decisions or recommendations, we first have to be cognizant of the type of task we're asking them to do. If it's more than simple calculation and classification, we need to ask to see the processes and routines the agents are using to make their decisions to determine if what they are doing is appropriate.[35] If you're responsible for managing people who are working with AI-powered machines as teammates, it is essential to make sure that you ask for and enable this kind of transparency so your employees or customers can have the confidence to work closely with the machines and follow their recommendations. And being transparent yourself when working with a machine is important to assure that the machine learns in a way that will improve your interactions with it over time.

Though you may think that such skills will become obsolete as digitally controlled, smart robots become more human-like in the way they interact with us, our own research, and the work of others, suggests that just the opposite is true. When robots act more like humans, we tend to treat them more like humans and that's where the trouble begins.

GETTING TO 30 PERCENT

Working with Machines

Developing a digital mindset means accepting that machines are not people even if they increasingly look and sound human. Getting angry or talking politely at machines is not effective! Instead, you need to learn how machines work, which means understanding the basics of AI.

- AI is the computer inside the robot. Today's cars, airplanes, thermostats, and even email filters all rely on artificial intelligence to perform specific tasks. When you interact with a machine by talking or writing it's through what's called a conversational user interface.

- Data, processing power, and algorithms are the three basic components that computer scientists use for developing AI.

- A technology stack is comprised of all the hardware and software systems needed to develop and run a single application. Typically, a technology stack includes a front-end system, a back-end system, and middleware.

- Machines mimic the "cognitive" functions of people by learning and problem-solving.

- Machine learning is a type of artificial intelligence that can generalize from examples and gain the ability to "learn" without being explicitly programmed by humans. Over time, machine learning enables computers to adjust their behavior to new situations based on the accumulated data to which they have been exposed.

- Advances in computational power paired with massive amounts of data mean that machines can make calculations much faster, more accurately, and at higher volumes than the human brain. For that reason, a digital mindset means becoming clear and intentional about the tasks you ask AI to perform.

- We cannot comprehend exactly how AI makes its calculations; we just give it instructions. A digital mindset means learning when it is and is not ok to trust the machine's results and also when to check to see that the results make intuitive sense.

Understanding the basic ways that AI works gives you a vocabulary and set of concepts that helps gauge how little or how much to trust the machines you will increasingly work alongside. When collaborating with machines, remember that AI will not respond to your emotions but only to the explicit directions that you program it to follow.

2

Cultivating Your Digital Presence

Being There When You're Not

You might think that working with other people is a cinch compared to collaborating with machines. We're all human beings, after all. In reality, working in a virtual environment changes how we interact with one another. When you're out of sight of your coworkers, managers, or clients, you can easily become out of mind and out of touch. Developing a digital mindset means learning to stay in sync with remote collaborators.

No doubt you can recall a time when you were perplexed by a remote colleague's behavior. Are they not answering your email because they are busy? Uninterested? Both? Maybe they didn't get your email? When we are not collocated with our collaborators, we make up our own accounts for their behavior and infer what their motives might be. We engage in this kind of behavior because the digital tools that make our physical separation possible lead to what Catherine Cramton, Professor Emerita of Management at George Mason University who has spent her career studying digitally enabled collaboration, calls the "mutual knowledge problem."[1] Mutual knowledge is the information that we need to achieve mutual understanding. It is the common ground that people need to reach. Perhaps your colleague has not answered your email because they have taken the day off. Or perhaps they had to attend to a pressing project or your email landed in their spam folder. Remote workers struggle to achieve common ground because even the slightest physical separation between people threatens their ability to establish shared understanding. Without mutual knowledge, collaboration suffers and teams begin to fall apart.

Establishing the close, collaborative working relationships that we all need to thrive in the digital age means developing a mindset that anticipates the mutual knowledge problem and learns strategies to compensate. We call these strategies *digital presence*. Here, you'll learn how to establish an effective digital presence. We identified these best practices by studying remote workers across different industries, doing different kinds of work, in companies that included Adobe, AT&T, Blue Cross Blue Shield, Cisco, FleishmanHillard, Hewlett-Packard, IBM, LogMeIn, Verizon Wireless, Tyco, and Wells Fargo.

When we compared people in the companies we studied who had excellent digital presence with those who didn't, we found that the primary way they cultivated that presence was by maintaining continuity in their relationship with others. These successful individuals made sure that there weren't long gaps in communication or big absences in how others experienced them. Although the schedules and numbers of hours they worked varied, the people who they worked with had the sense that they were sufficiently accessible. How do you keep people aware of you and thinking about you regularly? In three ways:

- Send updates; don't wait

- Create a sense of curiosity

- Communicate on their timeline, not yours

Send Updates; Don't Wait

After four years working as a software engineer for a large network hardware company, Jenna was asked to join an elite team of developers working on the flagship product. The team manager and a quarter of the team worked out of the company's Silicon Valley headquarters, but the team also included subject matter experts from all over the world. Jenna was the sole member from the company's North Carolina outpost. She loved the work, but she struggled collaborating at a distance. She remembers the difficult first few months of being 100 percent virtual. "It was the first time I'd worked in a scenario like this. Doing the work was easy, but I kept getting this feeling that things were going on without me, that my manager wasn't sharing everything with me."

Some of our work with *Fortune* 50 companies has shown that these feelings of being forgotten or overlooked are not uncommon in remote work situations because of the mutual knowledge problem. Although Jenna's company provided her and everyone else with multiple channels for communication—email, IM, internal social media, and other digital collaboration tools—Jenna still felt that her team often forgot she was there. The problem was compounded, and this is also typical, by the hybrid nature of the team, in which some people were collocated while others like Jenna worked remotely. The problem is exacerbated when the collocated people are working alongside the manager or if one person on the team is in a "solo" location. In Jenna's situation, both factors were in play.

At her performance review, Jenna was shocked to get the worst set of evaluations she'd ever received. When she told her manager that she had met or exceeded all her goals during the evaluation period, her manager told her that she was technically fine, but he just didn't have the sense that she was really excelling at her overall job. Jenna was upset by this vague answer. Upon reflection she understood him to mean that her absence might be misinterpreted when she was offline.

Jenna made one simple switch: "I decided to give updates about my progress and to be very forward about where things were going even when I wasn't asked." In practice, that meant that Jenna would copy her manager on emails to their consultants; she would mention him in the collaboration tool when she reached a particular product milestone; and she would write short direct messages to her manager and other teammates providing them with updates on her tasks. All these mini-updates helped to establish a sustained digital presence with her manager and teammates. At her next review, Jenna received her best evaluation. She remembered only one comment from her manager: "Jenna. You're everywhere!" Notice, though, that Jenna hadn't made substantive changes to her work. She only changed when and how people knew about her work, and that alone changed her evaluation from worst to first.

Like Jenna, professionals who excel in digital collaboration don't wait for managers or teammates to ask them what they're doing, how things are going, or what their thoughts are about certain matters. Instead, they're proactive in reaching out to others in order to establish and remain digitally present—even when insight into their projects and their performance is unsolicited. Those who are successful at digital collaboration tend to find it odd, at first, to constantly broadcast their work status and activities to others. It feels unnatural to provide small updates all the time. But over time, they learn to take proactive steps to describe what they were doing, without making specific requests of their teammates. As a result, their work participation is top of mind to their collaborators and managers.

Another common fear is that overcommunication becomes a nuisance to the receiver. But we were surprised to learn that none of the managers and collaborators who were receiving more communication had seemed to notice the increase in communication. In one case, we showed the manager of a large team the volume of communication he'd received from one of his individual contributors over the past two weeks and he was blown away: "I had no idea he sent me so many updates. No idea at all! But I'll tell you what, I knew he was working hard." Crucially, these extra, unsolicited messages didn't add to receivers' cognitive loads because the sender didn't ask anything of them. There was no call to action, and no need for the recipient to invest their time. The only purpose was to manage and maintain digital presence. But managers who learned, as part of the process, how team members were progressing on projects knew when to intervene if necessary. What's more, they could fully appreciate the work that team members were putting in. Everyone had learned to work in sync.

Create a Sense of Curiosity

"Are you around?" "I need to talk about something important." "You need to hear this. Message me ASAP." "I've got some news to share." "Can you call me as soon as you're available? We need to talk."

What do these message openers all have in common? Damon, a senior-level manager at a large telecommunications company, explains, "When someone reaches out to me like this—a little ambiguously—I can't get them out of my mind. It just makes me curious." Damon and other leaders, and colleagues react similarly to messages that pique their curiosity: they focus their thoughts and attention on the sender. Messages that begin this way don't always encourage people to respond more quickly, but they are another practice to remain digitally present to remote colleagues.

You've probably had it drilled into your head that clear and concise communication is the best form of communication, especially in work settings. That advice is undoubtedly correct when your goal is to update someone, provide timely insights, or make sure that your audience understands your message.

But if your goal is simply to be present, ambiguity—as opposed to clarity—has virtues that can be integral to relating to others with a digital mindset. University of South Florida professor Eric Eisenberg has spent the better part of his career studying how people can use ambiguity strategically when communicating.[2] He's found that when a message—whether an interpersonal message like email or formal communication such as a company's mission statement—is phrased purposefully ambiguously, two simultaneous effects occur. First, people think about the message more, trying to intuit meaning from it, and they focus their attention on the sender. Second, they begin making their own interpretations, forming opinions about what it means and what the important parts of the message are. In both ways, ambiguity captures people's attention and focuses it exactly where digitally minded strategic communicators want them to: on them.

Likewise, we find that these ambiguous messages create a sense of curiosity that amplifies attention in remote work.[3] Alena, a sales rep at a large bank who worked remotely from her team, described how she did this: "If I haven't had a lot of face time with someone and I want them to remember me, I might wait until I've got something I need to talk to them about and then just send them a message like, 'I've got something important to tell you.' You know, leave it at that. Without the details they get curious. When they get back to me they say, 'I've been thinking about you all day,' which is exactly what I wanted to happen." Alena is exhibiting a digital mindset. She is intentional about developing and using strategies for maintaining digital presence.

Of course, if every message was designed to provoke curiosity, your audience would begin to tune them out quickly. You may have experienced that tuned-out response to advertising that promises to give you the best and most amazing solution to some intractable problem—often, once you pay a substantial fee. So in addition to strategic ambiguity, it is important to be restrained in your promises and strategic about timing. Strategically ambiguous messages are most effective when they meet three conditions:

- *Payoff.* Messages designed to provoke curiosity have to come with some payoff for the recipient. If the buildup was for nothing, your recipient will be put off.

- *Timing.* Filling the recipient in too soon can undermine the establishment of your presence. If the goal of inciting curiosity is to make sure that people are thinking about you and focusing on you for an extended period every so often, relieving the tension too soon obviates the goal.

- *Frequency.* Don't send to the same person more than once every four to six months.

The takeaway here in developing your digital mindset is that when interacting primarily through mediated communication, thinking about someone and focusing attention on them in intense bursts, even if periodically, has the positive effect of making that person feel more immediately present.

Communicate on Their Timeline, Not Yours

One of the key reasons establishing presence is so important in the digital realm is because people's attention is being commanded by many other people and information sources. When you're out of sight, it's easy for all those other distractions to fill the space someone might have devoted to thinking about you. Advertisers and marketing professionals have contended with this challenge for decades.[4] Digital advertising has offered one solution to overcoming this problem from which we can all learn: timing influences when people are likely to be more or less receptive. Advertisers, who find it easy to track when someone engages in certain behaviors on their digital platform, routinely run data analysis on what's called digital behavior data to find out when people are most receptive to seeing an ad.

Mark Vadon, founder of the online jewelry retailer Blue Nile and Zulily, which began as a flash sale site for kids clothing, used digital behavior data to determine consumer buying patterns at his two companies. He found that most sales take place on Mondays and the fewest sales occur over the weekend. Claudia Lombana, a shopping specialist at eBay and PayPal, found a similar pattern when crunching the numbers on her site. Not only did she find that Mondays were the days that people bought the most, but they did so between noon and 1:00 p.m. in their time zone. It turns out people were quite fond of using their lunch breaks on Mondays—when they were already sitting in front of a computer—to buy all of the things they were thinking about over the weekend. These insights spurred a flurry of advertising during the lunch hour to catch people when they were most likely to be in the mood to shop.[5] Google AdWords cost more during the noon–1:00 p.m. time frame as advertisers jockeyed to be in front of people who were primed to buy. With the explosion of mobile purchasing in recent years, those consumer behavior patterns have changed and advertisers are subsequently having to perform ever more intricate data analysis to find the right time to serve ads to people, but the fact remains that timing makes a difference when it comes to receptivity.

People's receptivity to your messages is also time dependent. If you want to reach someone whose attention is under assault from many other sources, you have the highest odds of doing so when *they* are primed to listen to your digital communication. Our work has shown, however, that most people do just the opposite—they communicate with others when it's easiest for themselves, not when it's best for others.

Chances are that some of the people you work with are in different time zones. Even slight differences in when you begin and end your day can create opportunities for what we call attention misalignment across work sites. Take for example, Syneca, an analyst at a large health-care insurer. Her office was located on the West Coast, but she regularly worked with her team in Chicago, New York, and Boston. It was typical for Syneca to start her day by messaging her team about issues still pending from the previous day when she arrived at work at 9:00 a.m. But by this time, her East Coast colleagues were on their lunch break. They would typically respond once they returned, but by that time, Syneca had moved on to other tasks. By contrast, when Syneca worked with people in the same time zone, she had lively back-and-forth communication in near–real time with her colleagues. Not surprisingly, her West Coast colleagues felt that Syneca was present to them while her East Coast colleagues did not. As one of her colleagues in Boston commented, "Syneca is fine to work with. I don't get to interact with her live much, but she's solid." In other words, Syneca had not established a strong presence with her colleagues in a different time zone.

Disappointed that she was not able to build strong connections with her team on the other side of the country, Syneca decided to make a change in the timing of her messages. As she recounted, "I started holding some of our action items for an hour or so after the start of my day so the folks on the East Coast would be back from lunch. Things changed fast when I did that. Instead of me sending a message and waiting, they responded right away and we really got that back-and-forth going that makes things happen." Small adjustments, such as waiting an hour or so to send an email, can make a big difference in how your digital communications do or do not establish presence with your remote coworkers.

Like Syneca, people we've worked with who shifted their mode of communicating to consider when their messages would be best received by their intended audiences were able to establish their presence despite the fact that their communication partners were inundated. A senior VP at a major computer manufacturer put it plainly: "You just get a feeling that someone is there for you or not. I guess part of that feeling comes from the fact that you know if you reach out they're there. If you have lots of experiences where you just seem to be missing each other, it's hard to really feel like you're connected and you sort of stop trying."

Social Lubrication for Digital Tools

Productively and intentionally interacting with collaborators and managers through internal social media tools that have radically reshaped interactions in the workplace is another key part of developing a digital mindset. Daily workflows can include participating in multiple chat messaging threads with several different groups, clicking on links a team member has sent to you, getting pinged about new activity in a group to which you belong, jumping on a brief screen-sharing session, co-editing documents, and reading a companywide posting alerting you to a change in, for example, parking policy. These communication methods have developed recently and rapidly. When the Covid-19 pandemic hit in 2020, internal social tools became ubiquitous, replacing email and phone communication in many cases.[6]

But the meteoric rise of internal social tools in the workplace does not necessarily mean that companies and their employees know how to use them optimally. When organizations attempt to go digital, they often reach straight for the technology and then try to figure out how it can fit into their organization. Michael Kanaan, director of AI and machine learning for the US Air Force, calls this thinking "techno-solutionism." He asserts that the logic is inverted. Companies instead need to determine what their specific goals are first, and *then* think about how specific digital tools can help them achieve these goals.[7] And this doesn't go just for executives, of course, but for managers and employees as well. As part of a six-month study at a large financial services firm, we talked to people and leaders of both large and small organizations about how they used internal social media platforms. We identified three best practices that maximize their use to meet company goals:

- Articulate the purpose

- Look to learn

- Get personal

Articulate the purpose

You, your colleagues, and your employees need to be aware of the purpose and potential of the internal social media tools in the workplace. You need to know that when used productively, internal social media tools can strengthen relationships and increase knowledge sharing.[8] This feature of digital collaboration tools may be less intuitive than their obvious usefulness for fast and accessible online communication, but it's what makes digital collaboration tools so powerful for organizations. More specifically, internal social media tools serve a crucial purpose because in addition to the actual information you receive you also learn who sent it and where the information came from. We call that contextual information *metaknowledge*, and it's the prequel to people's ability to connect with one another.[9] Connecting in turn leads to more information sharing and collaboration for problem-solving or innovation.

Leaders must demonstrate the power of enterprise social networks to employees. They must explicitly state that the purpose is to strengthen employee relationships in order to improve communication and collaboration. Otherwise, employees assume that online social activity that is non-work related is an impediment to productivity instead of a boost. It's an understandable assumption to make when "socializing" at work—especially online—is traditionally characterized as a distraction. For this reason leaders can model the behavior they would like to see. When they notice a good idea streaming on the company's social tool, they should publicly engage the person who posted it. And when employees share information that's not related to work, leaders should chime in with interest. It takes a critical mass to make internal digital collaboration tools useful, and this is difficult to achieve when people disengage from the site for fear of reprisal. Thus, leaders need to clearly model and explain what employees—and the organization as a whole—stand to gain through these new technologies.

Look to learn

Reagan, an IT technician at a large atmospheric research lab, was quietly surfing her group's social site one morning. She often started her day by perusing chats that might have taken place here and there. One exchange caught her attention. Her colleague Jamie had sent a message to another technician, Brett, asking about how to fix a semantic key encryption issue. When she read Brett's response, her eyes widened with excitement. She had been struggling with the exact same issue that Jamie had asked about, and now she had an answer. "I'm so happy I saw that message," she said. "Jamie explained it so well that I was able to learn how to do it." Perhaps you have shared or learned this kind of information with coworkers in hallway conversations or emails. Social media tools make such information sharing possible for remote workers, but equally important, also allow the exchange to become visible to a larger group rather than remaining trapped in one-to-one exchanges. Because Jamie and Brett's chat was visible to others in the lab, Reagan was able to find an answer to an ongoing problem without even explicitly looking for it. All three people had made productive use of the social site.

Social tools also can increase innovation if you borrow ideas and solutions from other parts of the organization and combine them in fresh ways for your own purposes.[10] Tim, an employee in the consumer finance division of a financial services firm, was working out the details of a new loan program. He couldn't quite figure out how to make his idea work. But then inspiration struck: "I suddenly remembered that I'd seen a communication exchanged between these two guys. . . . One of them who's in the pricing department mentioned something about rate variation depending upon risk factors. That caught my eye, so I read the history of the conversation he had, and it included some key ideas about risk that helped me. I sent him an email to see if I could learn more about it, and it made sense. So I developed the program around it, and it's been pretty successful so far—really innovative, so it made me proud." Tim not only monitored a previous conversation to access the information he needed but as a result of using his company's digital collaboration tool learned "who knows what"—the person he could email to find out more of what he needed to know. Tim's director was happy, too. The product came in on time and under budget and carved out a new niche for the company in a crowded market.

Developing a digital mindset means becoming aware that social media networks can facilitate knowledge even when the information isn't in clear sight. Consider Amanda, a marketing coordinator at the same financial firm as Tim. Her manager asked her to analyze trends in an enormous data set, but Amanda was unsure how to do it. She tried to figure it out herself, but to no avail. So she hopped on to the company's social platform, and still couldn't find an answer. But she did see an exchange between two employees in marketing—Rick and Alicia—who were discussing the same issue. Rick recommended that Alicia contact Mark, in the analytics department, who could write the script. Amanda eagerly left Mark a voice mail. When she didn't get a response, she tried again the next day. Still nothing. Fortunately, by observing the conversation between Rick and Alicia, Amanda had learned not only "who knows what" but also "who knows whom"—a crucial form of metaknowledge. So she asked Rick if he would broker an introduction. Minutes later, she was on the phone with Mark, who wrote the script and saved Amanda nearly a week's worth of time on her project.

The lesson here is that it's to your advantage to keep an eye out for information that may be useful.[11] Developing a digital mindset means understanding that social tools can be used not only to uncover necessary information but also to prevent duplication of work by allowing everyone in an organization to learn about existing projects and initiatives, thus freeing up time and money to generate new knowledge.

Like Reagan, Tim, and Amanda, employees who observe others' communications pick up bits and pieces of seemingly unimportant information over time. Eventually, they begin to form a picture of who knows what and whom. Tech writer Clive Thompson compares using digital collaboration tools to staring at a pointillist painting.[12] No dot by itself makes much sense. But when you step back to see all the dots together, you comprehend a rich image. That's also a rich metaphor for what it's like to develop a digital mindset. The slow process whereby people see the individual dots makes it difficult for them to realize they are learning. That's why it's crucial for managers to explicitly highlight the potential for knowledge sharing and skill building when rolling out digital collaboration tools—and have developmental conversations with employees—otherwise people may underutilize or even abandon them.

Get personal

Millennials "breathe" social media, as one senior executive at a large insurance company puts it. They are digital natives who grew up on Facebook, Twitter, Instagram, Snapchat, and Reddit. Online dating is not an oddity for them; it's the norm.[13] Unsurprisingly then, managers often look to millennial employees to set an example with technology, expecting that they will be pioneering users of digital collaboration tools at work.

But that's a mistake. In our research, we've found the opposite to be true: about 85 percent of young professionals said they struggle with digital collaboration tools at work. Ironically, about 90 percent of older professionals viewed these tools simply as new and useful modes of communication.

Developing a digital mindset around social media tools can present different challenges depending on your previous experiences. This can play out in how the digital collaboration tools are presented. In too many rollouts senior executives—trying to provide a cognitive link to a familiar technology—have referred to digital collaboration tools as "Facebook for the company" or "Twitter for the company." But after hearing that from a manager, a twenty-two-year-old data analyst at the insurance company asked, "Why would I want to use Facebook at work? I don't think I necessarily want my manager knowing that I went to a party last night." Therefore, leaders need to think carefully about how to frame digital collaboration tools—they need to signal that the casual tone of social media chats and activity are welcome and encouraged, while clear lines between professional life and personal life should be maintained. Social media interactions at the workplace can be casual—and often non-work related—while still being productive and also distinct from personal life. Chats about sports, Netflix, and cooking are good examples of such a balance.

No matter which generation you belong to, developing a digital mindset means understanding that friendly, non-work interactions on digital collaboration tools are productive because they will increase your networks for knowledge sharing.[14] That's what happened when Jose, a marketing manager at a telecom firm, parlayed his coworker Alex's love of soccer into a productive partnership. Their initial chats about the Euro Cup sparked other conversations about shared work issues in their respective departments. They hatched an idea to apply Jose's marketing expertise to develop a new branding campaign for one of Alex's projects in the e-commerce division. Their collaboration ended up increasing customer retention by more than 200 percent. Alex said, "No one from my department had ever worked with marketing before. Who knew we could complement each other so well?"

A key motivator to engage with your company's digital collaboration tools should be shared interests and hobbies *outside* of work. That's true for people of all ages and ranks. It's hard to strike up a conversation with someone you don't know well. It's even more difficult to ask that person for help or a favor. You will feel better equipped for such exchanges when you have gained personal insight about your coworkers by watching them communicate on internal digital collaboration tools.[15] Our analysis of the telecommunications company where Jose works, for example, revealed that employees who do so are three times as likely as others to get pertinent *work* information from colleagues.

By watching colleagues talk about hobbies and pastimes on internal digital collaboration tools, you can also assess whether coworkers are likable. An engineer at a large e-commerce company told us that he often did this to "size people up" and determine how "safe" they were to approach. Others made similar comments. How coworkers responded to people's queries or joked around suggested how accessible they were; it helped gauge what we call *passable trust*—whether somebody is trustworthy enough to share information with. Trust is crucial because asking people to help solve a problem is an implicit admission that you can't do it alone; it can make you feel vulnerable, especially if you're afraid of developing a reputation for lacking certain knowledge (true for in-person as well as digital interactions!). Sometimes developing a digital mindset is a matter of knowing that it doesn't have to change how you feel and behave.

Digital collaboration tools bring the greatest benefits when you are exposed to ideas and insights from people across the organization—particularly people you wouldn't normally encounter. The challenge, however, is that focusing attention on content coming from multiple departments—many of which have different goals and may seem unrelated to your own work—is difficult and time-consuming. For this reason, organizations tend to deploy digital collaboration tools within departments. But if patterns of communication are too insular, the expanded network that digital collaboration tools promise won't materialize. Just as organizations must be sensitive to both sides of the equation when implementing digital collaboration tools, it's helpful if you can balance your attention between your immediate coworkers and others with whom you might want or need to interact. Internal marketing campaigns, one-on-one sessions, and group trainings are effective ways that managers can help users navigate these dimensions and develop a digital mindset that can get the most out of online interactions with colleagues.

Focus on the Right Data

Despite the vast amount of information digital collaboration tools expose to users, not all that is visible is important or useful. Sometimes social content leads people to focus—and act—on the wrong data. To illustrate, let's return to the atmospheric research lab. A reorganization brought together IT technicians who had never collaborated before. At first, they relied on seniority as a proxy for expertise. But when they implemented a digital collaboration tool for the department and people began reading messages between coworkers about solutions for IT problems across the lab, it became clear that Jill—the most junior technician—was also the most knowledgeable. People started turning to Jill with questions. Digital tools' inherent ability to flatten an organization's hierarchy to allow the best ideas and information to surface is often a positive force for collaboration and innovation. However, in this case, one outcome was not so positive: Peggy, the group's most senior technician, quit after several months. She was frustrated that her coworkers no longer seemed interested in her input. Her colleagues were very clear about why they had shifted from Peggy to Jill: Jill's messages and posts were chock-full of useful technical details. One coworker noted, "Jill just seems to really know a lot about the issues I face." Jill, we might add, had done a fine job of achieving virtual presence.

The IT director was not sad to see Peggy leave. He reasoned that the digital collaboration tool had exposed the fact that she was not as knowledgeable as everyone had thought, and he was pleased that his employees were now going to the "smartest" and most virtually present person for help. Yet, barely two months after Peggy's departure, the IT department's evaluations from scientists across the organization plummeted. Peggy might not have been the most technically sophisticated employee in the department, but she had the most cultural and political knowledge. She knew which scientists' problems should be highest priority, and she knew what preferences various scientists had for technology in their labs.

Although the group had embraced online information sharing, they'd overlooked the low-tech relational skills and cultural knowledge that Peggy offered. They had not valued the presence she'd achieved among the department scientists. Sometimes, a digital mindset can mean knowing when to integrate low-tech with high-tech. Because the technicians were thinking of expertise solely in terms of technical knowledge, Peggy's value to the group was hidden. To salvage the department's customer satisfaction scores, the IT manager hired Peggy back at a 30 percent premium and began to encourage her and others in the department to diversify the types of knowledge they shared on the site.

Across all the companies we studied, the most visible information and knowledge were perceived as most important. You need to understand that if your contributions and strengths are not showing up in your posts or messages, they are likely to be overlooked. Not only does that put you at a disadvantage, but the organization is unable to benefit. Our findings support the old adage that what gets recorded gets remembered. Whether in one-to-one emails or postings to social media sites, establishing a digital presence requires what may at first seem like extra or awkward efforts, but know that over time you will become more comfortable with a digital "self" that can communicate intentionally and collaborate productively.

Remain "In Mind" When "Out of Sight"

Working remotely, as so many of us have now experienced, it's easy to fall out of sync as well as out of sight.[16] We lose many of the benefits related to face-to-face interaction that we rely upon for social bonding, such as nonverbal communication and the ability to have spontaneous communication. Such interactions create a shared experience, represent commitment to the interaction through physical presence, and allow both parties to focus their attention on the interaction. In the absence of col-location, developing a digital mindset means learning to employ new practices to successfully achieve virtual presence with both your imme-diate coworkers and, if possible, the larger organization.

A digital mindset means recognizing that teams relying heavily on digital technologies to collaborate will inevitably face the mutual knowl-edge problem, make wild attributions about each other's behavior and, eventually become out of sync. If you are a manager of a remote or dis-tributed team you need to think about your role as working to actively be present to your team and to make sure that they are present to each other. We define presence as the state of being noticeable to others such that focal actors are salient. When you are present to somebody, they think about you and their actions are affected by you. Even though you are out of sight, you are very much "in mind." Thus, managing pres-ence and building social lubrication is about making sure that you are making yourself more or less noticeable to others depending on the nature of your relationship and learning about them in ways that can help you to ask the right questions and get the information that you need.

GETTING TO 30 PERCENT
Establishing Digital Presence

Digital technologies that enable virtual work change how people collaborate. In remote work, you lose the benefits of nonverbal communication and spontaneous communication that create shared experiences and understanding crucial to social bonding. This is called the mutual knowledge problem.

Developing a digital mindset means learning new practices for achieving digital presence with your collaborators, managers, clients, and the broader organization.

Best practices to lay the foundation for digital presence:

- **Send updates; don't wait.** Let your team know you're making progress, whether or not you might need course correction, and that you're engaged.

- **Create a sense of curiosity.** Don't be afraid to use ambiguity to pique your teammates' interest when necessary, but don't overdo it.

- **Communicate on their timeline, not yours.** Keep your teammates' schedules and time zones in mind when you reach out to them.

Best strategies to use internal social media for digital presence:

- **Articulate the purpose.** Interactions on social media help you see how your teammates fit into the organization, what roles they play, and how they contribute.

- **Look to learn.** Keep a lookout for helpful information. Social media platforms open up dialogues that would otherwise remain trapped in private email exchanges.

- **Get personal or social.** Don't be afraid to socialize with people on social media platforms, even when the subjects aren't work-related.

Casual chats with team members build natural rapport that leads to better collaboration.

- **Focus on the right data.** Keep a lookout for less visible forms of knowledge—for instance, knowledge of the organization's politics and processes.

- **Remain "in mind" when "out of sight."** Stay active on the platform! Let others know you're out there.

Establishing the close, collaborative working relationships that we all need to thrive in the digital age means developing a mindset that expects the mutual knowledge problem and learns strategies to compensate. Establishing a digital presence is key!

PART TWO

COMPUTATION

3

Data and Analytics

What Is Counted Ends Up Counting

As Michael Lewis chronicled in his hit book *Moneyball*, general manager Billy Beane made the perennially underfunded Oakland Athletics competitive against teams with deeper pockets. How? By being one of the first Major League Baseball managers to run statistical analysis on the troves of data collected about player performance. He appeared to perform a near-miracle by using the data to strengthen the Athletics' talent recruiting methods and in-game decisions. When Lewis's book hit the market, it spawned a public debate among baseball enthusiasts about whether analytics or more traditional means of scouting and recruitment, which relied on people finding and then offering star athletes enormously high salaries, could help identify the best talent. Data have largely won. During the two decades that followed, most baseball teams hired full-time analysts. In the 2020 season, the Tampa Bay Rays were widely considered the most adroit users of analytics. They reached the 2020 World Series with a payroll of just $28.2 million, the third lowest of the thirty teams in Major League Baseball.

The success of data analytics in transforming how teams form and perform is one example of how powerful data can be if we have the digital mindset to use that data wisely and—as you will see—how misleading or frustrating data can be if we do not understand how they really work.

Nick Dalton is a self-proclaimed "nerdy math guy who likes sports" who read *Moneyball* and wondered if he could attempt to apply Beane's methods to improve the performance of the men's high school basketball team he coached. Dalton floated the idea by a couple of his friends, one of whom pointed him to an article that Lewis had written for the *New York Times Magazine* about basketball analytics.[1] The article profiled Shane Battier, a 6-foot-8-inch guard for the Houston Rockets and former first-round draft pick out of Duke. He was a solid player. But he never excelled on any of the traditional basketball metrics, such as games played, field goals made, free throw attempts, rebounds, or assists. His talent could not be easily measured. As Lewis wrote, "His greatness is not marked in the box scores or at slam-dunk contests, but on the court Shane Battier makes his team better, often much better, and his opponents worse, often much worse."

"That piece was like a revelation to me," said Dalton. "One of the things that stuck with me the most was how Battier was good at forcing players to shoot in their 'zones of lowest efficiency.' I just thought if I could figure that out—like what our opponents' 'zones of lowest efficiency' were—and share those data with my players, maybe they could start directing them to those spots and forcing a shot and we'd get an edge. You know, find the 'moneyball' for high school basketball." Dalton, who also taught math at the high school, thought he had an ace up his sleeve because one of the star players on his team had read Lewis's article and also happened to be a star student in Dalton's AP Calculus class. "I thought it was going to be a slam dunk—pun not intended—because I happened to have some kids that were strong in math on the team that could actually take some of the stats and make use of them.

"Boy, was I wrong."

After tracking down that year's box scores for most of the high school teams in the division and running some simple stats to compute things like whether players missed more field goals in the second half of the game than the first and from which zones on the court players were most likely to miss shots, Dalton started to coach his team on how to read the statistics. "It was a disaster," he said. "They were so good at math in the classroom, but they couldn't handle the applied nature of the stats. I would ask them what action they thought we should take based on the stats, but they just couldn't translate it. So, I tried just walking through the data with them. Some of them seemed like they got it and were interested, and others just dismissed it because they were convinced that their intuition was better. I couldn't convince them that the numbers were accurate." In other words, just because Dalton's students were strong at math didn't mean they had developed a digital mindset capable of making productive use of data.

After some failed attempts, Dalton did finally convince some of his players to try to use the analytics in their playing strategy. "That was maybe the worst disaster of all. We'd do just what the stats suggested we do and the guy would make the shot anyway. I'd explain to the kids that it was just probabilities, but probabilities are hard to grasp—even if you're good at more abstract math like calculus." Again, without a digital mindset it can be difficult to fully integrate the concept that a statistically probable win doesn't mean that changed behavior will result in the right outcome every time.[2] More importantly, as Dalton realized, "I'm not even sure that the data that I got from the division was that accurate to begin with. So, I might have spent all that time doing the analytics and coaching the kids to use it, and the data on which I made those predictions was just wrong to begin with." After trying to "moneyball" his high school basketball team for three years, Dalton gave up. "I just do fundamental skills coaching and play calling now," he remarked. "I think it's best to leave the analytics to the pros."

• • •

The power of analytics is replete with stories about successful teams like the Oakland Athletics, successful players like Shane Battier, or giants like Amazon or Facebook. They have been able to win more games, improve their on-court performance, and increase product and ad sales exponentially by mining data patterns and using them to make predictions about people's behavior. In fact, you can hardly walk into a sports franchise front office or a corporate boardroom without hearing someone saying something like, "The real moneyball would be . . ." or "We need to find the moneyball for . . ." Even if you're not a sports fan or an analytics expert, you may have seen the movie starring Brad Pitt and Jonah Hill and sensed that most major league sports and countless industries are changing how they operate as the result of advanced analytics.

But you're not likely to have heard many stories like Nick Dalton's—stories in which well-intentioned individuals try to use analytics to their advantage and fail. Yet in our experience, failures like Nick Dalton's are more common than successes like that of the Tampa Bay Rays. To be clear, that's not because the promises of analytics are overhyped. It's because seeing the world through an analytics frame is difficult for people who aren't trained in data science, who aren't used to probabilistic reasoning, or who don't have the money to hire people who can do the job for them.

Developing a digital mindset means you have to become comfortable with analytics and to learn from Dalton that just saying "I'm going to use analytics" isn't enough. Even deploying them isn't enough. At the very least, you need to know what questions to ask of the data and what to look for when you or someone else analyzes them. It also helps if you can anticipate potential consequences of analytics, including errors, and the effects different modes of data representation can have on others. We will devote chapter 4 to the key statistical analysis that you will need to understand; here we will cover how to avoid pitfalls like Dalton's by becoming proficient in basic issues inherent in working with data. By demystifying the nature of data, you will be able to see what it can and cannot do.

In our work with global tech giants in software like Microsoft, in finance like Discover, in defense contracting like FLIR, and in mining like South32, as well as in interviews with hundreds of employees facing the challenge of making sense of data produced, collected, and computed, we've identified three key practices that help people to develop a digital mindset that allows them to see, think, and act analytically. They are:

- Learn where the data came from

- Open the black box of data categorization and analysis

- Match your data visualizations with your audience's needs

Learn Where the Data Came From and How They Got There

One of the most important things to know about data is that they are not natural substances. They don't exist in the wild. Data are created. They serve as representations of some thing or some process. This means that they are, at the most basic level, inherently subjective.

Think of it this way: At some point, someone thought that a natural phenomenon like wind could be depicted in a variety of ways—how cold it is, how fast it blows, how dry it is. To depict wind in these ways, devices were invented to measure those qualities, and those measurements were recorded and stored. Such measurements—what we call data today—represent wind in a number of ways. But they are not wind. Nor do these data objectively describe what wind is or how it feels. They're simply ways to explain wind.

It's somewhat of a misnomer to say that data are *collected*. It is much more accurate to say that data are *produced*.[3] In fact, keeping in mind that data are not simply to be collected like shells, but rather are always the *product* of technological capture and social categorization helps us to keep a critical focus on the role that data play in our decisions—it's a contrivance, an agreed upon conceit that doesn't exist independent of us. Wind exists independently of our measurements, but not the other way around. We could, conceivably, decide we want to measure wind with a new category—say, "strong enough to blow off a hat," and produce the corresponding data.

Understanding this concept means that you are less likely to blindly trust in data's truth or facticity. We tend to find data credible, or factitious, especially if we don't entirely understand what they represent. Keep in mind that just because it's data doesn't mean it's necessarily accurate or true.

From paper ledgers to barcodes—flexibility vs. accuracy

The oldest form of data production is manual input, which means data production started when people began to write things down. For example, scraps of ancient Greek musical notation are forms of data production, as are ancient religious scrolls. For data production in the more recent past, think of a bookkeeper for a domestic goods store in the 1800s logging sales and inventory entries into a ledger. The bookkeeper would likely record price and quantity of the items bought and sold, date of purchase, and other useful information. Perhaps they produced data about what the weather was like when the delivery was made or who the delivery person was.

In early bookkeeping, the bookkeeper exercised broad discretion about what he or she recorded; therefore those manual entries would vary widely from one bookkeeper to the next. One may tally and record goods sold over an entire month, while another bookkeeper may do the same for each day of the week. There was no standard.[4]

Today, most merchants don't produce such data manually. Items come with barcodes that are scanned and data about the item are automatically populated into a software program that describes the item in terms set and favored by the vendor (such as color, weight, and dimensions) and with data points designed in by the software provider (such as the time the scan was made, and so forth). Many companies are moving or have already moved to even more automated processes in which radio frequency identification (RFID) tags automatically trigger data entry into software programs upon arrival in a warehouse, without the need even for a manual scan by a person.[5] But still, it's just data being *produced*.

A digital mindset means that you comprehend the risks that undergird the automated processes we use today to produce data. Regarding inventory and sales, the use of more advanced technologies makes the data production process more accurate: it's much less likely that the scanner or RFID tag will record the wrong data about an item than a person would. However, it also removes the degrees of freedom that individuals have to determine what data they want to produce. The scanners and RFID tags in use in many high-end retailers and distributors come preprogrammed with data fields, as does the software that records the figures produced by the scans. Unless the hardware or software was designed to be configurable by the user, producing the data you want requires negotiating with various vendors.

Becoming analytically nimble means that even with this lack of flexibility, you will find opportunities to produce new data sources from prepopulated fields for your own use. For example, if the software used to track incoming merchandise records a delivery date and a sales date, it's relatively easy to calculate how long the merchandise sat as inventory before it was sold, thus creating a new data point that can be useful for understanding specific facets of the business.

Garbage in, garbage out

Automated data are not free from error or consequence. Computer scientists and data analysts use the phrase (attributed to IBM programmer and instructor George Fuechsel) "garbage in, garbage out." Flawed, useless, or nonsense data produce flawed, useless, or nonsense output: garbage. Having a digital mindset means keeping an eye on the "data in" to make sure they're not garbage.

What's more, in highly automated data production, the consequences of putting garbage in can quickly spiral out of control. For example, in the fall of 2004, an employee logged on to a computer system run and maintained by appraisal officials in Porter County, Indiana, to check on the value of a property in rural Valparaiso. The data were used by a standard algorithm to automatically adjust property appraisals based on values entered by county officials. The property was a twelve-hundred-square-foot, two-bedroom house. No one's quite sure how it happened—the user probably hit the wrong key—but the assessed value of the house was changed from $120,000 to $400 million.[6]

That was the simple garbage in. The garbage out was more complex and consequential than you might imagine. It started with a property tax bill for $8 million received by the homeowner a year later. The homeowner flagged it and got it corrected to the proper amount, a more modest $1,500. Still, before the error was discovered, the assessor's office ran a standard calculation using the data on assessed home values to calculate property tax revenues for the county. This calculation would be used in annual budgeting. The county budget, in turn, was used by eighteen taxing districts in their own budget-planning processes. By the time the data entry error was discovered and corrected, those eighteen taxing districts had already begun to spend their annual budgets. But the budgets they were spending were much higher than was real, because that one house value made it appear they would be collecting much more in property tax than they would.

Officials were forced to return to the county an advance of more than $3 million on funds that were never collected! As a result, the city of Valparaiso had to cancel important infrastructure restoration efforts to complete street resurfacing and sidewalk repairs.

When you recognize that all data are produced by machines and continually touched and reconfigured by people as they go about working with it, you can't help but begin to see that the way we collect our data and how we provide access matters tremendously. Nick Dalton discovered this principle when he realized that the high school basketball player stats from the box scores he collected were not always accurate, making his analytic models useless.

A first step in building analytical insight is to recognize that when we are presented with data, we need to ask how those data were produced, who had access to them, and how well they represent the behavior or activities we hope to understand.

Data are increasingly produced through sensors—think of how your Fitbit or Apple Watch produces data about the number of steps you take or your heart rate, or how heavy mining equipment now comes with an array of sensors that can document how many hours a drill has been in operation or how thin the rubber is on a tractor's tires. Professional sporting leagues are investing heavily in sensors and cameras to collect granular behavioral data on players.[7] The National Basketball Association (NBA) implemented a system with multiple cameras in all of its arenas that can capture granular data on players' movements. These photo- and sensor-based technologies are allowing the NBA to do much more than collect data on free throw attempts and rebounds; they can now track whether players make a break by leading with their right or their left foot and how much their speed has increased or diminished throughout a game. Think of what players like Shane Battier could do with such refined data.

Data are also being produced about us continually as we engage in actions online. As we will discuss in chapter 6 on experimentation, our behaviors and activities online leave a digital exhaust that companies like Google, Amazon, and many others use as data about our viewing patterns and purchasing decisions. Although the behavior and activity collection methods are certainly more sophisticated than manual book-keeping, the data produced today are still prone to the same kinds of errors and misinterpretations that bookkeepers of long ago faced. And they're as vulnerable or more vulnerable to accidents like the one in Indiana, as well as hackers.

Despite data's wondrous potential and power, a digital mindset also respects its fallibility. Learning where the data came from and how they got there means recognizing not only that that data can be flawed or inaccurate, but that we tend to perceive data to have what's called "high facticity." Numbers, especially long strings of numbers automatically generated, can feel true and objective even if they are not. We are all prone to accepting data-driven conclusions, especially if we do not understand the nuances and details of how data work. Better is to develop a digital mindset that recognizes data's limitations and fallibilities.

Open the Black Box of Data Categorization and Analysis

Facility with analytics such that you develop a digital mindset means understanding that data alone don't do much beyond providing description. Description is useful for understanding patterns and trends, like which employees are most productive or when demand for certain products is at its highest.

Data have even more use and power when they move from description to prediction, and then to prescription. The Oakland Athletics used data to predict talent contribution and to prescribe on-field strategies to beat other teams. A school system might use data about its city's real estate sales to predict future student demographics and prescribe students' educational needs. But unlike description, in which the way that data are aggregated into patterns and trends is relatively straightforward and easy to understand, prediction and prescription require data classification, manipulation, and computation that often goes unseen. To most people, the data analytics process is a black box. Data go in one side and out the other side come descriptions and predictions.[8] Building an analytical mindset requires making the black box of analytics as transparent as possible, so you're able to have confidence in the predictions.

In our conversations with people who regularly produce or consume the predictions and prescriptions of the analytics process, we've learned that seeing into the black box means understanding both how data are categorized and how the algorithms that sort data into causal models are constructed.

One of the under-recognized facts of data analytics is that data don't exist apart from the systems we use to classify them. When you think about data as a human invention, created through conceptualization, measurement, storage, and public negotiation, it's easy to see that data carry some political ramifications. One of our favorite examples, as reported by professors Geoffrey Bowker and Susan Leigh Star in their book, *Sorting Things Out: Classification and Its Consequences*, is the publicly reported data that show that Japan has one of the world's lowest rates of fatal heart attacks.[9] Many people point to this statistic to suggest that low levels of fat in the Japanese diet help to reduce heart disease. However, a number of epidemiologists suggest that an alternative reason for such a low rate of fatal heart attacks is that in Japan many heart attacks are actually classified as strokes. As Bowker and Star note, heart disease "is a very low status cause of death within Japanese culture, suggesting as it does a life of physical labor and a physical breakdown. Accordingly, what Americans would call heart attacks often get described as strokes, since an overworked brain is more acceptable there." If we reclassify some or all of Japan's stroke data as fatal heart attacks, the country's low rate is no longer a viable statistic—and the Japanese diet may not be as crucial in reducing heart attacks as we'd like to believe. Developing a digital mindset means thinking hard about how the data you use are classified. Basic data literacy means learning how to ask the right questions to ascertain details about what exactly is going on inside that black box.

Count what is being counted

Albert Einstein once said that "not everything that can be counted counts, and not everything that counts can be counted." When it comes to classification, we might add to this adage that what does get counted ends up counting and, of course, what we don't count often doesn't end up counting. Whether things count or not has consequences. Basketball analysts agree that players like Shane Battier that excel in areas not captured (and thus not valued) in traditional categorization schemes lose significant money during salary negotiations throughout their careers because they can't point to data showing areas in which they contribute to the game. Even though someone like Shane Battier might be, as Michael Lewis called him, a "No Stats All-Star," in the conventional data categorization regimes in which basketball operates, he couldn't take that title to the bank. Conversely, some players may land big contracts based on what's in box scores that more modern analysis suggests isn't that important. In other words, what gets counted may count more than it should.

Again, this brings us back to facticity. Because data can easily and often feel innately objective to us is all the more reason to develop a digital mindset that helps us see inside the black box to question its objectivity. As these examples reveal, even though we might do our best to be accurate in how we measure and collect data points about behavior, the way we classify the data we collect is always a socially informed decision and therefore subjective rather than objective. Today, we largely leave the classification process up to the companies that create the software that tracks the data we input. But those classification schemes are neither natural nor neutral. In fact, they are often the source of much conflict and consternation for data scientists. A contemporary case in point is Netflix's *Napoleon Dynamite* problem.

Understand categorization schemes

Netflix is well known for its advanced use of data analytics. Because Netflix can't sustain monthly subscription pricing if a customer only watches one or two movies or shows a month, they have to get customers to realize that many appealing options exist on the streaming service. Netflix's success in doing so is largely attributable to its early machine learning recommendation engine called CineMatch. CineMatch analyzed customers' viewing habits and recommended other content that the customer might enjoy. If you viewed a dystopian action movie, Netflix would recommend other dystopian movies, other action movies, and other dystopian action movies. If you viewed an animated release from Pixar, Netflix would recommend other animated movies—and so on.

At the core of CineMatch's analytic architecture was an algorithm that classified movies into various categories (action, dystopian, animation, Pixar, and more) representing a film's attributes. This categorization scheme was then submitted to machine learning algorithms that performed a technique called "singular value decomposition." The technique worked by comparing the categories that two movies had in common and correlating those categories to ratings given by users in order to make a prediction that a viewer will like the recommended movie because he or she liked a similarly categorized movie in the past. The analytics were quite robust. Singular value decomposition had a much higher likelihood of predicting what movies a person would decide to watch than simpler techniques like "collaborative filtering," which basically recommended movies to you liked by other people who've liked some of the same movies as you.

But singular value decomposition had flaws and weaknesses. In 2007 Netflix launched a competition, promising to award $1 million to the person or team who could improve its categorization scheme enough to make CineMatch's predictions 10 percent more accurate. Len Bertoni, a computer scientist who lived outside Pittsburgh, solved part of the problem by figuring that if he could predict whether you'd like the movie *Napoleon Dynamite* as accurately as he could for other movies, he would get closer to winning the prize. *Napoleon Dynamite* was a 2004 cult hit that people tend to either love or hate. Its 2 million Netflix reviews are polarized between many five-star scores and many one-star scores, with far fewer scores in between.[10] It is a quirky film and doesn't hew to many traditional categorizations, thereby making it difficult for CineMatch to produce recommendations for viewers who liked it. Bertoni wanted to figure out an algorithm for *Napoleon Dynamite* that could correctly categorize all these factors.

The CineMatch improvement contest concluded in 2009, and Netflix now uses a group of newer, more advanced algorithms, but the categorization problem still haunts the company as well as many others who use data to derive predictions and descriptions that will affect people's behaviors. As confusing as the process is, the lesson for developing a digital mindset is rather clear: Seeing inside the black box of analytics requires understanding how things are categorized, why they are categorized that way, and when categorization simply won't work. Once you understand the categorization schemes that are being used to build predictive and prescriptive models, the next step to seeing inside the black box of the analytic process is to have a sense of what kind of statistics are being used to establish correlational and causal relations between categories and activities. We'll discuss how you develop this competence in chapter 4.

Beware of bias

A corollary to the garbage rule is "bias in, bias out." Looking inside the black box is also essential for making sure that the predictions and pre- scriptions you're making are not inherently biased. The most well- intentioned engineer can build a model for an algorithm intended to serve society as a whole but end up reinforcing structural inequalities that are embedded in the data sets used to build the model. For example, the city of Boston used a well-designed app called Street Bump to solve the city's persistent pothole problem. The app records accelerometer data from smartphones as a resident drives, producing data that suggested the car just hit a pothole. However, since the residents with smartphones tended to be of higher income, it only was identifying potholes in more affluent neighborhoods. When Boston's Office of New Urban Mechanics discovered the data bias problem, the approach was immediately adapted to represent the city as a whole—not just its wealthy.[11]

In another example, MIT Media Lab researcher Joy Buolamwini and Timnit Gebru, who was a doctoral student at Stanford University at the time, published a study called "Gender Shades" that revealed the inher- ent gender and racial biases within facial recognition software built on data predominately representing white males.[12] IBM's system, for instance, was more than 34 percent worse at determining gender for dark-skinned women than light-skinned men. The findings shattered IBM's claims of the system's accuracy, along with similar claims from Microsoft and others (see figure 3-1).

Sarah Brayne, a professor of sociology at the University of Texas at Aus- tin, spent nearly a decade tracing how the Los Angeles Police Department (LAPD) used advanced data algorithms to identify "hot spots" where crime typically occurred or predict where crime was likely to occur and also to identify "chronic offenders" and target them for surveillance.[13]

Operation LASER, or Los Angeles Strategic Extraction and Restora- tion, maintains an ongoing list of community residents to monitor by cre- ating "Chronic Offender Bulletins" for so-called persons of interest.[14] Each of the sixteen LAPD divisions using the program is required to maintain at least a dozen bulletins, intended to help officers identify the most active

FIGURE 3-1

Gender bias in facial recognition software

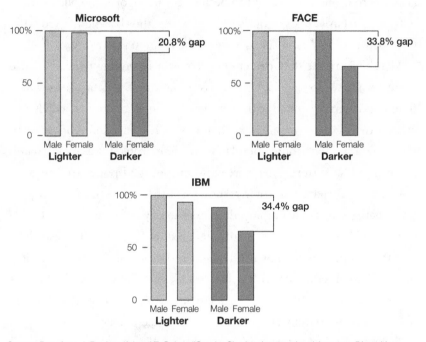

Source: Data from J. Buolamwini and T. Gebru, "Gender Shades: Intersectional Accuracy Disparities in Commercial Gender Classification," in *Conference on Fairness, Accountability and Transparency, PMLR* (January 2018): 77–91.

violent chronic offenders in a given geographical area. It's easy to believe in what looks and sounds like an accurate and reasonable strategy.

However, that identification process has two stages. In the initial screening phase, a crime intelligence analyst subjectively decides whether the police records, like arrest reports and field interview cards, associated with an individual are "relevant" enough to move them to a "workup" phase. This is where human bias begins to influence the so-called objectivity of data; clearly, not all crime analysts will reach the same subjective conclusion about which individuals are or are not relevant enough to include. The second stage, the workup, involves software provided by a data analytics company called Palantir that pulls data from multiple sources on identified people's criminal history and affiliations, their social media networks, and other sources. It uses that data to create a "chronic offender score" for the individual. As Brayne observes, when the data analytics algorithm directs officers to specific areas, such as a low-income area where crime is predicted to be higher, the algorithm collects more data points than it does in more affluent areas, thus biasing the model in favor of directing them back to low-income areas in the future.

Here's where the data can create a circular reasoning process. Police presence in low-income neighborhoods results in more data points, which then puts them in contact with more low-income individuals, which creates more police records, which then have a higher likelihood of accumulating into the chronic offender score. The problem was exacerbated by economics. Austerity measures also encouraged police to find ways to be more efficient with their resources, which led to the LASER program being selectively employed across the city. To save money, LAPD never used LASER in the most affluent areas of LA, which have the lowest crime. This means that residents in those neighborhoods were less likely to have interactions with police, less likely to show up on the LAPD's watchlists, and less likely to have a chronic offender score than people in low-income neighborhoods. The vicious cycle persists.

Brayne's findings starkly illustrate how subjective data analysis can be because of its reliance on human bias. Yet the complexity and multistep process of the analysis can make bias difficult to detect. Developing a digital mindset, as Brayne did, means having the patience to tease out the details of who is doing what part of the analysis and how bias and its unintended consequences can lead us to faulty conclusions.

Machine learning analysis can perpetuate human bias. The department also uses a data analytics service called PredPol, which relies on a machine learning algorithm much like the ones used by Facebook and Amazon for advertising purposes. It's a mathematical model that inputs three variables: where a crime was committed, when it was committed, and what type of crime it was. The model is used to calculate hot spots in a 150-square-meter area where, theoretically, certain types of crimes are more likely to be committed on a given day and which patrol officers use to plan out their daily routes.

These biases in the collection and analysis of data have major consequences for prediction that demonstrate how technologies like PredPol can reinforce racially biased policing patterns and practices. To test this bias, researchers William Isaac and Kristian Lum used a publicly available version of PredPol's algorithm of reported crime data from Oakland in 2010 to predict where crimes would occur in 2011.[15] Then they compared their prediction map to what actually went on in Oakland. If the data weren't biased, the maps would be similar. But in fact, the test using PredPol directed police to Black neighborhoods like West Oakland instead of zeroing in on where drug crime had actually occurred.

The researchers also compared PredPol's map to a map of where Oakland police arrested people for drug crimes. They found that the maps were very similar. Regardless of where crime was happening, predominantly Black neighborhoods had about two hundred times more drug arrests than other Oakland neighborhoods. In other words, police in Oakland are already doing what PredPol's map suggested—over-policing Black neighborhoods—rather than zeroing in on where drug crime is happening. "If you were to look at the data and where they're finding drug crime, it's not the same thing as where the drug crime actually is," Lum said in an interview. "Drug crime is everywhere, but police only find it where they're looking."

As you can see, the social and political ramifications of bias in reading and using data can be enormous. Would police practice change if they were made to review the difference between PredPol's analytic model and the maps created to show where drug use actually occurred? Perhaps, but it would require a developed digital mindset that could understand both the human bias that plays into data production and the consequences of relying on data produced from that bias.[16]

Match Your Data Visualizations with Your Audience's Needs

Every urban area in the United States with a population of more than fifty thousand is required to establish a Metropolitan Planning Organization (MPO), which produces comprehensive regional plans that municipal governments approve. While these plans are not legally binding, they serve as a guide for regional governance that concerns transportation and land use development.

We spent over two years working with two MPOs in different regions of the United States, which we'll call Oceanside and Mountainside. Both were embarking upon a new data-intensive process using simulation models to make predictions that would inform their regional plans. Both regions adopted a new algorithmically based simulation technology called UrbanSim.

UrbanSim was developed by UC Berkeley professor Paul Waddell and his colleagues to make predictions about the effects of policy choices, and to do so through analytic models that were as transparent as possible, thereby avoiding concerns commonly voiced in urban planning that "black-box" models were so complex that their logic could not be explained to policy makers or the public.[17] The comparison of these two regions illustrates another point someone with a digital mindset understands: Data don't speak for themselves. How you present the results of your analytics matters immensely in whether people believe them or not and whether they're willing to trust them or use them to make decisions.

Oceanside planners brought UrbanSim to the center of their discussions with community groups by showing the technology's 3-D visualizations. With the click of a few buttons, planners could show a simulation of areas detailed enough to show specific buildings. It could show how regions changed over time. The visualization put viewers in the heart of the action. It was common in meetings for community members to blurt out comments such as "I know that street" or "That's my neighborhood" as they watched the animation play. As one community member noted after seeing the model in action: "Those changes are amazing. You can just see them happening. I feel like I'm right there. I can't wait for those improvements. The city is going to be so much better." The richness of the visuals of the UrbanSim animations immersed viewers in them. (See figure 3-2.) And for many spectators the model stopped appearing as though it represented a possible future that could happen (if the right policy changes were made and the assumptions embedded

FIGURE 3-2

Oceanside approach: Still shot from 3-D animation of model produced by UrbanSim

Source: Courtesy of UrbanSim, https://urbansim.com.

in the model were accurate) and started appearing as though it were the future that would come to pass. Although in this case people were responding to visual rather than numerical representations of data, again it demonstrates our tendency to believe in data's facticity; if the data *seem* convincing they must be true.

The level of detail combined with the sensory 3-D experience immersed viewers in the projection and evoked embodied, emotional responses. If the projection looked less dense than they feared ("not at all like Manhattan") they were soothed, but if the high-rises they disliked appeared, they reacted with negative emotions. Planners repeatedly brought up the challenge of managing emotional outbursts at public meetings. The simulation of high-rise buildings, what one anti-density activist called "stack-and-pack housing," elicited a strong, embodied response from stakeholders. Furious people from diverse backgrounds filled public comment periods to complain about anticipated school crowding, traffic jams, and depleted water resources.

FIGURE 3-3

Mountainside approach: Graph derived from data from UrbanSim model

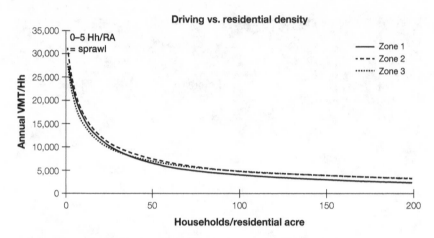

Driving vs. residential density

Source: UrbanSim, https://urbansim.com.

Mountainside chose not to produce 3-D animations for their meetings. Their stakeholders saw only charts, graphs, and tables, such as the graph presented in figure 3-3. A transportation modeler described his work to us as "mostly charts and graphs. I like charts and graphs, but 90 to 95 percent of my work can be monotonous, just looking at spreadsheets a lot, managing stuff, cleaning stuff up."

Mountainside planners had very good "people skills," but their charts and graphs lacked the richness, intrigue, and logical sequencing of 3-D visualizations. As one stakeholder from a tribal community group noted, "The planners do their best, but you kind of lose your attention. It's just boring looking at all those numbers." Planners understood this sentiment well. As Alison, a Mountainside planner, commented, charts and graphs were inherently limiting because they lacked a sense of intuitiveness that other visuals could provide. In addition, making charts and graphs of specific issues of concern (such as the relationship between housing density and driving distance illustrated in figure 3-2) artificially isolated what were actually many interdependent issues. Viewers of charts and graphs had to try themselves to integrate multiple data points and often had difficulty doing so. As one community member noted, "When you see so many different graphs you don't really know how they all go together and I don't really feel like I see what's going to happen." Unlike in Oceanside, people here didn't see the future of their community through UrbanSim.

You might read this description and conclude that Oceanside's 3-D representation of algorithmic models was more successful than Mountainside's because it resulted in higher levels of stakeholder participation. Yet our finding shows the opposite. At Oceanside, stakeholders were highly engaged but about issues that planners did not feel were productive. The high levels of granularity and immersion offered by the models focused people's attention on very specific issues as opposed to big-picture issues that needed public comment and reflection. At Mountainside, where, by contrast, models were not granular or immersive, stakeholders found it difficult to comment on and react to specific outcomes in the model, so they moved their discussions to a higher level of abstraction and asked big-picture questions about the overall plan and its objectives.

Research on what psychologists call *construal levels* points to why such a paradox existed and why it endured.[18] When individuals are psychologically distant from something, they construe that object at a higher, more abstract level than they do if they are psychologically closer to it. This dynamic is also true if an event is hypothetical. One study by Cheryl Wakslak, a professor at the University of Southern California, and her colleagues found that when people were asked to think about an upcoming camping trip, they grouped the objects they would pack for the trip into much more specific and concrete categories if they were told the trip was very likely to happen than if they were told the camping trip was unlikely.[19] Oceanside residents felt a closer psychological distance to what might happen. Indeed they experienced a future they literally could see and were more likely to believe it would happen. They found themselves lost in the details of their response in a forum that was meant to guide a higher, big-picture discussion. In contrast, Mountainside residents were free to imagine important issues such as density in any way they chose. They weren't reacting to a single, visible future. So they felt a more distant psychological distance to hypothetical changes, making those predictions seem less likely, and could therefore engage in more abstract discussions.

What this means, and this is key for developing a digital mindset, is that *presenting more or more detailed data isn't always better.* It may create the wrong discussions and distract from the important analysis.[20] This is especially crucial as technology makes it easier and easier to collect and present enormous quantities of data in visceral detail, as the Oceanside planners did.

More specifically, professor Batia Wiesenfeld, a management scholar at New York University, and her colleagues have speculated that it may be easier to move from more abstract mental representation, as Mountainside urban planners did, to the more concrete representations that Oceanside planners presented than the other way around.[21] This means you may need to figure out ways to encourage participation when your data model representations are less immersive at first so as to help people operate at abstract levels and then shift, over time, to representations that are more immersive and that activate concrete response and discussion.

You've taken an important step in developing your digital mindset by thinking about data, a topic that might at first seem basic and unimportant. Data are just numbers and stuff we store in computer files, right? No. Data are an artifice. Something we produce. And once you think of it that way you see its power and pitfalls much more clearly. You're able to think critically about data and not fall prey to their facticity, or the sense that it must be true because it's numbers.

You're ready for the next step, thinking about the math behind data—thinking about statistics.

GETTING TO 30 PERCENT

Constructing Facts

Data and their use permeate nearly every facet of life. Understanding the basic principles of data analysis is key to developing a digital mindset:

- Data are *produced* and are the product of what we choose to capture and agree to categorize.

- Errors in what data we input can have unintended consequences; the tiniest of errors can sometimes create enormous failures.

- Data classification is a socially informed decision. Because discrepancies in classification can lead to misnomers or erroneous decisions, you need to think hard about how a data set is classified.

- Classification schemes that use complex algorithms to predict behavior, such as Netflix's singular value decomposition, are highly influential but not entirely accurate; here is where data scientists focus much of their attention.

- Developing a digital mindset that can critically analyze the data means becoming aware of how bias, existing in both humans and the machines who learn from the data we give them, can skew our notion of what is true and accurate. Data confirm rather than compensate for racial or other bias.

- Data don't speak for themselves. Tell the story of your findings so their meaning is clear and relevant.

- Technology provides us with sophisticated options for data sharing, so you want to think about how much or how little data you provide people in any given situation, and in what format. We have emotional responses to how data are represented. Learn to match your data representation with your specific audience.

Developing all these facets of a digital mindset helps you to work with data's inherent subjectivity and avoid the common pitfall of believing in what can feel like data's inherent and objective facticity.

4

Drunks and Lampposts

It's Time to Become Conversant
in Statistics

Imagine if the key to your extraordinary success could be found in data sitting right in front of you. All you need to unlock that success is to know the right questions to ask of the data and to understand the responses they give.

Developing a digital mindset means using data to advance your goals and develop an intuitive sense of underlying patterns in data that can work for you. *Having* data isn't an issue. There's an abundance of it that would be hard for previous generations to fathom. *Interpreting* the data and drawing conclusions from them are what you need to do. You want to use data as evidence that drives sound decisions and strategies.

Often, this requires statistics. Even if you are not conducting statistical analyses, you need to know how that's done so you can provide directives to the team that will help you uncover the right information you need in your work. In this chapter, we will provide the minimum threshold of computational material you need to understand about statistics to develop your digital mindset.

Historically, statistics has gotten a bad reputation as something people use to twist data into saying what they need it to say. There's a famous saying, often attributed to the Scottish novelist and folklorist Andrew Lang that's a good reminder of the perils of statistical reasoning. It goes, "Statistics are used much like a drunk uses a lamppost, for support, not illumination."[1] Of course, that's the very antithesis of having a digital mindset. While it's true that numbers can be twisted or misinterpreted, resulting in erroneous conclusions, or manipulated to bolster weak arguments, that's all the more reason for you to have a basic understanding of it—to spot the distortions and mistakes. You don't need to become an expert statistician, but once you have collected data, statistical analyses can be a powerful tool to make sense of what is otherwise a confusing morass. If you are one of the many people who believe that the study of statistics is overly confusing, boring, or intimidating, we are here to tell you not to worry. Statistics is just this: math used to analyze numerical or quantitative data. Understanding what types of statistics are available for what purposes will enable you to glimpse the reality of what interests you. You may even find it fun.

Whether you choose to learn how to run statistical analyses or not, there is one key prerequisite to developing a digital mindset with statistics: you must think like a data detective. Good detectives ask the right questions to get the answers they need. Good detectives observe what they see and pay attention to details. Sometimes you might need to come up with a reasoned conclusion from a hypothesis, which will require you to ask for certain types of data collection. Other times, you will need to take observational data and work backward to a plausible hypothesis.

To get to 30 percent with statistics, let's start by understanding two types: descriptive statistics and inferential statistics.

Descriptive Statistics: What Are the Underlying Patterns in the Data?

Suppose you started a streaming platform: How would you learn how your customers use your service? You might begin by collecting data about your customers' usage preferences, including when they logged in and for how long. This information would give you a measure of your service's performance. Spotify, a Swedish audio streaming and media service, measures performance in this way. But it's the use of statistics that enables the company to detect answers to questions about *how* their customers use their service. For example, is usage going up or down each month and by how much? How does it differ from last year? Spotify used statistics to learn that in 2017, their users played an average of 630 audio streams per month (up from 438 in 2015).[2] In 2019, average revenue per user (ARPU) was $5.32 USD (down from $5.51 in 2018).[3] To discover this information, Spotify needed to run some *descriptive statistics*.

Descriptive statistics summarize the features of a data set. They describe the data.

Once you are able to see the patterns of the raw data, descriptive statistics can represent that data in useful ways. You may have experienced descriptive statistics in assessing an organization's past performance, since that is an area where they are commonly used. Key performance indicators (KPIs) across all aspects of a business, from sales to human resources, are descriptive statistics in action.

Amazon uses descriptive statistics to determine the demographic characteristics of its customer base and then measures those findings against averages of the overall population in order to determine the average customer age and the average customer income. They can build a profile of the typical user and keep building it to see how it evolves and how it compares to other groups. In a November 2019 report, the data showed that Amazon customers tended to be younger and have a lower income than the average US consumer.[4]

Spotify and Amazon were able to understand their customers' characteristics and needs by analyzing descriptions of their past behaviors as collected in the data. Such statistics could then inform all sorts of business decisions and initiatives.

The trick with descriptive statistics is to know which ones matter. There are plenty to create and analyze, and plenty will look like they might mean something you need to know, but not all do. To figure out what was statistically important, companies like Spotify use summary statistics that focus on two main features of a data set: *central tendency* and *dispersion*. Let's look at each in turn.

Central tendency

These statistics describe where the values of a data set tend to land. The most common measure of central tendency is the mean, or the average of a data set (each value of the data added together, then divided by the number of values). Other measures are median (the value that falls at the midpoint of all your data), and the mode (the most common value in the range of data). In the examples above, both Spotify and Amazon analyzed for central tendency statistics. For example, Amazon looks at average or mean number of purchases in a time period. Spotify looks at the most common genre streamed (the mode).

Dispersion

These statistics analyze how the data are spread out. Measurements of dispersion can be as simple as the range of the data (the difference between the highest value and the lowest value). Other more complex measurements are variance (an estimate of the distance of each value from the mean) and standard deviation (a measure of how spread out the data are from the mean).

For example, suppose you wanted to know how engaged your employees were at work. The 2018 Gallup poll defines employee engagement by asking employees the extent to which employees are involved in, enthusiastic about, and committed to their workplace.[5] They found that the annual percentage of engaged US workers in the past two decades has ranged from a low of 26 percent to a high of 34 percent in 2018—a measure of dispersion—and averaged out at 30 percent, a measure of central tendency. Ultimately, they used these statistics to show that the higher percentages in employee engagement are associated with higher business performance for the organization.

In developing your digital mindset around statistics, remember that descriptive statistics are a method of finding the underlying patterns in data. Depending on what you want to know, the same data can be used to answer many different questions. Spotify could also run the numbers to describe which song was downloaded the most frequently, for example, or compare which song was most frequently downloaded depending on the season. Amazon could analyze the same data to describe the range of incomes of their customers or compare that range with geographical data to describe which locales tended to have the most customers. The possibilities are nearly endless.

Inferential Statistics: What Conclusions Can We Draw from the Data?

While descriptive statistics summarize the underlying patterns of data that have already been collected, inferential statistics examine the data from a relatively small subset of the total population—called a *sample* set—that might reflect the nature of the broader population. For example, the Gallup poll about employee engagement only asks a tiny fraction of all US workers how they feel, but then draws inferences from those responses that apply to the entire population.

In order for a sample to reliably represent a bigger population, the people that comprise the data set must be selected randomly—that is, pulled from the overall population without any preconceived criteria. For example, you could ask a sample of 500 people that you see in the mall if they like shopping at the Apple store. If 250 people say "Yes," and 250 people say, "No," you can *infer* that 50 percent of the population in all malls like shopping at the Apple store.

Think of inferential statistics as the method that allows you to draw statistical conclusions and make predictions without collecting data from everyone you are trying to understand. The auto insurance company Geico wanted to determine the level of risk for a potential customer. One of the first questions that the company website's risk calculator asks is marital status.[6] A married driver is considered a lower risk and given lower premiums. How did Geico reach this conclusion? Their policy is based on inferential statistics—the available data show that married people on average get into fewer accidents than unmarried people. Geico used the sample set to infer that this average reflects the population as a whole.[7]

What if your company wants to determine the likelihood that consumers will buy from you? Inferential statistics are often used for this purpose. Consider the work of startup Embr Labs, which produces an innovative wrist-wearable device that regulates an individual's body temperature.[8] The estimated demand for the product was initially based on statistics from a UC Berkeley study that analyzed the relationship between people's personal comfort and room temperature. Relying on the statistical evidence from the study's sample data, Embr inferred that demand for a product regulating body temperature would be high for a population of consumers much broader than those actually studied at UC Berkeley.[9]

We make inferences all the time. If rain is predicted, we infer we will need an umbrella when we go out. Learning to use numerical insights to inform a digital mindset means fine-tuning this natural way we think. Technically speaking, there are two main approaches used to draw inferences from a sample: *confidence intervals* and *hypothesis testing*.

Confidence Intervals: How Reliable Is My Inference?

It's easy to say that because 30 percent of people say they're engaged at work in a survey that means 30 percent of *all* workers are engaged at work, but how sure are you that what a few people said in a survey applies to everyone?

That's what confidence intervals are used for: to assess the reliability of our inferential statistics. They are used in market research, risk assessment, or budget forecasting. Election forecasts derived from polled sample sets of the voting public are an inference we see regularly in politics that have confidence intervals attached to them.

Another way to think about it is that a confidence interval describes the plausibility of the range of values of summary statistic like an average in the overall population. If you were completely certain that our inference would play out in a broader population you would have a 100 percent confidence interval. Conversely, if you think your inference is wrong, you'd have a 0 percent confidence interval. A 50 percent interval is effectively a guess.

In practice you don't see confidence intervals like this. The most commonly used confidence interval is a "95 percent confidence interval" because this number represents a comfortable balance between precision and reliability. A 99 percent confidence interval may appear to be more reliable, but it would necessarily have a much wider range of possible values and therefore be less useful.

For example, we could say with 99 percent confidence that the average age of MBA students is between eight and eighty, but that wide a variance in ages wouldn't be saying much, would it? Alternatively, we could calculate a 90 percent confidence interval indicating that the average age of MBA students is between twenty-seven and thirty, but there is a greater possibility that this range is inaccurate because it's too narrow; some students may in fact be twenty-five or thirty-two or thirty-five years old. The range of a confidence interval depends on the variance in the data set. Higher variance in the data—as in our theoretical MBA population of students aged eight to eighty—limits our ability to draw inferences about the greater population, and results in a wider range of values for the confidence interval. Variance in the data that is too low also limits our ability to draw meaningful inferences.

Consider the example of a McKinsey study on the business value of diversification—companies entering into new industries. From a sample of over forty-five hundred companies, the study found that diversification in emerging markets led to a higher average value for companies than did diversification in developed markets. Note, however, the confidence intervals for each of these averages. The -0.2 percent decrease in average value for diversification in developed markets has a relatively tight 95 percent confidence interval, while the 3.6 percent average value increase for diversification in emerging markets has a much wider 95 percent confidence interval. In other words, the study is *more* confident that the statistics showing a small decrease of value (0.2 percent) in developed markets are true for all companies across the world, and *less* confident inferring that the larger increase of value (3.6 percent) in developing markets is actually true for all companies across the world.[10]

Becoming comfortable with the statistical insights a digital mindset affords is more about having the vocabulary to understand the different relationships between numbers than memorizing percentages or specific numbers. Having the vocabulary to describe these basic concepts means you will be able to discern, for example, if you have cause to doubt statistical conclusions that have been drawn from a sample size because it has too wide or too narrow a confidence interval.

Hypothesis Testing: How Do I Compare Statistical Evidence?

A digital mindset informed by numerical insights can also ask questions by comparing two or more pieces of statistical evidence. Are people more likely to purchase your product in the winter or the summer? Do teams that contain an equal number of men and women do better than teams that contain an unequal gender distribution? To answer questions like these using statistics requires that you use a methodical process called hypothesis testing. The basic format for hypothesis testing compares two summary statistics (or *parameters*) in a set or multiple sets of data. The test starts with what's called a *null hypothesis*, most often a conservative position that assumes the status quo. It then proposes an *alternative hypothesis*. If there is enough statistical evidence to support the alternative hypothesis, the null hypothesis is rejected in favor of the alternative. However, if there is not enough statistical evidence, the null hypothesis remains.

Let's create a hypothesis test for the actual average age of Harvard MBA students based on the data from a sample of thirty students. Let's say the average age of the sample is twenty-six, and you come across an article online stating that the average age of MBA students at top business schools is twenty-eight. Does this mean that the average age of all Harvard MBAs is actually different from the overall average of MBAs at top programs? Not necessarily—remember, the sample set represents only a portion of the Harvard MBAs; the overall student body may actually have an average age that is different than twenty-six.

Indeed, as the statistic found online seems to imply, the average of the overall MBA student population could very well actually be twenty-eight. That average comes from a much bigger sample set (students at multiple MBA programs rather than just the thirty Harvard MBA students), so let's take twenty-eight as the baseline assumption and test it. A hypothesis test can assess the likelihood that the average age of the thirty MBA students is twenty-eight or in fact different, as your sample set indicates.

First, formulate a null hypothesis: "The average age of Harvard MBA students is twenty-eight." Then, propose the alternative hypothesis: "The average age of Harvard MBA students is NOT twenty-eight." Now calculate the probability of seeing the average age in your sample set—twenty-six—*under the assumption that the hypothesis test is true.* In other words, you are asking how likely it is that you would see an average age of twenty-six in your sample set of thirty Harvard MBAs if the average age of all Harvard MBAs is actually twenty-eight. If you find that probability is very low, you can reject the null hypothesis in favor of the alternative hypothesis. However, if, for example, you calculate a 2 percent chance of seeing an average age of twenty-six in your sample set of thirty students if the actual average of the overall student population is twenty-eight, that's some pretty convincing statistical evidence in favor of your alternative hypothesis. You may conclude that, statistically, the average age of a Harvard MBA is likely to be twenty-eight, in keeping with the larger sample size. Again, hypothesis testing is a very specific method of statistical analysis. Understanding how such a method can provide numerical insights is part of developing your digital mindset.

A classic use of hypothesis testing is *A/B testing,* a methodology used in marketing and product development for digital products such as apps and websites that we will discuss more in chapter 6.[11] A/B testing compares user response to two variations (A and B) of a specific product in order to determine which version is more effective. In a standard A/B test, the null hypothesis would be that versions A and B have the same usage rate. The alternative hypothesis would be that version B (an experimental variation of the product) attracts more users than version A (the current version of the product). The test would then calculate the probability of observing the usage rate of version B under the premise that the null hypothesis is true. Let's take a look at two examples of how A/B testing has led to highly successful marketing campaigns and products.

Electronic Arts (EA) is one of the largest video game companies in the world. Their *SimCity* games allow players to build cities from scratch. For *SimCity 5*, released in 2013, EA used A/B testing to create an effective online marketing campaign. Version A of the game's web page offered anyone who bought *SimCity 5* 20 percent off a future EA game purchase. Version B of the page did not offer the discount on future purchases but did give users the ability to preorder *SimCity 5*. Surprisingly, the version *without* the discount incentive performed 40 percent better than the preorder version. The A/B testing showed EA that *SimCity* customers, contrary to the alternative hypothesis, were not as interested in other game options as some might expect; most customers were there specifically for the *SimCity* franchise.[12] The null hypothesis remains. In this case, the testers were digitally minded when they compared customer responses to the A/B offers. The marketers were also digitally minded when they relied on the results of A/B testing to guide their selling strategy.

In another example, HubSpot, a software development company specializing in marketing, sales, and customer service software products, used A/B testing to determine the best design for a search bar at the top of its web page. The test was composed of three versions of search bars (A, B, and C). In Version A, the search bar included the text "Search by Topic" and provided results from across the entire HubSpot site. Version B had the same text but provided results only from within the blog instead of the entire site. Version C changed the text of the search bar to "Search the Blog" and provided results for only the blog. The results of the test showed that usage rate was highest in Version C.[13]

In the *SimCity* and HubSpot examples, the data, once collected and analyzed, offered evidence for the best possible choice. EA could conclude that there was no benefit in offering customers a discount on future games when selling the new *SimCity*. HubSpot could conclude that search bar text "Search the Blog" would lead to higher usage than the other two versions. If you were reviewing these conclusions, you would also want to ask how high or low the numerical difference between the data results has to be before rejecting or accepting the null or alternative hypothesis. In that case, you would want to know about the *p-value*, which refers to the probability of observing the statistics in a sample data set if you assume that the given null hypothesis is true. A smaller p-value means there is stronger evidence in favor of the alternative hypothesis, while a *significance level* is the designated threshold that marks the maximum limit that a p-value can be before you say it is too high to reject the null hypothesis in favor of the alternative. A common significance level is 0.05: if the p-value is below 0.05, then you reject the null hypothesis in favor of the alternative. If the p-value is above 0.05, then you reject the alternative and retain the null.

Possibility of Being Wrong

We love how Larry Gonick and Woolcott Smith describe the possibility of being wrong when making statistical inferences. You can never say you are "100 percent confident" about a data sample representing the properties of an overall population precisely because you want to acknowledge the fact that you could be wrong. Gonick and Smith use the analogy of smoke detectors to describe the two types of errors that you can anticipate in hypothesis testing and significant tests. They call the first a type I error, an alarm without fire (or a false positive). The second, referred to as type II error, is fire without an alarm (a false negative). "Every cook knows how to avoid a type I error: just remove the batteries. Unfortunately, this increases the incidence of type II errors! Similarly reducing the chance of a type II error, for example by making the alarm hypersensitive, can increase the number of false alarms.[14]

Type I error: An alarm without fire

Type I error is an outright rejection of the null hypothesis when it is actually true. Consider the ramifications of this error in the example of EA's *SimCity* video game sales page. What if the null hypothesis that favored the presale offer page (version A) was actually true after all? Then EA would lose potential sales revenue by choosing version B, which seemed more effective based on available (and apparently misleading) data. If we want to reduce the likelihood of committing a type I error, we can lower the significance level (for example, to 0.01), making it even more difficult to reject the null hypothesis. However, this cautionary approach increases the likelihood of a type II error.

Type II error: Fire without an alarm

Type II error is failing to reject the null hypothesis when the alternative is true. For example, let's imagine that HubSpot's A/B test for the search bar on its blog page led to the mistaken conclusion that their original design and functionality for the search bar remained the most effective. This mistake would prevent HubSpot from adopting the new version of the search bar, which in fact had a higher usage rate. To reduce the likelihood of this error, we can raise the significance level (for example, to 0.10) to make it easier to reject the null hypothesis. However, this more flexible approach increases the likelihood of committing a type I error and moving forward with data that are actually meaningless or misleading. See table 4-1 for a breakdown of these errors (H_0 is "null hypothesis" and H_A is "alternative hypothesis").

This possibility of error, either in reasoning or numerical calculation, and the fact that we must make decisions with the knowledge of their possibility is perhaps what gives credence to the quote about "lies, damned

TABLE 4-1

Outcomes based on four hypothesis scenarios

	Fail to reject H_0 (null hypothesis: no fire)	Reject H_0 (null hypothesis) in favor of H_A (alternative hypothesis: fire)
H_0 is true	Correct decision	Type I error
H_A is true	Type II error	Correct decision

lies, and statistics." A digital mindset means accepting the fact that numbers don't lie but the humans interpreting the numbers may make mistakes. The real error might be in expecting 100 percent accuracy from statistical analysis. Your decision-making will be guided by understanding that the likelihood of each type of error is affected by the relative value of the significance level. Raise it and you increase the chances of a type I error. Push it down and chances of a type II error increase.

Predicting Outcomes with Regressions

A statistically informed digital mindset requires a general understanding of predictive modeling, which could be described as using statistical models to predict outcomes. A common model used to make predictions is the *linear regression* model.[15]

You don't need to run regressions, but you need to understand how they function and when they are important to use. For now, you just need to remember that a regression analyzes the relationship between two or more variables or factors. It is an essential tool for predictive analytics to forecast potential outcomes, opportunities, and risks. Regression is also used to increase operational efficiencies, from product development to hiring practices.

For example, McKinsey wanted to examine if an organization's demographic diversity, defined as "a greater share of women and a more mixed ethnic/racial composition in the leadership of large companies," had an impact on financial performance.[16] The study's model used financial data and leadership demographics from hundreds of organizations and thousands of executives. By placing each organization's financials on the Y axis and its leadership demographics on the X axis, the study sought to determine if higher X values (how diverse the company was) were matched by higher Y values (how well the company was doing).[17] Based on the model, the study found a positive association between a more diverse leadership and financial performance: more diverse leadership teams were in organizations with better financial results. On a chart the dots plotted would literally trend up and to the right. Diversity and performance rose together.

Linear regression is a powerful tool in predicting future sales and demand for a product. For example, if a sales manager can map product demand on customers' annual salary, the manager could then predict the demand of the product based on a specific salary of an individual consumer. A customer with a salary below a certain value would presumably be less likely to buy a particular product. Additionally, too high a product price might lower customer demand.

Another manager could use linear regression if interested in the actual price of kids' shirts as a function of a given year to predict values for future years. These concepts of supply and demand and their relationship to price points are fairly intuitive and have been in existence since before computers came on the scene. With a digital mindset, however, you can access computational power and large data sets to run linear regression models to make predictions that have more accuracy and granularity.

Regression is also a key tool for improving business processes across all aspects of an organization, from operations to human resources. For example, a product developer might use a regression model to determine a possible relationship between the number of software developers on the team and the effectiveness of the product. Questions to ask include: Is there an optimal number of people on such a team? How many software developers are too many? How many are too few? To find the answers requires plotting the number of team members on one axis and a measure of product effectiveness on the other axis and then looking for relationships between the two. The model would help determine how to organize the team to maximize its performance. Or a hiring manager might use a regression model to explore a possible relationship between job candidates' background and qualifications for a role. The model would help refine the manager's search for the right pool of candidates to interview for the job.

Bear in mind, also, that you want to be intelligent about the variables you plot on the X and Y axes. If you were to, for example, use a regression model to conclude your best employees all had names that began with the letter *S*, you would not have optimized meaningful data for future job candidates. Even if that were true, it's random and doesn't inform you about the future. Again, it's a matter of what questions you ask and what you want to know. As is so often the case when using a digital mindset, what's important is to understand the stories the numbers can tell you rather than computing the numbers themselves.

P-value in regression

In the McKinsey diversity study cited above, 366 companies were in the sample set. The analysis shows the statistical significance of the relationship between diversity and financial performance for companies observed in the data. For the executive teams in the data of 366 companies, the EBIT ("Earnings before interest and taxes," a measure of financial performance) margin is predicted to increase by 1.6 percent for every 10 percent increase in the gender diversity metric. The p-value of 0.01 tells us that there is only a 1 percent probability of seeing that coefficient or measure of strength of the relationship between financial performance and gender diversity on the executive board if in actuality there was no relationship between them. In other words, ninety-nine times out of a hundred when you get this result it means diversity correlates to increased performance. The same model was applied to boardroom diversity (as opposed to executive teams) and again found an even stronger connection: EBIT margin should increase by a factor of 3.5 for every 10 percent increase in the gender diversity metric in the boardroom.

However, the corresponding p-value in this case was 0.11, meaning that there is an 11 percent chance of seeing this result even when there was no correlation.

Remember that the lower the p-value, the greater the reliability of the statistical conclusion. In other words, while the predicted increase in financial performance for gender diversity in the boardroom is much higher than it is for gender diversity on executive teams, this prediction is much less reliable.

Correlation vs. causation

In discussing their findings, the authors of the McKinsey diversity study draw a crucial distinction: "The relationship between diversity and performance highlighted in the research is a correlation, not a causal link."[18] Put more simply, the study's regression model can only show that financial performance increases as the level of diversity in leadership increases by a certain factor, on average; it does *not* show that diversity in leadership actually *causes* financial performance to increase. There are many other elements involved (what statisticians would call "confounding variables") that must be considered. Perhaps, for example, more diverse companies tend to be in more developed markets where the EBIT for executives would naturally tend higher. Whenever building a regression model to explore the relationship between two variables, businesses must be wary of mistaking causation for correlation. Fortunately, a relationship does not always have to be causal to be insightful; in most cases, a strong correlation is more than sufficient evidence for drawing valuable insights in business and pursuing a course of action.

Integrate Statistics into Your Digital Mindset

So, that wasn't so bad, right? Just by reading and reviewing this chapter, you have already begun to inform your digital mindset with a basic understanding of statistical concepts and the vocabulary for statistical analysis. You encounter statistics regularly in annual reports, decision-making documents, and in newspaper articles. People often use statistics as evidence to bolster their arguments or to make suggested strategies credible. Developing a digital mindset that can integrate statistics means becoming conversant enough in the language of statistics so as to understand the conclusions drawn from data sets and to form conclusions of your own. As a detective who can ask questions using statistical data, you are likely to put together clues that take some of the mystery out of, for example, product marketing and sales predictions. Statistics can also be used to pose and answer questions about the relationship between data sets—for example, diversity hiring and organizational performance. Sound critical reasoning plays a role when distinguishing between the stories that numbers tell, as in not mistaking cause for correlation or in remembering to scrutinize for p-value. You need statistical analysis to make proper and useful sense of all the data that surround us. Finally, it's important to remember that while numbers don't lie, people make mistakes, especially in the numbers we input or in the way we interpret results. As you continue to develop your digital mindset you will become attuned to the many and various ways that statistical analysis can help drive your success.

GETTING TO 30 PERCENT

Statistical Reasoning

Statistics are tools for analyzing underlying patterns in data. Developing a digital mindset means operating like a curious detective who asks the right questions and recognizes the stories that statistics can tell. Understanding a few basic concepts and terms will go a long way.

Descriptive statistics identify patterns in data:

- Central tendency statistics describe where the values of a data set tend to land (mean, median, mode).

- Dispersion statistics analyze how the data are spread out (range, variance, standard deviation).

Inferential statistics allow you to draw conclusions about a population from a sample set of available data.

Confidence intervals are a range of values that estimate the accuracy of a statistic about a population from the available data.

Hypothesis testing is the process of comparing two assumptions in order to assess the likelihood that a data sample actually reflects the overall population:

- The null hypothesis is the assumption of the status quo (there is no actual difference in the sample set and the overall population).

- The alternative hypothesis refutes the null hypothesis (there in fact is a difference in the sample set and the overall population).

The measurement for assessing these two hypotheses is the p-value:

- A smaller p-value means there is stronger evidence in favor of the alternative hypothesis.

- Significance level is an acceptable threshold for a p-value, past which point we can say that the null hypothesis is more likely than the alternative. A common significance level is 0.05.

Predictive statistics use statistical models to anticipate outcomes.

Regression models analyze the relationship between two or more variables by plotting them on an X and a Y axis.

Distinguish between *correlation* and *causation*, but remember that in business, a strong correlation is more than sufficient evidence for drawing valuable insights and pursuing a course of action.

You don't need to become an expert, but keep in mind that statistical analyses are a necessary and powerful tool to interpret data that can otherwise be confusing or useless. Statistical reasoning is more intuitive than you might think at first glance.

PART THREE

CHANGE

5

Cybersecurity and Privacy

Why You Can't Just Build a Castle

On a warm spring day in 2012 in Dhahran, Saudi Arabia, a computer technician on the information technology team of Saudi Aramco (officially the Saudi Arabian Oil Company) opened an email and clicked on a link. Nothing happened, and he went back to work. A few months later, during the Islamic holy month of Ramadan, when most of the company was away on holiday, a few people at the company began to notice that their computers were acting strangely. Files were disappearing and some machines shut down without any explanation. Within a few hours, thirty-five thousand of the company's computers were partially destroyed. In a rush to mitigate damage, Saudi Aramco's technicians began ripping cables out of the back of computers and servers at data centers across the world. Every office was physically unplugged to prevent the virus from spreading farther. The financial toll of lost connectivity on the world's seventh-highest-revenue company began to stack up quickly. Although oil production continued, domestic trucks seeking refills had to be turned away, and the company's ability to supply 10 percent of the world's oil was suddenly at risk. For weeks, the company resorted to analog communication—typewriters, snail mail, faxing—and eventually began giving away oil for free to keep it flowing within the region. In the end, it took Saudi Aramco five months to build out a new system that they felt confident could be opened to the world. During this time, they flew representatives around the world to buy every computer hard drive coming off production lines. The company paid higher prices to cut in line ahead of all other potential buyers, temporary halting the supply of hard drives to the rest of the world and driving up prices.[1]

Saudi Aramco's crisis was due to a computer virus named "Shamoon" that was ultimately traced to a fairly routine security breach that we will explain later in the chapter. Although not every security problem will have consequences as dire as putting 10 percent of the world's oil at risk, our research and work with companies has taught us that a digital mindset must accept a broad lesson about security in the digital age: You *will* experience security problems. Full stop. Although there are ways to plan in order to reduce the likelihood that computer viruses will infiltrate your systems, that your data or the data of your users will be harvested by third parties, or that records of your transactions will be manipulated, sooner or later there will be a failure and you will have to deal with it. People with a digital mindset will understand this and be prepared to deal with the inevitable security crisis when it occurs. Two of the major questions about digital security you should be asking are: "When will a problem happen?" and "How can I be prepared to respond to it?"

When we ask people to describe how to keep valuables secure, they usually suggest something akin to building a castle. If you want your belongings—say, your gold and silver or most cherished documents—to stay secure in the castle, you make sure the castle walls are tall and well fortified. You need a moat and a drawbridge. You should have armed guards manning a strong portcullis over the main entrance. If you anticipate a security threat, you can deepen the moat or double the guards. In short, if you are like most people you can easily envision beefing up the castle's defenses and—most importantly—you assume there are a finite number of entrances and securing them against most threats is just a matter of good planning.

However, the castle analogy is not useful or accurate when thinking about cybersecurity. For one, data are stored on digital networks that have more than a few ways in and ways out.

Second, the castle analogy might be useful in an analog world where the castle builder owns the thing. But digital ecosystems don't operate that way. You might have tilted up the castle walls by yourself, but you likely bought prefabricated panels from one vendor and placed them atop a foundation that you bought from another vendor. You are likely to employ some of the castle guards, but others you contract from a security vendor who trains them differently. And the water in your moat isn't in your control. As it ebbs and flows, over time it changes the contours of the shore and, sometimes, begins to waterlog the soil on which your foundation rests. In other words, the digital castle is so complicated and the infrastructures on which platforms are built are changing so quickly that even if you could create the ideal defense plan for today, it would be useless tomorrow.

Having a digital mindset means retiring the castle analogy and learning about the dynamism and decentralization of digital ecosystems. It also means recognizing that for all of your best intentions to keep things secure, you have much less control over your own security measures than you think. To understand this process and to develop the right mindset to deal with it, we discuss three key areas of security concern and how you should approach each one in ways that will increase your ability to navigate data security in the uncertain digital world. They are:

- Embrace ecosystem interdependence

- Design for privacy

- Assure data integrity through blockchain

Although you don't have to become a security expert you do need to understand different ways that data can become vulnerable to outside threats so you will be able to make smart decisions that make it less likely for breaches to happen and so you can respond quickly and effectively when they do. We will spend most of this chapter discussing the third area of security concern—data integrity and blockchain—because this is one of the areas in which you have the most control to make proactive changes, and it's also a digital technology about which many people are confused.

Embrace Ecosystem Interdependence

As we discussed in chapter 2, most of the technologies in your stack and all those in the broader ecosystem access your data. It's like your castle has tens or hundreds of entrances that all need to be manned and monitored in different ways. What's more, because the technologies are always changing (and also changing in relation to other technologies they work with), new doors can accidentally open where you didn't expect them, and often they open without anyone noticing. And all of those problems don't even account for the fact that roughly 20 percent of all security vulnerabilities are accidentally created by a company's very own employees who change something in the software configuration or in the stack without fully understanding the repercussions of what they're doing.

Appreciating security requires you to retire another common misconception: digital systems aren't just pieces of hardware or products that are final once they're in use. We've found that most nontechnical people think of digital systems as if they are like desks. Once a desk is built, you probably assume it will be useful and without the need for change for ten to fifteen years no matter the room it's in, how it's used, or how much stuff you put on top of it. Digital technologies are different. Imagine if the material for one leg of the desk was changed every year. If the wooden leg became plastic, the fastener that attaches the leg to the slab would likely not work anymore. Also, the new plastic leg might be less sturdy, which would require installing a brace on the table to keep it steady. What if you wanted to stay with your wooden leg to avoid all that bother? You might not own the leg and would therefore not have much choice. You could possibly find a new leg provider who probably doesn't build legs in your exact size anyway, so you'd have to make other adaptations to the desk. You get the idea!

All digital systems constantly evolve, often in ways that you cannot control.[2] That's why it's important to think of a digital system as an ecosystem consisting of a technology stack that changes and is managed by you and your partners, who change, too. When different companies or businesses control different parts of the stack or different technologies upon which your stack is dependent, you will see the technologies provided by those companies change often—they have to in order to stay relevant and to keep up with the competition. That means that everything you've built on those technologies or built to connect to those technologies will need to be updated too.

To give you an example of how these interdependencies play out, let's look at Twitter, which has had a remarkably strong record for securing its own data and the data of its users but nonetheless has run into a number of problems because of the complexity of its technology ecosystem.

When you take a photo, your smartphone tags that photo with geolocation data indicating where the picture was taken. Twitter does not post this geo data with your pictures or share those data with partners for obvious security reasons. But a bug in the company's iOS app accidentally and unknowingly introduced by programmers who were trying to fix another problem in the software temporarily sent the precise location data of a Twitter photo to a third party.[3] Once the bug was discovered, it was quickly fixed. A second vulnerability occurred when engineers who work on the Android mobile platform were updating code to adjust for the leap year, but somehow the documentation for how to do so wasn't correctly followed, and updated code was misconfigured. Twitter's own internal security measures dictated that if an improper date and time were used in a server call, it should be rejected for fear that the system was being hacked. So, when the Android update went live, Twitter rejected anyone on Android who tried to connect. For sixteen hours, more than two thirds of the Twitter user base on Android were logged out and barred from logging back in.

It would be easy to conclude that Twitter simply didn't fortify its grounds well enough, but consider just some of the players in those ecosystems that affected the security problems: there's Twitter technology itself and its own developers; there's iOS, controlled by Apple; Android, controlled by Google; the people who wrote documentation for the leap year change; also the companies who make the photo apps and the engineers who developed the GPS technology used to tag photos. And on and on.

The reality is that digital companies like Twitter can never secure all their entrances because those entrances are constantly moving. Again, to be digitally minded is to accept that the data you work hard to secure are inevitably going to become vulnerable at some point. It's not a question of if, but when. When you come to terms with this fact, you have to begin to treat security as a risk assessment problem. How much risk are you willing to take on if you rush the development of your product? How much risk are you willing to take on if you buy a component (hardware or software) from a vendor instead of building it yourselves? How much risk are you willing to take on if you don't prioritize updating certain components of your software in favor of building out new functionality?

In addition to making calculated decisions at these choice points, it is important to conduct periodic risk audits to determine where vulnerabilities are or might arise. Making calculated risks is half of the equation. The other half is being prepared to respond to security breaches once they do occur. Developing a plan ahead of time for how resources will be allocated to fix problems, how security breaches will be communicated to customers and stakeholders, and how to be transparent about the problems are all best practices we've seen in our work with successful digital companies to assure that when security problems do eventually arise, you can deal with them responsibly. Which brings us to technical debt.

Budget for Technical Debt

People with a digital mindset understand that you need to constantly update and integrate software with changes made in other parts of the ecosystem. The maintenance of these components in the ecosystem is what engineering managers often refer to as *technical debt*.[4] Technical debt is a phrase originally coined by software developer Ward Cunningham, who in addition to being one of seventeen authors of "The Agile Manifesto," is also credited with inventing the wiki.[5] He first used the term to explain to nontechnical stakeholders at his company why they needed to budget resources for reworking their older technology investments.

That kind of budgeting is not very exciting for most companies who want to invest the money to build new features or products, rather than continually upgrade or future-proof the current offering. It's like home renovations. We'd much rather install new countertops and appliances than spend our money on updating the plumbing or electrical. But if we keep spending our money on the fun stuff and don't invest in the maintenance, eventually pipes will break and circuits will short and we'll have to take on debt to fix the infrastructure emergency. Technical debt is the plumbing and electrical. Good product and engineering managers have long budgeted time and money to update core components of the product on a regular basis so that they continue to work well and the company doesn't find itself one day in a situation in which they are encumbered by so much technical debt that they'll have to stop building out the product to fix things that have been neglected for too long.

To stay on top of technical debt, AppFolio, a successful SaaS company that builds property management software, regularly holds "demolition derbies" where product engineers pitch projects for updating (usually proactively) portions of the stack that they control and fixing known problems in their core products. These demolition derbies, which can sometimes last up to two weeks, are a tool to stay on top of updates that are key to a healthy system. But as VP of engineering Eric Hawkins observes, "Nearly every time we do a demolition derby, several of the teams say they don't need to participate because they've kept on top of their technical debt. They've just been taking care of it in the normal flow of work. That's music to my ears. We make sure to budget time to constantly stay ahead of changes we know we're going to need to make even if it sometimes means slowing down the pace of new software development. If you don't pay your technical debt you're going to have major problems down the road."[6]

Additionally, you have to constantly think about how you are going to stay on top of changes in the systems provided by others on which you're dependent. If you need an example of how technical debt can quickly accrue, look no further than Apple's App Store. Each year thousands of apps introduced in the prior few years fail and vanish from the platform. That's because you can't just build an app and expect it to live forever. As the platform provider, Apple constantly changes its requirements for application performance. The mobile operating systems on which the apps run change, too. So does the hardware in the phones or computers on which those operating systems run. All of this means that app developers have to constantly refactor (a term software developers use when they refer to rewriting parts of the code in an application) and redesign their systems in order to keep the app working.[7] Many app developers aren't cognizant of the needs for these changes or don't budget to keep up with them all along. They eventually incur so much technical debt that they have to abandon their app like a house condemned because the pipes burst and electrical isn't up to code.

The speed with which the Shamoon computer virus was able to wreak so much havoc on Saudi Aramco was partly attributable to issues of unresolved technical debt. The virus's creators found and exploited weaknesses in code controlling the interoperability between computers—they created their own entrances into the castle Saudi Aramco thought was so heavily fortified. Since that attack, the virus's creators have become more sophisticated. In 2017 the same virus was responsible for shutting down several petrochemical plants in Saudi Arabia. The virus exploited vulnerabilities that arose because the systems operating between multiple companies had not been simultaneously updated—one company had made changes that affected the systems of another company, leaving unnoticed gaps in security that the hackers infiltrated. The hackers attempted to shut down controllers across the various plants that regulate tasks like voltage, pressure, and temperatures. Security experts believe that these attacks could have resulted in massive explosions.[8]

The higher up the problem is in the technology stack, the easier it is to understand and appreciate the consequences of technical debt on product or business performance. But for changes that occur lower in the stack, it's often more difficult to conceptualize because the changes normally don't have an immediate effect. However counterintuitive or unglamorous it may seem, it's extremely important to understand that in a digital world you often have to make investments to set your product or platform up for future success by making changes to products that today work just fine. The time between today and that future for most digital businesses is constantly shrinking. Leaders of digital companies need to be proactive in allowing budget and time to make updates in the technology stack that will allow them to get ahead of ecosystem changes. In the world of digital business, if you wait until you need to make a change in your technology infrastructure, you've waited too long.[9]

Design for Privacy

In 2013, Cambridge Analytica, a British political consulting firm, announced the release of an app called "This is Your Digital Life," which was developed in conjunction with data scientist Aleksandr Kogan and his company Global Science Research.[10] The app presented users with a series of questions about their behaviors and digital technology use. Cambridge Analytica used those data to build psychological profiles that could be used, among other things, to predict voting behavior. To get access to the data they needed to construct these profiles, the company teamed up with Facebook, which required them to follow an informed consent process for research. The agreement stipulated that Facebook users would complete a survey in return for payment and their data would be used for academic purposes. In reality, the app did much more than simply collect surveys from informed users; it also collected personal information from other people in the survey respondent's network (their group of Facebook friends), without the knowledge of informed users or their friends. Cambridge Analytica then used these data to construct a massive database of psychological profiles that were used to create targeted political ads. When news of the data leak went public,

Facebook shares fell more than 24 percent within ten days, about a $134 billion loss. In 2019, the US Federal Trade Commission announced that Facebook was to be fined $5 billion for its privacy violations.[11] The UK's Information Commissioner's Office also found Facebook guilty of exploiting users to a "serious risk of harm" and levied a substantial fine.

Privacy is a security concern. Data are valuable to a company for many reasons, but above all because they often contain confidential or proprietary information. Sometimes that information was generated or assembled by the company; other times it was given by customers in exchange for services. Either way, a digital business must secure those proprietary data not only to protect its customers, but to protect its own competitive assets. Our own individual data are also becoming increasingly valuable and important. Technology companies like Google, Facebook, and LinkedIn make the lion's share of their profits by collecting data about our behaviors, using AI to make predictions about what we are likely to want to buy, and selling those predictions to third parties who try to sell us those things through targeted advertisements.[12] Thus, making sure that the data we deem valuable remain secure is of the utmost importance.

Data privacy is linked to one of the most profound shifts enabled by digitization—the intensification of behavioral visibility. Each activity you conduct through digital technologies leaves traces that make your behavior visible to people you never intended to see it. In the digital age, visibility is tied to the amount of effort people must expend to locate information. As former director of Xerox PARC John Seely Brown has argued, if people perceive that information is difficult to access, or they do not know what information exists for them to access, they will likely not seek it out. In this regard, information about people's work behaviors, tasks, knowledge, or whatever else, though it may be theoretically available for people to uncover, may be, for all intents and purposes, invisible.[13] Yet digitization reduces the effort required to make one's own behaviors visible, or to see the behaviors of others. Although digital technologies by no means cause behavioral visibility, the increasingly intense amounts of data about people's behaviors means that we no longer live in a world where people are invisible and need to work to make themselves visible. Rather, we are always—through traces of us left in data—already visible to others. How visible and in what ways we are visible are the important questions about privacy and consent.

Facebook made behavior visible to Cambridge Analytica after users were expressly told that their data would remain the property of Facebook. Privacy is a tricky concept in the digital world. No user of Facebook or any social tool can expect that their online behaviors will only be seen by people in their friend network. All it takes is a simple click by one of those friends, and a post, a reaction, a photo, or a meme that you send can be propagated to an entirely new network comprised of people you may not know.[14] You probably understand that this risk exists on sites like Facebook. But what you may not count on is that companies like Facebook might harvest your data and transfer it to other companies.

One major way that companies make our behaviors visible is through what's called *algorithmic ordering*.[15] At the simplest level, algorithms sort, rank, recommend, and categorize information so that it is more easily understood and useful. But algorithms also produce visibility. Microsoft researcher Tarleton Gillespie argues that algorithms do not make all behavior visible, nor do they make different kinds of behavior visible in the same way.[16] For one, not all data are technically available to be inputs to algorithmic processing. Also, an algorithm's human programmers decide what is likely to be relevant. As a result, the algorithms position some behaviors as visible while others are not. Algorithms do not treat everyone equally; behaviors made visible through algorithmic ordering are not uniform for all viewers. Search engines like Google regularly present different rankings to different selected classes of users to determine what kinds of content users will respond to most favorably (via clicks) and then, through comparative assessment, make further determinations about how to modify the core algorithm.

In practical terms, algorithmic ordering impacts your privacy and consent for how your individual data will be used. For example, if you actively provide information about yourself in hiring forms, surveys, and the like, you probably know the company has and can use the information. But when you use digital tools that collect seemingly innocuous records of what you do online to create a behavioral profile, you often don't know that your data are being collected and made visible—even if you agreed to it when you signed an employment agreement or a technology use consent form.

In our extensive work with companies who collect and analyze digital data, we've distilled some best practices about how to appropriately respect employees' or customers' rights to privacy when they are using digital tools. Understanding when and how your private data can and cannot be harvested is part of developing a digital mindset. If you are a manager or involved in setting privacy protocols, the best practices below function as general guidance. If you are an employee who is concerned that your company is "spying on you" or encroaching into territory that should be private, these best practices can serve as a reality check on what your company may or may not know about your digital behaviors.

Follow best practices for privacy

First, transparency is a must. If amassing digital data, employees and customers should be asked to sign an agreement indicating they understand that their patterns of interactions on company-owned tools will be tracked for the purposes of analyzing their behavior. Full disclosure and employee consent is the only option. We've also uncovered some additional moves to get ahead of privacy concerns:

- *Employees should have access to whatever digital data are collected about them.* We recommend providing it at least annually. The data can include a map of the person's own network, a summary of their transactions or key behaviors. For example, a report could provide an employee with a score about how much time they spend using particular features of a software application compared to others.

- *Provide clarity about the level of data collection.* The level that is most basic—and the least prone to privacy concerns—is generic pattern analysis. The analysis might show, for example, that someone is an outlier in their online social network, but not identify specifically why that person isn't better connected. Or the analysis could show that a certain percentage of teams within an organization are the most innovative, but not identify which teams.

  The second level identifies which specific people have certain kinds of preferences. Scores may provide predictions about whether a person's behavior is likely to make them an influencer or whether their departure from a company would make the organization vulnerable. Although this level of analysis provides more value, it singles out individuals.

  The highest level pairs digital data collection with machine learning. In this scenario, data are collected about whom employees interact with and about the topics they discuss. A company might examine the contents of emails and posts on social networking sites to identify who has expertise in what domains. This information provides the most specific guidance for leaders—for example, about who is likely to develop good ideas in certain areas. This most advanced level obviously also comes with the most privacy concerns, and senior leadership must develop deeply considered strategies to deal with them.

If you work for a company building digital technologies, privacy should be much more about simply having good policies. Having a strong digital mindset means incorporating concerns for privacy into everything you do, even how you design your digital tools. One popular approach to making sure user privacy is protected is a framework called "Privacy by Design" (PbD) developed by Dr. Ann Cavoukian, Ontario's three-term Information and Privacy Commissioner. PbD is a framework for "protecting privacy proactively by embedding it often and early in technology" instead of treating it as an afterthought that is simply responding to regulatory demands.[17] PbD is based on seven foundational principles:

1. Be proactive, not reactive—preventative, not remedial.

2. Lead with privacy as the default setting.

3. Embed privacy into design.

4. Retain full functionality: "Both privacy and security are important, and no unnecessary trade-offs need to be made to achieve both."

5. Ensure end-to-end security: "Data life cycle security means that all data should be securely retained as needed and destroyed when no longer needed."

6. Maintain visibility and transparency.

7. Respect user privacy—keep it user-centric.[18]

The PbD principles are not only the right thing to do for individual privacy, but the research suggests that companies that follow a PbD process when building new digital technologies have fewer material data breaches and happier users. Here's how Deirdre Mulligan of UC Berkeley and Jennifer King of Stanford's Center for Internet and Society define the inherent privacy issues with which our data-driven, digital era must reckon:

> Understanding privacy as a human process requires companies to solicit and understand the context-dependent privacy expectations of affected individuals. This requires a conceptual and empirical inquiry into privacy's meaning. This form of PbD begins with value-centered and human-centered processes. It requires a new set of privacy experts. Ensuring that a company accurately describes its privacy-related activities in its terms of service and provides appropriate mechanisms to capture consumer acceptance of them is a task for lawyers. Understanding the values at play and privacy requirements in a given context requires a separate set of skills. It requires research

to understand and document what individuals bring to the table—their naivete, their uninformed and ill-conceived notions of how technology works, their mental models based in prior brick and mortar interactions, and their cognitive biases, to name a few. It demands attentiveness to context and human experience, the very attributes that companies, through privacy notices, attempt to disavow and make irrelevant.[19]

A good example of using PbD for consent management comes from HERE Technologies, a Netherlands-based company that uses AI to provide companies with mapping and location data generated by GPS systems in people's vehicles. HERE Technologies' director of data science, Dr. Michael Kopp, says that just four location data points are enough to reveal a person's identity in 80 percent of cases.[20] Given the highly sensitive nature of such data, HERE has taken a proactive approach by building a platform that offers a neutral server (a remote and secure server where data can be accessed securely without allowing third parties access) for people to exchange location-related data across industries that can be used for machine learning models. The fact that the server is neutral hinges on a consent management system—which allows users to determine exactly what data to share and how. Users can thus use others' location-based data without it ever revealing personal information on either side of the transaction.

What's exciting about PbD and HERE's approach is the proactivity. The conventional wisdom is that technology is and must be inherently invasive and therefore its invasiveness is curbed by regulation. Not in this case.

Incorporating PbD also requires more than hiring a chief privacy officer or other compliance personnel. It requires far more than simply ensuring that the engineering staff have heard of the word *privacy*. Privacy by Design also requires that you, your colleagues, and your employees have the mindset to understand users' privacy concerns and expectations and who has the authority to advocate for you even when users' needs conflict with the company's goals. To develop a digital mindset, it is essential to remember that privacy has to be at the core of everything that you do. It can't be an afterthought; it must be architected into digital systems and developed into robust policies about how behavioral data will be collected, stored, analyzed, and used.

Assure Data Integrity through Blockchain

The global diamond market is valued at more than $90 billion a year. Experts estimate that each year up to 15 percent of that value—$13.5 billion—is lost to fraud. It's not difficult to understand how. Between fifteen and twenty intermediaries touch a diamond between the time it is extracted from the earth to when it is purchased by a consumer. With so many handoffs and transactions, it's easy for diamonds to disappear, get swapped, or misclassified. Prior to the year 2000, about a quarter of all diamonds were traded illegally. Until the United Nations set up the Kimberley Process in 2003 to ensure that "diamond purchases were not financing violence by rebel movements and their allies seeking to undermine legitimate governments," a diamond's path from mine to retail store was not closely tracked.[21] Although eighty-one countries have signed on to the Kimberley Process, it has not worked well, because tracking is difficult, since certification is done via digital ledgers that are shipped around the world. Although a good gemologist can discern a raw diamond's provenance and quality, as diamonds move up the value chain and become more refined, it becomes difficult for even the most seasoned professionals to determine if the diamond mined from its place of origin is the same diamond that is being presented to consumers. As Wuyi Wang, director of research and development at the Gemological Institute of America, observes, "Despite the concern from the public and within the industry . . . there is no scientific or technical way to tell where diamonds came from once they are cut."[22]

The diamond supply chain serves as an apt metaphor for the importance of data integrity. Without data integrity, too many things can go wrong when multiple people act on and manipulate data concerning an agreement, relationship, or asset without other people knowing what is being done. Data integrity is a global problem that affects a wide range of industries, such as luxury goods, clothing, food products, pharmaceuticals, and more. Proving or disproving the authenticity and quality of an asset can be a challenge because traditional supply chains are long, complex, and lack transparency.

This is where blockchain comes in as a potential solution to this age-old, stubborn problem.

A company called Everledger works with the major diamond certification houses in the United States, Israel, India, and Belgium that grade and certify each diamond for the market.[23] Everledger takes this data and creates a digital "DNA" record comprising the 4Cs (color, cut, clarity, and carat weight), fourteen other metadata reference points, and a unique identification code for each stone. With this information, Everledger knows who owns which diamond and where it is. It can even trace each diamond as it moves into retail stores and onto ecommerce platforms. In short, it ensures that the data about a diamond are kept secure so that no diamond fraud can occur. A digital mindset means that, in addition to security and privacy, you must also focus on data integrity. To help keep digital systems secure, we have to make sure that the data in them are not corrupted or changed to benefit certain parties and disadvantage others.

Although still in its infancy, the development of blockchain technologies represents an important step forward in assuring data integrity. Thus, understanding how blockchain works is important to building a strong digital mindset. Because of this, we're going to discuss in very simple terms what blockchain is, and we will provide examples of how it can be used to enhance data integrity. Overall, blockchain is a very good security technology for verifying the integrity of data. Also, processes where maintaining data integrity is crucial (say, real estate transactions, medical credentialing, supply-chain tracking) that used to take weeks or months to secure can be cut to seconds when blockchain is involved.

What is blockchain technology, and what is it used for?

You probably have heard the term blockchain. Perhaps you thought that's something too complicated to understand or something that only concerns coders. Neither is true, and you should get to know the basics because blockchain is only going to gain in importance.

A blockchain is simply a ledger; it's just a super secure and non-repudiable one. Like a traditional ledger, blockchains record data regarding transactions: who owns what, who bought what from whom, who is allowed to make certain decisions, and so on. In an office, a ledger is kept private. Once it was locked in a safe box and used only by certain people. Today it's likely a highly secure software system. But this is where blockchain differs, cleverly. The digital ledger is distributed. This means that blockchains function as a network of shared databases that any authorized party—whether inside or outside of an organization—can use to verify the particulars of a transaction and terms of engagement.

An easy way to understand this is to imagine a magic world in which you could make records in a ledger, and when you did, your records magically showed up in a thousand ledgers around the world—with no one party controlling all these ledgers. Anyone can show up to that place and access the ledger, provided they know the password. If they don't have it, the ledger literally won't open. If they do, they can not only look; they can record their own transactions, too, which will show up in all the other magic ledgers.

Finally, once you add a transaction to the ledger, it can't be undone, and it never goes away. The ledger just keeps growing.

That's how blockchain works. The real keys to it are the immutability of the transaction history and its decentralization.

Unlike a more traditional database where data are stored in tables, with blockchain—as the name suggests—pieces of data (blocks) are linked to one another to form a chain. The amount of digital data that any one user has on the blockchain, then, is tracked across a web of interconnected transactions, with each transaction (or exchange of currency) building upon the last one. This chain structure makes it so that changing any one block of data would require altering each linked block as well, a process that would take an infeasibly high amount of computing power. This means that once a transaction has taken place using blockchain technology, there is no going back, except through a new transaction. Such permanency also ensures data security, as it's nearly impossible to tamper with this system.

Decentralization means no one party has control over a blockchain ledger. This differs from how we typically operate, where a third party like a bank has to verify that everything is in order before we can purchase goods from a vendor, for example. With blockchain, the technology design itself is the guarantor so multiple parties can exchange payment for services or goods directly without the need for third-party intermediaries to act as guarantors. This is because transactions over blockchain take place between blockchain addresses, which are unique to each user. In other words, virtual currency is held in a kind of digital, personalized wallet, rather than a bank.

Moreover, everyone can see these addresses, but they can't unlock them. This is part of a system known as public-key cryptography and is also what makes blockchain so appealing for data security. Because each user has a unique address that is shared across the blockchain, other users know that they're transacting with the user they actually think they are. Each user also has their own unique private access code that allows them to access the contents of what's called their personal digital wallet. In this way, users can be confident in knowing their payment is going to the intended party—without the need for a central power to tell them so—and that their digital wallet is secure from outside parties.

Because transactions occur in this way—between unique accounts and without the need for verification from a central authority—they can occur rapidly. The information pertaining to these transactions is also updated across the blockchain and made available to each party instantly. This makes transactions not only more transparent, but also more secure, as it adds further blocks to the chain, thus increasing irreversibility. This combination of immediacy, transparency, and security makes blockchain particularly useful for large transactions that need to be done quickly and safely (like a large asset exchange), or for foreign exchange transactions.

Because it is particularly well suited for tracking complex information across systems and assuring that these important data are not tampered with, organizations have begun using blockchain technology to create streamlined, internal record-keeping systems, which can keep track of things from IT equipment to tax and voting records.[24] MedRec, which is part of the MIT Media Lab, is seeking to use blockchain technology to create a medical records system to give patients a transparent and easy-to-understand view of their medical records across providers.[25] Blockchain technology is also being used to track, trace, and record the movement of goods across various industries. IBM, for example, is using blockchain as part of their Food Trust initiative to track the origins of food shipments not only to increase the efficiency of supply chains and decrease waste, but also to isolate potential outbreaks of contamination.[26] A number of industry giants have joined since the project's inception in 2017, including Walmart, Carrefour, Tyson, and more.[27]

Blockchain is also promising to facilitate more revolutionary applications that will displace well-established models and institutions. For example, new peer-to-peer marketplaces may emerge that would make centralized hubs like Amazon obsolete. Such applications might someday take the place of existing models, but they will require a high degree of coordination before they can do so.[28] Cryptocurrency systems like Bitcoin, Ethereum, and Ripple, the aspect of blockchain technology that has perhaps received the most media hype, also fall into this category. Although cryptocurrencies could technically replace physical currencies, doing so would require a high degree of complex coordination as financial institutions across the world would have to agree to adopt them before they could be of widespread value.

One of the most transformational applications at present is the "smart contract" that can clearly delineate and enforce in real time the breakdown of things like royalty payments for digital content. Smart contracts are already finding use in the music industry, where this process had otherwise become extremely tedious, murky, and costly. In 2018, the

British musician Imogen Heap, for example, launched the blockchain project Mycelia, which aims to create a new way for musicians to manage their projects and metadata. She also released the first song that sends out payment to each creative party involved automatically through a smart contract with each listen.[29] By quickly and transparently divvying out payment at the appropriate times automatically, these smart contracts aim to eliminate the need for lengthy negotiations that eat up both time and money. Beyond royalty payments, smart contracts can also be used for the execution of wills, deeds, leases, or even parking tickets.[30] This sort of application is one of the most transformational, as it will fundamentally change how we devise and handle all sorts of contracts by reducing or eliminating the need for attorneys, brokers, or other third-party mediators. It is also, however, one of the more difficult to implement, as it requires us to rethink how we go about these deeply entrenched processes.[31]

Elsewhere, some companies, particularly in financial services, have started to create "localized" applications, such as private chains that facilitate quick and secure transactions between frequent partners.[32] Interstellar, for example, has partnered with organizations like Nasdaq, Visa, and Citigroup to develop enterprise-level blockchain applications that will make it easier to track assets.[33] One such network is Stellar, which IBM has used to create Blockchain World Wire, a blockchain-based payment system aimed at facilitating the transfer of value across different currencies and financial assets.[34] A system like this would eliminate the transfer time needed to settle and clear transactions like large asset exchanges, which banks like Santander estimate will save up to $20 billion annually.[35]

Preparing for a future that will rely on blockchain

Our colleagues, Marco Iansiti and Karim Lakhani of Harvard Business School, argue that blockchain could create as profound a shift in how we live and work as another foundational technology: the internet. Retrospectively, in our current digital age, it is obvious to see how revolutionary the internet was, but at the time of its inception, it was met with widespread skepticism. In the 1960s and 1970s, for example, many telecommunications companies doubted that data could be sent—let alone voice or video connections—across the early architecture that would one day underlie the internet. In fact, they were in the business of operating in a non- (or yet-to-be-) digital landscape, and they made quite a bit of money doing so.

This skepticism, paired with the time it took for the proper technology to be developed, had a direct effect on the value of the early internet. Just like with any network, much of the utility of the internet is rooted in the size of its user base—more users means there is more you can do.[36] It took years for many of the internet's greatest benefits to be realized, because the user base grew gradually. Nevertheless, even in the early stages, simple applications like email drove an increase in interest and use, which thereby paved the way for further innovative applications. In this analogy, Bitcoin is like email: an application that wasn't particularly novel and that didn't require a lot of infrastructure to coordinate, but that provided a better, more efficient way of doing something that was immediately valuable to those who used it. And, to continue the analogy, it is applications like Bitcoin that will gradually convince more organizations to become users, which will allow the full potential of blockchain to be realized.

As blockchain is already beginning to revolutionize systems and pave the way for new solutions, Lakhani and another coauthor, Saïd Business School's Teppo Felin, urge companies to start thinking about how they can best make use of the technology rather than passively become late adopters.[37] You may be interested to know that to do so, they suggest considering three unique aspects that can make a company's use of blockchain its own: the company's strategy, its capabilities, and the problems it can solve for its stakeholders. One simple way to do this is for people to start with itemizing and noticing the everyday problems you may be facing and brainstorm how blockchain's fundamental bent toward recording, tracking, verifying, and aggregating data can be best put to use. At present, this might be a simpler, more straightforward application, something like an internal record system that does not need a large number of users. Over time, expect more innovative and disruptive solutions to emerge, but for now, the key is to anticipate the coming change and begin thinking about how to integrate the technology into your regular workflow. If you are in a position to do so, you may want to change your business model and invest in developing the technology that will enable this future transition, before it's too late.

Strive to Reduce Rather Than Eliminate Security Problems

Computer viruses, Facebook profiles, and the journey that diamonds make from mines to retail stores each represent a particular kind of security threat that is common in today's digital environment. You cannot avoid security problems, but a strong digital mind knows to ask, "When will a problem happen?" and "How can I be prepared to respond to it?" Although you do not have to be a security expert, if you can embrace ecosystem interdependence, pay off technical debt, design for privacy, and understand the emerging uses of blockchain to assure data integrity, you are well on your way to reducing, if not eliminating, security problems large and small.

GETTING TO 30 PERCENT

Security

Developing a digital mindset means letting go of the idea that data security is like securing a castle with fixed access points; dynamic digital environments are inherently interdependent, complex, and bound to change. Accept that it's not a matter of *if* your data become vulnerable, but *when*. Privacy is another security concern. Plan proactively with security and privacy top of mind:

- Budget for technical debt continually and deliberately by updating old infrastructure and future-proofing existing infrastructure.

- Each activity you conduct online leaves traces—digital exhaust—that make your behavior visible to people you never intended to see it. These clues can be pieced together to form behavioral profiles.

- You should be able to opt in or out of the collection of your personal data.

- Companies need to design for privacy as the default setting, embed privacy into all aspects of design, and be transparent about data collection.

- Blockchain refers to an array of distributed ledger technologies.

- Blockchain technologies are capable of recording data for complex transactions quickly and securely. Transactions performed using blockchain are permanent and irreversible, and they can be processed immediately without the need for a third party.

- Speed, security, and the ability to facilitate direct peer-to-peer transactions make blockchain ideal for cryptocurrencies, efficient record-keeping systems, the tracking of goods across supply chains, and more.

- Blockchain functions like any network—its value increases as more users adopt it—and promises to be a foundational technology that will revolutionize business and society.

Understanding when and how your private data can and cannot be harvested is part of developing a digital mindset. Remember also that digital systems are always evolving, which can bring about both intended positives and unexpected vulnerabilities.

6

The Experimentation Imperative

You Won't Know Until You Try

You've probably seen the TV ads featuring yellow and black checkered dummies sitting in a car as it's pushed at high speeds into a wall to demonstrate the vehicle's safety. Those ads were modeled after actual crash experiments done by automotive engineers.[1] By the early 2000s, one US-based automobile company with a long history of such experiments had made a strategic move to reduce the number of physical experiments it ran. It moved the majority of crash tests to digital platforms.

The move made great economic sense. It cost over $750,000 to build and crash one preproduction vehicle in the lab. But it cost only pennies (once the infrastructure investment in software and computing power had been made) to run experiments digitally. And you could run many more experiments in a fraction of the time it took to smash a vehicle. An audit in the early 2010s suggested that the company was saving close to $100 million a year in testing with its switch to digital experimentation.

Granted, this was a tremendous change in vehicle safety testing. However, as this chapter will show, simply switching from physical to digital experimentation is not enough to truly bring about a digital mindset—and its tremendous benefits—in the *people* who work at an organization.

Enter Balaji and Davide, two engineers at the automotive company. In 2014 they were running digital experiments to determine the best way to redesign the front of the company's bestselling small SUV so it would achieve a coveted five-star crash rating. They had crashed 1,247 digital models of cars into digital walls. Each simulation was only marginally different from the ones that preceded it. As Davide recounted, "The major advantage of being digital is you can do so many experiments that you start to see a trend. So, then you just do a little tweak to see if the trend continues in the direction you want, and you do another, and then another and then all those experiments really add up."

One day at lunch Balaji and Davide were discussing the designs of their vehicles with some colleagues. Balaji thought from what his colleagues were saying that the design of the front rails (an important structural component underneath a car's engine compartment) of their vehicles sounded quite similar. He asked one of his lunch partners how many experiments they'd done to arrive at their design. "Oh, maybe 2,300 or so" was the quick answer.

Back at his desk, Balaji said to Davide, "This is ridiculous. We're working on two different teams and we're both doing all of these experiments for our own vehicles and coming to the same conclusions. It's like everyone here is learning from their experiments for their own projects, but we don't know if there are any global design solutions that work for everyone." He knew that because all of the experiments were digital and stored on the company's servers, the results of *all* experiments—both the successes and failures—were just sitting there waiting to be mined. "What we need to do," Balaji said to Davide, "is do some experiments on all our experiments to see what really works."

Davide saw Balaji's point. But both were well aware that their flash of insight went against the company's usual way of doing things, and they feared a negative response from their boss if they raised the idea with him. But as they continued to talk about how they might experiment with the data, their excitement won over their reluctance to ask permission. They met with their boss and received a vehement "No." The boss's rationale? Balaji and Davide's job was to design *their vehicle*, not to think about the optimal design rules for *all vehicles*. "We've got a group of subject matter experts who advise on best practices for design," the boss explained. "That's their job responsibility, not yours. I'm surprised you'd even come to ask me about this. What if it doesn't work? It would be a total waste of time and it would reflect poorly on the team. It just isn't a good use of your time." The two engineers returned to their desks, defeated.

Throughout our research and work with nearly thirty companies trying to embrace experimentation, we've seen this scenario repeated many times. Without a properly developed digital mindset, even the people who know the advantages that digital experimentation can bring—like the senior manager of the auto company—don't see the world through an experimentation frame. We've also seen that managers and employees like Balaji and Davide who intuitively embrace experiments don't always have the right vocabulary or frame of reference to successfully push their ideas. Both are reasons why a digital mindset for everyone on a team or organization is essential for creating a healthy culture of digital experimentation.

The idea of experimentation as a core business practice isn't new, but the complex, data-intensive nature of experimentation is.[2] With digital innovations requiring the integration of software, hardware, and organizational layers, products and services are becoming highly integrated and computationally driven. Such complexity makes the experimentation process both more complicated and more essential for success in the digital age. Recent research suggests that organizations that can create a healthy culture of digital experimentation grow at least eight times faster than global GDP.[3] Microsoft attributes annual revenue increases of 10 percent to 25 percent to monthly improvements that it makes on its Bing search engine through constant experimentation. One large bank that we worked with saw a 30 percent increase in revenue over a two-year period from the introduction of new financial products honed through digital experimentation.

The capacity to reap the benefits of rapid prototyping and data analysis to improve internal work processes, products, and services comes from a culture that embraces the digital mindset in experimentation. Developing that mindset requires understanding four core approaches:

1. Develop a learning agenda that will set the tone for experiments and provide a framework for making sense out of them.

2. Turn the digital exhaust generated by user behavior and system logs into digital footprints that can be systematically analyzed to create the design of future experiments.

3. Prevent current organizational structures, such as how work is divided among people or departments, from stymieing experimentation efforts.

4. Build a culture of psychological safety in which experimentation is not just encouraged but expected (even when it's experimentation about experimentation).

These approaches are significant whether or not you are actually doing digital experiments. Understanding their basic concepts plays into key technological processes that affect our work and our lives.

Create a Learning Agenda

Our colleague, Harvard Business School professor Stefan Thomke, one of the foremost scholars of experimentation, argues that the need for an "ethos of experimentation" is so strong in today's digital era because of the speed and scale of change.[4] The rapid development of digital products and services, the increasingly fickle habits of customers, and the immense leaps in computer processing power and data storage capacity power made annually are among some of the reasons why today's customers, companies, and markets are in a constant state of flux. When change is constant, it's difficult for hunches (which take time to form) or theories (which take much longer to form than hunches) to help chart the best course of action.

But you can't just start throwing experiments out there. Creating a learning agenda helps you experiment intentionally rather than willy-nilly; it entails creating a learning document and becoming comfortable with failure.

Experiment intentionally

Successfully using digital experimentation, especially to guide important decisions, means intentionally determining in advance what potential business question an experiment could be designed to answer and then deciding what metrics you will use to evaluate the experiment.

Take for example Dropbox, a company whose dramatic growth owes a great deal to founder Drew Houston's mindset toward digital experimentation. Early on, Houston created a three-minute demo of the interface and feature set for Dropbox, which he then posted to a popular online forum for developers called Hacker News. Because his questions were about which specific features resonated the most with them, he designed the demo to yield detailed, measurable feedback from potential users about what they liked and didn't like about the new tool.[5]

In this process you should be open to discoveries that defy common sense and your initial hunches. For example, Dropbox data analysts experimented on the optimal size of free storage given to users by doing A/B testing and by running analytics on how much space current users were using. The triangulation of these data points showed that the number of gigabytes of storage made available for free was not the best measure of value for Dropbox users. Consequently, Dropbox reduced the available storage space that it advertised and provided to its users while simultaneously decreasing its costs.

As he grew the company, Houston worked to build the ethos of digital experimentation into its culture. Teams experimented with display ads and affiliate programs, as well as placement of features and the scope of product offerings, to see what attracted users and what did not. They used A/B tests to fine-tune page layouts. Based on the measurable results of these experiments, they made a number of key business decisions that increased customer acquisition and decreased cost.

Experimenting haphazardly, or giving the appearance of doing so, is one of the reasons Balaji and Davide's boss was against their proposal to experiment on the company's existing crash simulation data. As brilliant as their idea might have been, they didn't articulate a clear rationale for doing the experiment or a plan for how the company might learn from it as part of a learning agenda. Likewise, in the companies we've worked with, the most successful experiments are ones that are accompanied by a learning agenda.

Create a learning agenda document

This short document outlines:

- The questions you're looking to answer

- The steps you'll take in the experiment to answer those questions

- A rationale for why the experiment will help to answer those questions

- A description of how you'll evaluate the experiment to know whether what you tried achieved the outcome you wanted

People who consistently learn from their digital experiments are able to answer these questions *before* they begin to test. It's important to do this work ahead of time because doing so helps you to decide whether it is worth committing the time, effort, and resources to launching the digital experiment. But perhaps even more importantly, it provides you with the ability to develop a digital mindset capable of learning from your experiment.

Here's how Nadine McHugh, senior VP of omni media, strategic investments, and creative solutions at L'Oréal, explains success in experimentation with digital advertising and marketing:

Anything that we test has to be something that we think can really make a difference at scale. . . . To make sure that we're staying on track and getting the biggest bang for our buck, every test has to have what we call a "learning agenda." That's where we outline what questions we're looking to answer, what new insights we'd like to uncover and the steps that we'll take to get there. Once we're clear on that, we'll look at upcoming campaigns and select brands or products that we think are best suited to testing our hypotheses. From there, testing is constant and iterative. Throughout, we're looking to see what effect it is having on a handful of important metrics. For a YouTube ad campaign, that would include things such as viewability, reach, scale, brand suitability, and sales lift.[6]

Incidentally, L'Oréal, founded in 1909, and still one of the world's most successful cosmetic brands, is testimony to the fact that you don't have to be part of a twenty-first-century software company like Dropbox to develop a digital mindset around experimentation. It helps that L'Oréal has always embraced experimentation and sought to learn from small experiments before launching major products or promotions. Digital experiments have resulted in innovations such as Snapchat filters and YouTube partnerships that have paid off across its portfolio of more than thirty brands. In 2016, sales at NYX Professional Makeup (a subsidiary of L'Oréal) had quadrupled in two years, and L'Oréal Paris was named the world's most valuable and powerful cosmetic brand for the third year in a row.

Become comfortable with failure

In most cases, the experiments we try don't yield optimal results. While it feels great to learn from success, it's actually more important to learn from failure. We know this in part because Peter Madsen of Brigham Young University and Vinit Desai of the University of Colorado were able to analyze company data from 1957 to 2004 to examine when an organization was likely to learn from their successes and failures, and when they were not.[7] Their results showed that organizations whose experiments failed in one time period were more likely to be more successful in a future time period. More surprisingly, they found that organizations whose experiments failed in the *first* period improved their likelihood of succeeding in a future period more than organizations that succeeded in the first period. They concluded that "experience with failure allows organizations to improve their performance relative to their own previous baseline, but that experience with success does not generate similar levels of improvement." Moreover, they did not uncover any evidence that organizations that were successful early on were able to replicate that success in future periods. In other words, becoming comfortable with failure, and recognizing its value, is paramount. People in the organizations that we studied were able to learn from their failures when they had mapped out a clear learning agenda before beginning their experiments.[8] That learning agenda helped them to interpret their findings and to build from them so they could design new digital experiments that would attempt to overcome the problems identified in earlier experiments.

Turn Digital Exhaust into Digital Footprints

Every time you, your colleagues, or your employees send emails via Outlook, post messages on Slack, initiate a video conference in Zoom, like someone's post on Jive, form a team in Microsoft Teams, or assign someone to project milestones in Trello, digital technologies record that action as metadata. If you are like most office-based employees today, you conduct slightly more than half of your communications digitally, record a quarter of your meetings, and document how you approached a particular work task 10 percent of the time. If you are among the many who shifted to remote work arrangements in the wake of the Covid-19 pandemic, you understand that remote knowledge work is enabled by digital technologies that allow you to communicate via text, audio, and video and to share and edit data and documents in real time. In fact, within a month of the start of the Covid-19 pandemic in the United States, Zoom's daily active user base grew by 67 percent, the number of daily active users of Microsoft Teams grew from 20 million to 44 million, and Slack added 7,000 new paid customers—roughly 40 percent more than in each of its previous two quarters. The metadata captured from all this user activity grew accordingly.

And all of those numbers are just about people communicating and interacting through digital technologies. If you also consider internet activity and the increasing number of e-commerce transactions (1.92 billion people purchased goods or services online in 2019[9]), and the number of people on social media (3.8 billion as of January 2020[10]) and mobile services (5.19 billion people by the end of 2019[11]), it's easy to see just how much of our lives are recorded and stored as metadata.

These metadata are often called *digital exhaust* because they are by-products of other activities, like setting up a meeting, running calculations, searching the web, buying products, or communicating with friends. For example, if you, your colleague, or an employee start work late one day (as recorded by VPN login times), spend an unusually short amount of time working with information in a portal (as recorded by server time stamps), and are unusually quiet in a meeting (as recorded by total seconds of talk time in a Zoom session), none of these pieces of digital exhaust by themselves tells us much. But when the digital exhaust of these behaviors is combined and examined over time, then compared to other employees' patterns, it can start to create inferences that an employee is, for example, disconnecting from the organization.

Digital exhaust can be immensely useful, and understanding how it works and its value to experimentation is key to developing a digital mindset. In our own research, we've documented how digital exhaust can be used to help employees reduce work duplication and increase innovation, develop more accurate organizational metaknowledge— knowledge of "who knows what" and "who knows whom"—and apportion work tasks more effectively. Leaders who collect and analyze digital exhaust created by employees can create efficient systems for knowledge transfer, more effectively implement strategy, and identify individuals whose networks are optimized for certain roles.[12]

Become aware of digital footprints—yours and others'

Developing a digital mindset around experimentation means you are able to think about putting these pieces of digital exhaust together to construct *digital footprints* of employees, teams, subunits, products, or internal innovation processes. Digital footprints are collections of data that represent some *thing*—a team, or a person, say. They are the mathematical representation of everything a company knows about that thing, and they are used to make predictions about its behavior. Digital footprints are constantly updated as more digital exhaust is produced. As you develop a digital mindset you are likely to become more aware of your own digital footprint and think about what tiny snippets of information your digital exhaust entails and to what purpose.

You may be interested to know that AI and machine learning algorithms have progressed far enough to make meaningful predictions based on these digital footprints—and we're surely just at the beginning of this trend. Although in the past many companies were ready to analyze data at scale, they didn't have enough of it to analyze because most employees' actions were not recorded and stored. Today, enough data exist that companies use algorithms to sift through the digital footprints collected as employees, partners, and customers create digital exhaust through their purchases, communications, and work activities. Of course, with the ability to sift through our digital exhaust comes the need for careful regulation of people's privacy.[13]

The most advanced companies that we've studied are just beginning to use AI to combine these patterns with new data sets (like employee turnover or performance data) to test assumptions about certain relationships, learn autonomously from these tests, and make predictions about behavior. Using machine learning and AI to turn digital exhaust into the digital footprints that can predict future behavior is one of the keys to experimentation in the digital age.[14] Even if you are not part of a team that is running such experiments, you—or more accurately, your digital exhaust—are likely to be part of an experiment.

Develop vocabulary to describe digital exhaust

When Balaji and Davide went to their boss to propose their experiment on the digital exhaust left from thousands of vehicle simulations, they did not have the vocabulary to describe how they would do it and what it would yield. If they did, their boss would likely have understood that running experiments on those digital footprints could lead to fundamental design principles that would improve all of their vehicles.

They needed to be able to explain in ways like this: digital models run algorithms—carefully defined procedures that take inputs and manipulate them based on certain assumptions—in ways that simulate the dynamics of complex environments. In SaaS companies, model inputs represent users' behavioral patterns culled from their digital activity. In organizations such as automotive companies that produce hardware or that model environmental systems, sensors such as accelerometers, barometers, and air-quality monitors collect analog data and convert them into digital data that can be classified, analyzed, and rendered into equations that represent assumptions about how the system will work under various conditions.

As product and service offerings become more intricate and embedded, digital models that simulate the dynamics of nonlinear, complex systems will likely be key to doing the kind of experimentation that leads to successful innovation. You don't necessarily have to understand the mathematical details of everything that goes on "under the hood," but it helps if you understand the basic ingredients of creating models, what constitutes input, and how the output may be analyzed.

Visual representations of digital data and the footprints they leave behind can often form the basis of a vocabulary that communicates complex metrics to a general audience. No doubt you saw visuals produced by various media outlets throughout the coronavirus pandemic to map, for example, infection rates, virus spread, and hospital ICU admissions. Again, these visuals were created by analyzing millions of data point inputs from health care and government data collections. Three economists who wanted to understand how different groups of people were spending or not spending US government stimulus checks were able to do so by analyzing anonymous digital exhaust combined from about a dozen credit card, payroll, and financial services companies to obtain information on consumer spending, employment rates, job postings, and other economic indicators. A key word here is "anonymous." Experimenting on data exhaust compiled from millions of people did *not* include individual identities or accounts. To communicate these complicated metrics to noneconomists they published an interactive visual.[15]

Safeguard privacy

As organizations increasingly make use of algorithms to sort through the digital exhaust they collect, it's important to recognize that employees and customers can sometimes be unfairly advantaged or disadvantaged by the way those data are turned into predictions. The vast amounts of digital exhaust produced through remote work arrangements can improve organizational behavior in many ways, but that exhaust also threatens to undermine some of the systems, processes, and institutions that make workplaces fair and equitable. How to safeguard individual privacy while reaping the benefits of digital data for experimentation is an ongoing discussion. Societally, this discussion is taking place in legal and in public policy realms to regulate how organizations can and cannot use digital exhaust. Privacy professionals and in-house compliance staff in many businesses are grappling with how to ensure the proper balancing of employee privacy rights and productive experimentation of data exhaust. Chances are your organization has legal and human resources in place to review and make recommendations about privacy, employee rights, and ethics. Having a digital mindset means that, at the very least, these are recommendations that you want to review. Developing a digital mindset means thinking through the implications of harvesting people's data and actively working with human resources and others to determine how to protect people's privacy.

You should understand that most of the digital tools organizations implement to help with remote work are cloud-based applications hosted by vendors whose contract rights give them access to some or all of the digital exhaust produced through them. Those vendors are able to use algorithmic modeling to create macro-level digital footprints of the behavior of people, organizations, and systems, and use AI to make predictions about their future actions. They sell those predictions to other companies that market to us and bid to consult with our organizations, and they use those digital footprints to improve their own technologies in ways that allow them to collect even more digital exhaust. Former Harvard Business School professor Shoshana Zuboff has written eloquently about how vendors monetize digital exhaust and use it to construct digital footprints that predict and shape our behavior.[16]

Don't Let Departmentalization Kill Experimentation

In the pre-digital world, it made sense to have separate departments dedicated to constructing experiments, running them, and analyzing their results. Before digital technologies made data plentiful and easy to access, it was a lot of work to set up an experiment and record its results. Now through A/B testing on digital platforms or the use of digital models, data and digital exhaust are abundant and the cost of running experiments is comparatively negligible.[17] If you are building products, making ads, and working with customers, chances are you are capable of participating in some form of rapid experimentation.

Today, it makes sense for the people closest to the products and the data to run experiments; however, many companies can't seem to move experimentation out of central analysis units or R&D labs and into the hands of designers, marketers, engineers, or managers. They have underdeveloped digital mindsets. Another way of saying this is that such organizations struggle to democratize experimentation. As Babson College professor H. James Wilson and University of Washington professor Kevin Desouza write, "If you don't democratize experimentation you lose the knowledge and skill of 85–90 percent of your organization's employees who do not work in the lab."[18]

Existing organizational structures can make it difficult to democratize experimentation and, in many cases, they lead to the death of experimentation.[19] To understand the dire implications of departmentalizing digital experimentation, let's dive back into Balaji and Davide's quest to experiment on the ongoing crash-test experiments in their automotive company.

Take initiative any way you safely can to try your experiments

Three months after his boss rebuked him for asking to experiment, Davide remained passionate about the idea and its promise. He convinced Balaji to join him at night and on the weekends to do the work on their own, without their boss's approval. "I was worried we were going to get in trouble for doing it," Davide remembers, "but it seemed like it was the right thing to do and we were doing it on our own time, so it didn't seem so bad." Like others with a highly developed digital mindset, they decided to take the initiative to try their own experiments.

They assembled a massive data set of all the experiments run in various parts of the organization. They enrolled in online courses in statistical analysis, machine learning, and design for six sigma (DFSS) methods. Then they started experimenting on their experiments.

After a month (Davide estimates that they spent roughly thirty hours on the project) their analysis suggested that there was indeed an optimal design for the front rails of the vehicle. By doing calculations on the work achieved on their own time, they estimated that if they had had the results of the experiment when beginning their vehicle designs, they could have saved more than twelve thousand people-hours of work time, which could have been repurposed to improving other design elements in the vehicle.

Still feeling timid, but emboldened by their positive results, Balaji and Davide scheduled another meeting with their boss. The boss expressed his frustration that they had pursued the experiment despite his advice at their previous meeting, but he agreed to look at the presentation. "I was really surprised by their results," he said. "The design parameters they developed make a lot of sense intuitively, but it's not what we were doing on most of our products. And I couldn't believe that we had the data internally to develop these insights. It just took their experiments to unlock the data. I had to eat some humble pie because I'm the one that told them I didn't think they'd get anything interesting out of it." Their boss was so excited about the findings that he scheduled a meeting with a senior VP for engineering to discuss the new insights Balaji and Davide had generated. Balaji and Davide were elated; their boss had finally appreciated and seen the value in their experiments.

Unfortunately, the meeting with the senior VP didn't go well. "I was thoroughly beat up," Balaji said after the meeting. "The VP told me that we shouldn't be doing these kinds of experiments in product development—that it wasn't our job. He said that it was up to the analytics and competitive benchmarking teams to look across all vehicles and try to synthesize insights for design parameters. Basically, he said let them do their job and you do yours." Much like Balaji and Davide's boss, the VP was stuck in old ways of thinking that relegated experimentation to one department. Without having developed a digital mindset, he was unable to comprehend the real potential inherent in digital experimentation and the real value that people closest to the products can bring to that experimentation.

Beware of organizational politics and develop a plan to combat them

About a year after their ill-fated meeting with the senior engineering VP, Balaji and Davide attended an open meeting held by the analytics and competitive benchmarking department. They were going to discuss the topic of front rail design.

At the meeting they listened to an engineer named Dan present the results of a recent study titled "Structural Enablers of 5-Star Performance." Dan's department was responsible for purchasing competitor vehicles, dismantling them, and analyzing them to determine the kinds of design solutions these competitor companies used to solve various problems. Dan mentioned that the department had spent roughly $4.5 million on the study.

During his presentation, Dan showed pictures of the front rails of vehicles that had earned five-star ratings on an important government safety crash test. Across a number of different manufacturers, the consistent trend was positive for vehicles that had straight front rails, with a long axial crush zone, allowing for an extended period of energy absorption. After Dan finished showing the competitor's rails, he showed a slide of his company's different vehicle platforms. "Here we thought we would put a picture together of our rails. We told [the VP of engineering] about this and he's going to recommend a major design change going forward."

As they left the room after the presentation, Balaji said to Davide, "I was about ready to vomit." Dan's department spent close to $5 million buying cars and taking them apart to arrive at the same conclusion that Balaji and Davide had reached for free, in thirty hours, with digital experiments on the company's own data. What's more, Dan's analysis relied on correlational evidence of a relationship between straight front rails and 5-star crash ratings, where the data-driven approach adopted by Balaji and Davide was able to provide causal evidence linking the two.

As you develop a digital mindset you may work in a company that has set up an organizational structure that centralizes analysis and experimentation, making it difficult for the people closest to the products and the data to have the legitimacy to run their own experiments. This is unfortunate because often people at the edges are the ones who can experiment the most quickly and cheaply and reap the biggest rewards. In our research, company leaders that were most successful at developing an experimentation mindset used one of two tactics to combat this problem. They either dismantled their centralized experimentation and analytics departments and incentivized people at the edges to experiment themselves, or they turned their centralized departments into consulting operations. In the latter approach, these departments provided resources that employees in engineering, product, marketing, and other functions could use to help them run experiments and analyze the data. Although Balaji and Davide were frustrated in their efforts, we can take heart from the fact that they did manage to change their boss's mind. As digital transformation becomes ever more pressing and as more people develop digital mindsets, we predict that leaders will inevitably realize the appropriate organizational changes.

Build Psychological Safety

Because experiments are only ever guesses, many—probably most—will fail.[20] Although using a learning agenda can help you convert those failures into valuable learning opportunities, many people don't do experiments because they fear that the stain of a "failed" experiment will haunt them and their companies. The leader at a large computer hardware company told us, "We have so much digital data and so many opportunities to try new things, but we're kind of reticent to do it too much. If we do an experiment and it doesn't work, it may be viewed like we didn't really do our homework well enough ahead of time." When senior leadership dampens the mood for experimentation like this, people eventually stop trying to experiment. In a survey we conducted of ten digital companies (totaling more than three thousand responses), the number one reason people said they don't consider doing experiments was because they didn't think their organization would perceive them well if they failed.

Balaji and Davide's reticence to ask their boss about conducting their experiment was for exactly this reason. It turns out they were right; until their hard and independent work changed his mind, their boss didn't want them to fail, in part because he thought it would reflect poorly on the department and, indirectly, on him.

If employees don't feel comfortable suggesting experiments, managers and departments cannot benefit from insights of those closest to the data. For example, a major airplane manufacturer that we worked with created a department full of subject matter experts (SMEs) to explore more effective product development practices. These SMEs were not the engineers who worked on the products, so we asked both SMEs and engineers to anonymously submit their proposed experiments to a panel of judges. The panel was three times as likely to rate the experiments proposed by engineers as most promising. But the SMEs were five times more likely to say they would propose their experiments than the engineers. The better ideas were far less likely to be proposed.

Unfortunately for the company, the missed opportunity to seek out experimentation at the edges was institutionally accepted. As the senior VP for product told us, "It's the SME's job to come up with process improvement; it's not an engineer's job. They should stick to their work." Engineers heard that message loud and clear. One said, "I wouldn't feel comfortable proposing a new experiment. It's not my job. If it didn't work, that wouldn't look good." Balaji and Davide's experience was not an isolated event.

Overcoming this fear of looking bad or going outside your job requires that you work in a strong culture of psychological safety, or that you build one for your employees. Our colleague Amy Edmondson at Harvard Business School defines psychological safety as a feeling that "people are not hindered by interpersonal fear."[21] They feel willing and able to take the inherent personal risks of candor. They fear holding back their full participation more than they fear sharing a potentially sensitive, threatening, or wrong idea." In other words, a manager, team, or organization that explicitly *asks* for people to share ideas that are potentially sensitive, threatening, or wrong (as Balaji and Davide did) will go far to reap the rewards of the experimentation frame.

Although digital technology was not involved, an example from Edmondson's research demonstrates how essential a culture of psychological safety is for experimentation to work. She and her colleagues studied sixteen hospitals that were implementing a new minimally invasive cardiac surgery (MICS) procedure.[22] They found that roughly half the hospitals were successful in implementing what was a relatively complex new surgical procedure and, in so doing, dramatically reduced cost and increased the likelihood of a full patient recovery. The other half of the hospitals in the study never successfully implemented the new procedure and reverted to their standard procedures. The hospitals that were successful engaged in lots of experimentation. The lead surgeons encouraged and empowered their nursing teams, who are historically lower in the medical hierarchy but who work closest with actual patients, to try different divisions of labor and to explore which surgical tools would work best to carry out the procedure. The teams were encouraged to keep the practices that worked and to jettison those that did not. By contrast, the nursing teams that failed to implement the new procedures did not work in an environment where they felt psychologically safe enough to experiment with trial and error; they simply tried to go about work as usual in the operating room, trying to fit the new procedure into their old routines.

In the rapid pace of the digital workplace, psychological safety is even more important for encouraging employees to experiment. In 2012, Google embarked on a large-scale study called Project Aristotle, to figure out why some teams were more successful than others at generating new product and process improvements.[23] Two years analyzing the data showed that the healthiest teams were most likely to propose and carry out experiments, fail, and retry. They had a high degree of psychological safety. Our own research with digital companies produced similar findings. As one leader of a large SaaS company told us: "We ask our teams to go out and try things. We don't know what's going to work, so we tell them to build some experiments and let the data speak. But that means they're going to be wrong a lot and their experiments are going to fail more often than they succeed. It's my job to make sure that they feel like that failure is OK. And it is: as long as it leads to some learning they should feel like they don't need to have all the answers figured out and they can't be afraid to tell me or the team when they don't."

So how do you incorporate psychological safety into a digital mind-set? There are several ways. First, it falls to leaders to set the tone. The surgeons in Edmondson's study and the SaaS leader introduced above made it an explicit cultural norm that failure on experiments is expected. Balaji and Davide's boss, by contrast, clearly believed that failure reflected badly on the team. Empowering your team to fail and to learn from those failures is easier to do when you create a learning agenda (as discussed above) that provides a framework for people to demonstrate, explicitly, how they have learned from their failures. When they're able to do this, a failed experiment is not a failure; it becomes a productive learning event. Framing experiments not as direct antidotes to problems, but as learning opportunities, goes a long way to supporting and developing a digital mindset characterized by the trust and risk-taking necessary for engaging experimentation.

For many digital organizations that have built a culture around rely-ing on data for decision-making and process improvement, measuring psychological safety is often useful. Since the completion of Project Aris-totle, Google employees are surveyed periodically to assess their psycho-logical safety, which they then discuss with their teams. Similarly, a leader of the tech practice at a large consulting firm told us, "We measure psy-chological safety and we report out to the team about it quarterly. It helps us get a sense of how we're doing. But more than that, the act of survey-ing people about it establishes it as an important metric and knowing that we have to report out on it keeps it in the front of everyone's minds."

GETTING TO 30 PERCENT

Experimentation

The speed and scale of change in the digital era makes experimentation a necessity. Developing a digital mindset means recognizing the value of running experiments large and small—to extract value from data, support constant improvement, and ensure continual learning. Some basic guidelines can help you to experiment with intention and intelligence:

- Begin with a testable hypothesis and a clear rationale for why and how an experiment should be done.

- Create a learning agenda by outlining an experiment's question(s), steps, and how to evaluate its outcome.

- If an experiment fails, think about lessons learned and how those lessons can be used to inform a future experiment.

- Recognize that the hundreds of millions of data points created as employees and customers use their digital tools can be turned into digital footprints that can form the basis of strong experiments.

- Remove organizational roadblocks by making resources and data available to teams across departments and rewarding teams for experimenting.

- Establish psychological safety by framing experiments as learning opportunities and emphasizing that failures provide valuable insights and lessons.

Using data and digital tools for running experiments is important at all levels of an organization. If you are building products, making ads, or working with customers, chances are you are capable of participating in some form of rapid experimentation. Best is a culture of digital experimentation, which can lead to increased revenue, cost-cutting, innovation, and employee satisfaction.

7

The Only Constant

Leading as Transitioning

As digital shockwaves accelerate, sending out wave after wave of
transformative disruption, digital will become the cornerstone of enterprise
and public services competitiveness and growth, bringing both opportunities
and risks. The business and social impacts of these shockwaves will
intensify competition in all industries, and will require the development of
new employee skills, new forms of security, and new business models.

**—Thierry Breton, former CEO of Atos,
European Commissioner for Internal Markets**

Thierry Breton's plan to transition the multinational IT giant Atos into a
global leader of digital services was massive and urgent. At the time, digital shockwaves, as he evocatively described them, were pulsing through
businesses across industries. No one was outside the seismic zone. Enter-
prises needed to rebuild from the shaky ground up, and Atos would provide the blueprints.

The scope of such a vision was nothing new for Breton. Neither was
its prescience. In his early twenties, at the very start of his career as a
tech entrepreneur and political adviser, he wrote a series of novels that

presaged cybersecurity as a field. The real challenge for him and Atos was strategy and implementation. What did such a transition look like for an IT giant with over 100,000 employees? What did "digital transformation" even entail for organizations? We have asked countless people this question, and answers have varied. Some refer to the mechanics of moving from analog to digital to enhance their systems. Others aspired to scale significantly with the adoption of specific tools like cloud or AI or began to reimagine their offerings. In every case, digital transformation remained a central concern to the vast majority of companies we have engaged, even if they operated in the tech sector. Years after Breton's announcement, digital shockwaves continue to surge, more rapid and sweeping than ever.

We define digital transformation as organizations redesigning their underlying processes and competencies to become more adaptive using data and digital technology, from artificial intelligence and machine learning to the internet of things.[1] While the tech-driven methods of this redesign are an essential feature that distinguishes digital transformation from other forms of organizational change, our focus is on the mindset shift that underpins it. Although this mindset shift ultimately happens on an individual level, the larger organization can support that shift to lesser or greater degrees. If we believe that an organization has "a mind of its own" or a "hive mind" then it's fair to also think about developing an organization's digital mindset. The first step in digitally redesigning systems and processes is to see today's digitally driven world through what we call a *transitioning* lens. In the digital age, change isn't something that happens periodically that you need to scramble to respond to. Your technologies, organizational structure, culture, and people systems are in a constant process of transition from what came before and to what is next. But you never arrive at what you thought was coming next because it will change before you get there. That is what we mean by transitioning—you're in a constant state of flux. That means that leading in the digital environment is no longer about navigating change when it happens, it means helping your coworkers, employees, partners, and customers to continuously prepare for what's coming next and to embrace that they live and work in inexorable transition.

This chapter is especially relevant for leaders and managers who will be implementing digital transformation as part of a greater organizational change. For readers who are the recipients of change, this chapter provides an understanding of the challenges that can help facilitate overall digital transformation. Everyone in an organization needs to, at least, have a sense of what is going on behind the scenes and how the leaders are making their decisions on helping to equip the enterprise. Doing so can only help to develop a fuller digital mindset and to be better at work. To that end we introduce what we call the *work digitization process* (WDP) and an *adoption framework* for the differing responses that leaders, managers, and employees may have to new digital tools and processes. We also detail how organizations have helped their employees learn and can continue to successfully upskill workers with in-house learning programs.

Accept and Embrace Change to Become Adaptive

In change management, *transitional states* are key. They are fixed periods of time in which an organization moves from a familiar set of structures, processes, and accompanying cultural norms to new ones.[2] This middle phase of the change process is characterized as the experience of being in-between.[3] People typically and understandably experience strong emotions during a transitional state because it requires us to accept new perspectives and behaviors. Let's say you, your colleagues, or your employees are nonnative English speakers who begin work at a company where you are required to communicate only in English. The transitional state would be challenging. Even if you are the manager, you might doubt your capabilities or fear repercussions if you or your employees are less productive because of having to navigate a foreign language. You might even find your perspectives toward authority and decision-making change—or not. The point is that you would expect to go through a challenging transitional period of gaining fluency, under the assumption that practice and effort would eventually have an end point. During this temporary state of ambiguity, everyone's task, regardless of their place in company hierarchy, is to negotiate between the organization's past and its future until the transition is complete.[4]

In a digitally driven context, however, there is no end point to the transitional phase. Leadership is the act of bringing others through transitions. Constantly. Digital technology—and its impact on organizational structures, job roles, people's competencies, and customer needs—is in constant flux. You master one software release only to have it replaced by a newer version that requires learning new features. Your department is reorganized to accommodate new ways of processing information—only to be reorganized again when the first effort fails. Your customer base expands because you can reach them with one medium, and then customer needs change because demographics shift.

Change has always been a constant in work and in life; the difference today has to do with the *pace* of change that digital technology entails. Digital shockwaves put us in a perpetual in-between state because the cycles of change are so rapid. Leadership that doesn't acknowledge that transition is constant will struggle.[5]

Seeing digital change as constant transition requires leaders at all levels to develop a mindset that can embrace both the dynamism and uncertainty of permanent instability. Within the transitioning, your task is not simply to adapt—it is to *be adaptive*. Much like the AI and machine learning solutions that drive digital transformation of business, you, your colleagues, and your employees must constantly be processing new data, analyzing it, and using the findings to hone a perspective for the next wave of data coming at you.

Digital transformation is not a goal that you achieve; it is the means to achieve your unique goals, which fall on you to define and pursue. AI isn't going to detect how much support you might need in accepting ambiguity. Machine learning isn't going to teach you how to explain new protocols to your teammates or customers. Simply put, an adaptive mindset cannot be acquired, regardless of how much you invest in digital technology, or how many "digital gurus" you hire. It must be attained. And it can be attained, provided you learn to become comfortable with ambiguity and learn to accept that there's no end point to transformation.

Although this may at first be uncomfortable or even frightening, as you develop a digital mindset, you become attuned to the thrills that digital transition provides for continual learning.

Create a process for transitioning

Digital transformation is not a one-off project, something you can hand off to the executive suite or an isolated wing of your organization. A global appliance manufacturer learned this lesson the hard way when the highly experienced executive they brought in to spearhead its digital transformation surveyed the organization and determined that its workforce was too set in its ways to change.[6] Had you been one of those people reluctant to change, you might have sighed with relief when this leader created a whole new business unit—separate from headquarters— comprised of fresh digital talent, allowing you to continue doing your job as usual.

For a while, that seemed to work for the appliance company. The new unit delivered with all the speed and innovation that digital promises. But the success was in a vacuum. At headquarters, the organization was in total disarray. Partners and customers were bombarding the company with exasperated complaints that the company's online channel was not linked with the traditional face-to-face business channels. The revenue from these channels started to drop, compounding the tension between departments. Once internal communication broke down, the new digital unit collapsed. Within a matter of eight months, the executive hired to transform the company into a digital player had instead sparked chaos within the organization.

The company's failure was not with the technology. In fact, the company's digital unit was an immediate success on its own. What the company lacked was a transitional process. Instead of taking the time to help everyone within the organization to develop digital mindsets that could learn to accept the frustration and fear that often accompanies transition, leaders sought an external cure and what they believed would be an easier fix.

On the second go-round, the company picked an insider who knew the organization and modeled a well-developed digital mindset. She was respected across departments, especially for her perseverance, willingness to learn, and adaptivity to new situations. She started by implementing a training program that guided everyone throughout the company, from the sales force to the executives, through each new step of the digital initiative so that they understood and bought into its potential (instead of fearing the unfamiliar). Then, she reconnected with customers on an individual basis, working to understand each one's specific needs and adapting her digital business model accordingly. Under her leadership, the majority of employees were able to develop digital mindsets and attain a transitional perspective. The company became a digital leader.

This transitional approach is also what guided Thierry Breton to succeed in his mission of *dual* digital transformation at Atos—undergoing radical change throughout the organization while helping customers through the process at the same time. Although it may sound surprising that an IT company needs help with digital transformation in its own ranks, that fact underscores our point about the constant and rapid change and the adaptive state a digital mindset requires. Just because you've mastered one technology doesn't automatically mean that you are ready to adapt to the next round. As the story of Atos and others throughout the chapter will show, a transitional approach to leadership must negotiate two main points of focus in order for organizations to fully achieve digital goals both for itself and, when necessary, for the clients it serves:

- Designing and aligning systems and processes

- Preparing people for a digital organizational culture

Each of these points, of course, impacts the other directly. From a transitional view, the task is for you to maintain alignment between them as the ground continues to shift underneath.

Design and align systems and processes

A digital mindset needs systems and processes that are designed to align and support. Leaders may have to reorganize teams to be rapid, agile, self-regulating, and collaborative. Here's a brief overview of how two companies did just that.

CEO Vincent van den Boogert realized the need to make fundamental transitions within his company, ING, a financial services company based in the Netherlands, when he noticed that existing internal processes were riddled with meetings, handovers, and other bureaucracies that were spread across functional departments, making limited use of data and digital technology to increase speed.[7] Plus, no one functional group assumed end-to-end responsibility for the customers, creating potential problems. When van den Boogert decided to upend the company's whole operating model, he looked to Silicon Valley, where agile processes were already established in digital companies like Spotify, Netflix, Google, and Zappos. He determined that ING needed to make the customer experience itself a commodity rather than presenting banking as just a service. As another executive put it, they needed to "unbank the bank." In order to offer this new customer experience, they first had to reorganize. ING moved to agile cross-functional team structures they called tribes. Autonomous teams started to use daily standups to address every pressing customer need, promote transparency, and achieve performance goals. They employed the Jeff Bezos "two-pizza rule" such that group sizes were small enough that two pizzas could feed everyone. Along with rescaled team sizes came completely new roles and the elimination of others, including middle managers. These new roles required a developed digital mindset aligned with the company's new scaled-down and digitally driven structures.

Similarly, Unilever, a ninety-year-old London-based multinational consumer goods company, needed to figure out how to adapt its sprawling global business for the digital age. As a multinational company that makes and sells over four hundred household staples in 190 countries, success was a delicate balancing act between the specificities of local markets and the broad scale of global operations. Unilever's solution, like ING's, was agile teams, which could focus on the demands of a particular last mile while simultaneously guiding their work with the company's digital capacities across multiple countries. Rahul Welde, Unilever's executive vice president in digital transformation and a thirty-year veteran of the organization, designed an agile team structure that allowed members to remain globally distributed while making strategic use of data for tailored initiatives within rapidly changing local markets.[8] Under Welde's leadership, Unilever formed three hundred ten-person agile teams that were remote, global, and able to operate at scale.

According to Welde, this strategy had three vectors. The first one involved the use of enabling technology and tools, which could reduce global-local divides. With digital platforms, brands could engage directly with customers in local markets on a vastly larger scale. The second was redesigning processes to adapt to new technology and tools. The last dimension was people. In the end, Welde recognized that people would be the change makers. Within eighteen months, Unilever had its three thousand agile team members deployed worldwide.

Follow data across silos—integrate!

Organizations must also use a transitional perspective to streamline communication across departments that were previously siloed. Moderna, an American biotechnology company made headlines in 2020, bringing out one of the first Covid-19 vaccines at breakneck speed. Integration across groups played a key role.[9] The cofounder and CEO, Stéphane Bancel, calls Moderna a "tech company that happens to do biology." Moderna exemplifies three of the main components of the current digital transformation. The first and foundational layer is its enormous access to data—the source of the company's value in developing vaccines and other therapeutics. The second layer is its reliance on the cloud—it is not only cheaper but faster and more agile than in-house computing. The third is its capacity for automation—building AI algorithms to perform R&D processes with an accuracy and speed impossible to achieve manually.

Historically, big pharma companies have been globally distributed operations of siloed units, but Moderna uses a fully integrated structure where data flow freely among different teams that work together in real time.[10] Juan Andres, the company's chief technical operations and quality officer in charge of production processes, says, "What's more important than having sophisticated digital tools or algorithms, is integration at all levels. The way things come together is what matters about technology, not the technology itself." When Moderna was tasked with the urgent need to develop the vaccine, they could accelerate the process because that integration was already in place. Bancel had hired Marcello Damiani five years before the pandemic to be in charge of both digital and operational excellence. Bancel did not separate the two roles, explaining that "enabling Marcello to design the processes was key. Digitization only makes sense once the processes are done. If you have crappy analog processes, you'll get crappy digital processes." Fully integrated systems and processes allow Moderna to source some preexisting digital solutions for the vaccine and build many others in-house, either designing algorithms from scratch or tweaking existing ones to perform deeper and more specialized analyses. By spring 2020, Moderna had roughly twenty algorithms in production and another twenty in development. Integration is what made development of those algorithms possible, and it is ultimately what made the speedy and successful vaccine rollout happen.

Identify and implement the right digital tools

Although we each develop a digital mindset individually as we learn to become adaptive, that can only happen if organizational leaders realize that *how* digital tools are deployed is a core part of digital transformation. Leading continuous transition means managers must be heavily involved in selecting and implementing the digital tools that support change. To do that, it's helpful to understand what today's IT department can and cannot do. Historically IT departments have been well equipped to handle large, enterprise-wide implementations of software and to make sure that the software undergirding a company's digital transformation works the way it should. This function of IT is still true for implementations of bespoke tools or, say, ERP systems. However, most of the technologies that companies adopt to enable digital transformation today are cloud-based tools that don't require costly implementation efforts and are updated frequently and unobtrusively by another company. In most cloud implementations, if you are a functional or project manager, director, or in another senior leadership position, your role is to simply buy licenses, download the software, and get started without ever looping in IT. Just to be clear, we're not advocating that you exclude IT completely. There are good reasons (e.g., cost, security, sustainability) to bring IT into any technology purchasing decision. But the stark reality is that a great number of SaaS implementations happen at the departmental or project level, without IT ever being involved. Ask any IT leader and they'll tell you that managing departmental flexibility with the need for corporate regulation is becoming one of the most difficult parts of the job.

It's important to deploy new digital technologies and manage implementations as a manager because these new technologies directly facilitate changes in the way people perform their tasks. These changes lead to new roles and responsibilities (such as when ING restructured into hundreds of ten-person agile teams), and they allow for new collaborative networks to open up within the organization (for example, Moderna's integrated systems and processes). These new networks are the real positive drivers for the organization. While IT is accustomed to managing support applications, the task of defining new roles and networks—and effectively reshaping organizational culture and goals—is best suited for business leaders.

Preparing People and Culture for a Digital Shift

If everyone can plan for a transformation by thinking about how they will actually interact with and use the new digital tools, they will be more successful in acquiring the adaptive mindset necessary for successful transformation. Likewise, if everyone understands how tools will help attain better results, they will see how they can become the means for greater organizational change and problem-solving rather than the new technology as an end unto itself.

In other words, becoming comfortable with transitional states involves shifting the organization's culture, its values, norms, attitudes, and behaviors.[11] As a leader trying to promote the transformation and develop digital mindsets, how do you ensure that people understand that a new day has dawned? You start with a *bold stroke*: an act that commands attention and prompts the organization to understand that a new direction is required.[12] Examples of bold strokes include a major reorganization, an acquisition, significant resources diverted, hiring a digital transformation czar who reports to the CEO, closures of legacy systems, or mandating that everyone learn some coding within a short time. A bold stroke has to be followed by a *long march*: the organized and enduring advancement toward new routines and behaviors.

Move from frustration to inspiration

A bold stroke is necessary but insufficient to gain buy-in. Any change provokes anxiety. With digital change, you, your colleagues, or your employees might be apprehensive not only about the unknown environment that will replace existing surroundings, but you may also worry about your own capacity to learn and apply the requisite technical material that you will need to perform effectively. These anxieties will affect technical and non-technical roles in equal measure. Engineers, for example, might not have the relevant technical competencies, as we discussed in earlier chapters.

We recommend a deceptively simple adoption framework that we have used to help leaders at many companies to influence people's behaviors so that they are motivated to engage with a change program that requires learning new skills.[13]

Do I have buy-in such that people believe digital transformation will be beneficial for them and the organization? And can I learn what I need to in order to succeed in this transformed organization?

FIGURE 7-1

Four types of employee responses with digital transformation

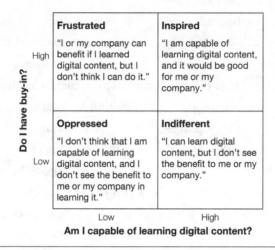

Mapping the answers to these two questions produces four types of responses you'll typically see and suggests what you need to do to make transformation successful. (See figure 7-1.)

The matrix of responses allows managers to locate where your team members might be. In the best-case scenario, people will be in the top-right quadrant, inspired by the change, believing that they have the capacity to learn digital content, and excited to go through the change. But, of course, you'll have varying proportions in the four quadrants.

The good news is that leaders and managers can move individuals from one quadrant to another. To shift people from oppressed or indifferent to inspired, you first must increase buy-in by helping everyone believe that learning digital competencies is good for them and their organization. Three factors are crucial to promote buy-in:

- Increase messaging from leadership that stresses the importance of digital transformation as a new and critical frontier for the company.

- Launch internal marketing campaigns to help employees imagine the positive potential of a company powered by digital technology.

- Promote a shift in people's identities; that is, encourage people to view themselves as contributing members of a digital organization.

After establishing buy-in, leaders can shift individuals from *frustrated* to *inspired* by boosting confidence in their capacity. Three factors contribute to people's confidence in learning digital skills:

- People's past experience with digital technologies—whether it was through education, employment, or work—tends to give them the confidence they need to succeed in this task.

- Vicarious experience of others, including peers and managers, influences beliefs in one's own capabilities.

- Persuasion and encouragement from managers and executives promotes confidence in employees.

Upskilling

Hiring digitally trained employees is an efficient way to bring your workforce into the digital age, but it is unrealistic to rely on hiring alone to accomplish your goals, given the war for talent. An expansive upskilling plan of existing talent must supplement the new talent.

Let's turn back to Thierry Breton from Atos. He spent his initial years as CEO doubling the size of company into a sprawling global enterprise with over 100,000 employees working in specialty IT areas like system integration, cloud, big data, cybersecurity, and others.[14] This strategy was designed to fend off a sea of global competitors flanking him— startups from Silicon Valley, India, and China—many of which were born digital. While Atos had not yet integrated AI and other data-driven services into their processes when Breton took over, competitors were emerging with digital strategy in place and had employees with digital mindsets and expertise from their inception.

Breton couldn't just acquire the skills to compete. He moved fast to upskill a large workforce comfortable with legacy IT and lacking the modern capabilities of a digital environment. In one survey, Atos had ranked thirty-ninth out of forty in digital maturity—the "continuous and ongoing process of adaptation to a changing digital landscape"—despite the fact that the company focused on IT systems.[15] The upskilling was an ambitious three-year plan that required employees to learn new skills in training sessions that took them away from their day-to-day responsibilities.

Others in the C-suite resisted, convinced that the only way for people to learn was on the job. There was also disagreement about what percentage and which parts of the workforce would need digital training. After intense debate, as competitors kept increasing market share, Breton made the call: he created a *digital transformation factory upskilling* certification program. The goal was to train about thirty-five thousand people, both technical and non-technical, in digital technologies and portfolios, including big data, AI, hybrid cloud, business accelerators, and cybersecurity.[16]

The upskilling program was voluntary. A significant internal marketing campaign was launched to motivate people to build their digital mindsets. In addition, a peer and managerial nomination system was instituted, along with rewards for achieving various benchmarks in certification completion. The belief was that employees who decided on their own to get certified would be more likely to internalize the new skills and shift their behaviors for the digital era. Executives throughout the company would encourage training or demonstrate specific needs that people could pursue. For example, one executive said to his group that he needed people with cybersecurity skills and asked who would be interested to get training in that subject area. Approximately 250 people raised their hands, and 80 of the people who entered the training went on to become cybersecurity experts.

The company created a full suite of certifications under the Atos University Academy. It designed its digital programs in partnership with heavyweights like Google, EMC, Microsoft, and SAP, as well as universities and corporate learning companies. Sessions were delivered virtually, which meant that any employee could take courses regardless of their location. In addition, the content of the sessions was designed to accommodate everyone from the most technical engineers and data scientists to sales and marketing professionals, whose functions had limited technical dimensions. On average, each course took between four and eight weeks to complete with approximately five to sixteen hours of learning per week. For example, the hybrid cloud architect certification program took sixty to eighty hours over the course of two months. Assignments included four case studies, a written exam, and two labs. Less technical roles such as sales were offered digital awareness courses that people could select from four categories: cloud, business accelerators, digital workplace codex, and cybersecurity. One course was called "Cybersecurity landscape and Atos's position"; another offering was "IoT solutions" within the digital workplace category.

Within three years, more than seventy thousand digital certifications had been completed. Every Atos employee had access to certification programs tailored to functional roles. Leaders at Atos saw that people were motivated to get certified because their jobs entailed some sort of a digital component. For example, salespeople had to be fluent in cloud computing or cybersecurity. Project managers needed to have a strong grasp of digital technologies' functions and applications, even if they didn't require an in-depth understanding of how the technologies worked. Those in technical roles, such as engineers or data analysts, needed to understand and operate new digital technologies with the same depth of expertise previously required for legacy technologies. Before long, it was clear to everyone that relevance and upward mobility at the company required a digital mindset that the certifications could help foster. Managers were also encouraged to take courses to build general awareness about digital offerings with emphasis on leading in a digital age.

Of course, Atos isn't the only company that has become aggressive in upskilling its workforce; even technical companies are seeing that teaching employees digital skills is an imperative. When Google moved from a desktop-first to a mobile-first and then to a digital mindset, skills had to be upgraded accordingly—especially among the engineers. The company introduced a "Learn with Google AI" training program as a fast-paced introduction to machine learning and trained more than eighteen thousand employees globally over two years, a third of its engineering headcount. And Amazon, the online retail giant, committed to spend more than $700 million to retrain a third of its US workforce to be better equipped to deal with digital transformation because it saw technology threatening to upend the way many of its employees do their jobs.

Key practices for employee learning programs

Companies that have successfully implemented employee training programs to upskill a workforce in a digital era have followed these six practices:

1. Set a companywide goal.

2. Design learning opportunities that include all functional roles.

3. Prioritize virtual delivery, making learning scalable and accessible to everyone.

4. Motivate people to learn through campaigns, nominations, and rewards.

5. Provide managers digital training to understand the offerings and motivate employees.

6. Encourage projects within the company to adopt digital components, leading to direct application.

It's important to note that organizations have to determine whether instituting a voluntary or compulsory program is best for them. In some companies, industries, and even countries, mandating learning might be the best approach. For example, Hiroshi Mikitani at Rakuten required his entire organization to learn how to code as part of his digital transformation objectives. This move was congruent with his mandate nearly a decade earlier that his Japanese-headquartered employees learn the English language for everyday work—a major initiative that he called

"Englishnization."[17] Mandating with a deadline works for a company like Rakuten. Every organization needs to consider its own context when determining how to influence their employees to develop requisite digital skills.

Autoworks: A Process for Leading a Transition to Digitization

A formal example of leading transitions to digitization is what we call the work digitization process, which has six phases (see figure 7-2):[18]

FIGURE 7-2

How to plan your company's transformation

By understanding how change naturally rolls out, you can start your planning with where you want to end up—identifying the gains in performance you can achieve with new digital tools—and work back from there to set company goals that employees will embrace.

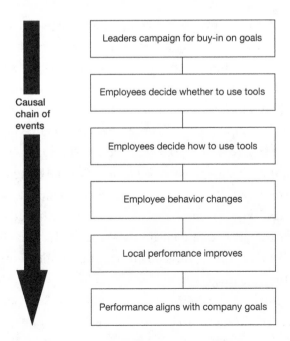

Source: Adapted from P. Leonardi, "You're Going Digital—Now What?" *MIT Sloan Management Review* (Winter 2020).

To illustrate the phases of this work digitization process, we'll use an example from a European automotive company we'll call Autoworks—a different company than the one Balaji and Davide worked for—which used the process to manage a digital transformation. Auto companies make great case studies because they have such complex physical products, but they have been at the forefront of digital transformation.

We'll describe how digital transformations tend to be experienced and processed by those on the ground and then show how reverse planning—working backward, phase by phase, to set broad corporate goals—leads to digital transitioning that sticks.

Most digital transformation efforts are launched with extensive roll-out plans that outline such activities as financing the transformation, reorganizing the company to make it agile enough to get the most out of digital tools, developing data-driven insights that allow the company to deliver more-customized products, and reducing time to market.

Phase 1: Leaders sell the digital transformation

Without widespread buy-in from employees, any major change initiative will wither and die. That's why the first step in a successful effort is to explain the benefits of digital change to the workforce.

The leaders of Autoworks understood this. Autoworks had embarked upon a digital transformation in the mid-2000s. One goal was to accelerate product development while cutting costs in resource-intensive areas. Eager to get started, Autoworks' senior leaders beefed up the company's supercomputing center and licensed a slew of digital design applications. The CEO declared, "We're going to be a digital company."

Senior leaders were vocal and clear about the change they wanted. Digital performance testing meant that product development could get done faster and cheaper. Directors heard "faster and cheaper" in their staff meetings, managers heard "faster and cheaper" in their division meetings, and engineers heard "faster and cheaper" over and over from managers, directors, and executives in training sessions, at conferences, during all-hands meetings, and in everyday work. "Faster and cheaper" became the mantra of the digital transformation.

Studies show that employees listen when senior leaders broadcast goals and announce bold initiatives for achieving them.[19] Early on, such pronouncements create frames of reference that people use to understand the technology they're being asked to implement. If you asked employees at Autoworks how they would know if new tools could transform the organization, they would (and often did!) answer, "I'll know if they help me build simulation models 'faster and cheaper.'"

Phase 2: Employees decide whether to use the new technology

With messaging and training in place, leaders then fully expect that employees will shift their work to the new applications. But there's no guarantee that will happen.[20] At Autoworks, roughly 40 percent of potential users decided *not* to use the technology, even when it was mandated by their direct supervisors.

That's a big number—big enough, in fact, to derail a digital transformation. So, it's important for leaders to understand why so many employees might make that choice. We've found that employees consider whether the technology enables *them* as individuals to carry out the goals announced by the company's leaders. At Autoworks, that meant that the engineers asked themselves, "Will this software help *me* develop new car designs faster and cheaper?"

As it turned out, not everyone thought it would. "Faster and cheaper" was more complicated rhetoric than Autoworks leaders had imagined. The phrase inadvertently encouraged people to *compare* the new tools with the old ones they knew inside and out and could already use quite efficiently. ("Faster" and "cheaper" grammatically are literally called "comparatives.") Top engineers, who served as early adopters, did just that—they compared the new with the old—and decided that the new software actually slowed their work down. While they could see that it had other distinct advantages for the *organization*, they rejected it for failing, in their experience, to be faster and cheaper for *them*. These engineers decided that it was in their company's best interest for them to stick with the tools they were already using. Making matters worse, the early experimenters had become negative influencers in the network of company engineers: other engineers decided that if a colleague they respected had rejected the new software, they didn't even have to give it a try.

Of course, senior leaders had intended that "faster and cheaper" would be seen as the broad goal of the transformation effort. They hadn't considered how those words might scan at various levels and influence granular decision-making. That's why senior leaders must take great care in crafting their rhetoric. If it doesn't match up with the reality of how work gets done, their prized new technology won't get implemented in the way they hope.[21]

Phase 3: Employees decide how they will use the new technology

Even if the new technology encounters a band of naysayers, the many employees who do make the switch will come to a second critical decision: *how* to use it. Almost any digital technology can be adopted in many different ways, intended and not intended.[22] In a digital transformation, the features people choose to apply are deeply consequential, since they determine what kind of data will be recorded, produced, or analyzed and how that data will be used.

Autoworks' leaders believed that data were a key benefit of moving design processes into a digital environment. The use of simulation tools would make it possible for engineers to run hundreds or thousands of iterations of tests for crashes, or noise and vibration, and many other types. By comparing all those results, engineers would be able to optimize a vehicle's design with far more sophistication than when the company ran a few dozen wrecks with crash test dummies. At least, that was the theory.

For one year, we tracked two departments that used the same digital tool for automating simulation designs. In one department, engineers engaged with the tool in widely varying ways, according to individual preference. In the other, every engineer used the same features in the same order. By the end of that year, the vehicles designed by the latter group were outperforming those created by the former by a 2-to-1 margin. The data produced by the engineers who had followed the same path had a uniform foundation and could be analyzed for patterns of effectiveness. The engineers who had followed their own paths produced just as much data, but the information arose from varying assumptions and choices.[23] These kinds of differences around the company made it difficult to create a set of best practices for the new digital tools. If a central value of digital technologies is the creation of data that can be mined for efficiencies and other valuable learning, shaping consistent usage patterns is essential.

Phase 4: New kinds of data change the way employees behave

In its pre-digital days, Autoworks vehicle design testing standard operating procedure went like this: engineers conducted crashes and various other simulations, collected the data, and passed it along to the data analysis group, where analysts tried to glean universal principles for good vehicle design. There were engineers; there were data analysts. The difference between the two was clear.

Remember those engineers who used the new digital simulation tools in consistent ways to produce comparable data? They started to change the status quo by slowly integrating analysis into their work. They could see the results of their own tests, of course, and could examine results in the aggregate. But then they started talking to one another about their results and thinking about them together. As one engineer commented, "Now that we've gone digital, our roles as design engineers are changing." Instead of being siloed away from one another while they ceded analysis to an equally siloed analysis department, the design engineers had become a collaborative team of data analysts.

Some "by-the-book" managers tried to curtail this empowerment by insisting on the separation between analysts and engineers. But this process of more and better data changing employee tasks, resulting in changed roles and relationships, is an inevitable by-product of digital transformations. At their core, relationships between people in different roles are based on data. When people start performing new roles because they have new data and information, they necessarily start interacting with different people. The result is the formation of new and initially invisible social networks. According to some research, these powerful new networks may be the most important ingredient in driving a digital transformation.[24]

Phase 5: Performance improves locally

There's often a dichotomy between the targets business leaders impose for their digital transformations and the benefits employees experience at a local level.

Once they were effectively using the new digital tools and comparing results with others in their emerging social network, Autoworks engineers started to see real concrete gains that they could appreciate. For instance, they found that it was becoming easier for them to optimize designs for key features like crashworthiness and fuel economy.

The process of moving from testing to final design solutions improved significantly, as well. In fact, according to our analysis, engineers who changed their roles to incorporate data analytics and shifted their social networks to interact with other engineers solidified the design of their vehicles 23 percent faster and with 31 percent fewer laboratory tests than engineers whose roles didn't change. In other words, engineers were working "faster and cheaper," after all.

That sounds like the kind of success Autoworks leaders had been hoping for. And it is. But there are two important caveats. The first, of course, is that 40 percent of engineers initially rejected the software because they hadn't found it obviously "faster and cheaper." The second is that those engineers who did achieve "faster and cheaper" gains arrived at them via metrics that mattered to them in their roles, like design quality improvements. If senior executives had customized their rhetoric early on to resonate with engineers' own experience of their work, they might have motivated more engineers to adopt the new digital tools sooner and secured even more significant gains.

Phase 6: Local performance aligns with company goals

A digital transformation gets traction when it meets key corporate goals by employing technologies that improve local processes and results.

One reason Autoworks chose to focus intently on vehicle design is that twenty years of robust statistical analysis had identified that process—along with supply chain, regulatory compliance, and manufacturing efficiency—as critical to reducing the time it took to get cars from concept to dealer. Better time-to-market would accelerate top-line growth.

Needless to say, the company was happy that the technologies led to "faster and cheaper" designs. Rather than sit on its laurels, however, Autoworks conducted a deep analysis of how the gains had been achieved. That's how they discovered the remarkable value of the social network that had been unleashed by the new design software: engineers who spent three times as many hours discussing vehicle design with one another as they spent instrumenting simulation models dramatically reduced the amount of rework that needed to be done in later stages of development. Sure, new software helped engineers speed up the delivery of a final, optimized vehicle design, but the dialogue spurred by the software accelerated things even more.

Autoworks Best Practices

By digging into its success, Autoworks uncovered two key learnings that could fuel further improvements in the years ahead. One focuses on the planning process and the other on whom you involve in the process.

Plan in reverse

The six phases we've just described illustrate the way change develops internally during a digital transformation. Now let's turn to how understanding this process should shape planning for your own company's transformation. This process can be derailed at any stage, so it is crucial

FIGURE 7-3

How to plan your company's transformation

By understanding how change naturally rolls out, you can start your planning with where you want to end up—identifying the gains in performance you can achieve with new digital tools—and work back from there to set company goals that employees will embrace.

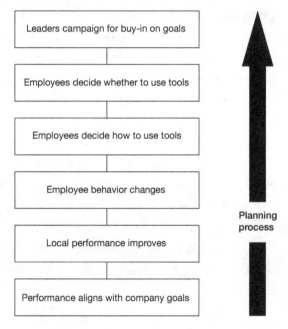

Leaders campaign for buy-in on goals

Employees decide whether to use tools

Employees decide how to use tools

Employee behavior changes

Local performance improves

Performance aligns with company goals

Planning process

Source: Adapted from P. Leonardi, "You're Going Digital—Now What?" *MIT Sloan Management Review* (Winter 2020).

to plan in a way that keeps everyone's experience front-of-mind. (See figure 7-3.)

The key is to plan backward, with the end goal first. One approach is to identify which local activities have the highest potential to transform, since this will inform the choice of digital tools and the direction of the digital transformation. To do so, organizations need to gather and analyze internal data on which local outcomes best drive larger organizational goals: this will highlight an area of improvement that can be targeted and facilitated with a digital tool. In the middle of this process, the organization must continue to gather data to see if the efforts are working, and whether behaviors within the organization are help-ing or hindering those efforts.

It is also key to foster an environment that allows everyone to meet their goals through the transformation, especially as their tasks and roles change in the process. Leaders can help facilitate this by understanding how information flows within the organization and by removing institu-tional obstacles that might prevent employees from embracing the change. Diagnostic processes like an organizational network analysis can be particularly effective.[25] This kind of analysis can show which groups of employees interact with one another, how they interact, and what kinds of new groups might emerge through the transformation process. This analysis can in turn help leadership facilitate the appropriate formal role transitions and identify key influencers to help champion the change.

Identify and recruit digital mindset influencers

Encourage those that are already further along in developing a digital mindset to become exemplars or beacons for those who are more reluc-tant. In addition, take the time to discuss the desired transformation with influencers who are trusted by others. That discussion may surface general concerns and ideas for improvements. Ultimately, you will want to ask influencers to help generate the messaging that would convey the benefits to the workforce. Hearing directly from trusted colleagues can significantly improve employees' willingness to embrace the change and the new technology. Holding training sessions, clearly establishing new targets, and even looking to hire new employees who already have the newly desired skill set are also part of digital transformation.

When campaigning for digital transformation, if you fail to explain the benefits of the desired change in terms that are meaningful for those who will be using the technology, you can fail to generate much-needed early buy-in, or even create misunderstandings about how the transfor-mation will take place at the practical level. Even when there is substan-tial buy-in, many may choose not to use the new technology if they perceive themselves to be better equipped at meeting desired goals with preexisting technology. People will find reasons to resist change if they can. For example, if the stated goal of the transformation is to make processes faster and cheaper, some people may feel that the best option *for them* is to continue using the tools they already are proficient at using. Moreover, even among groups who readily adopt the new digital tools, if a consistent pattern of usage is not sufficiently adopted, the efficacy of the new technology—as well as the analyzable data its adoption produces—can be diminished.

Transition to Continuous Learning

Continuous learning has become an economic imperative for people and organizations alike in the face of rapid changes in the digital economy.[26] Continuous learning environments work best if there is employee autonomy, tailored curricula, and psychological safety. And to state the obvious, these conditions have to align with the strategic combination of digital technology (AI- and cloud-enabled platforms, in particular) and effective leadership.

Successful continuous learning initiatives are ones that foster individual autonomy for learners to own the process themselves. That is, learning has to be decentralized and become a responsibility that each person owns. At Spotify, for example, all employees are responsible for their learning, although the company has a robust learning and development group called the GreenHouse to honor the company's focus on enablement. As a greenhouse does for plants, the group promotes the idea of watering and fertilizing growth. It also understands that in order to promote self-ownership, finding modular content online has to be easy for employees. Spotify built an in-house learning platform for delivering education that has the same functionality as a social media or entertainment platform (think Instagram). Other companies, like Philips, have adopted the *playlist*. Employees can share playlists of their tailored lessons with colleagues, thereby helping to enhance knowledge exchange from the ground up. Ultimately, an organization's ability to adapt through continuous learning is dependent on the motivation and commitment of its employees to engage in the process themselves. For continuous learning to be sustainable in the long term, learners must be internally motivated.

Tailored curricula are the core of continuous learning initiatives. Instead of generic training programs applied to the whole workforce, customized learning plans are designed for specific roles and functions based on the skills and credentials necessary for each. Software engineers might learn a new coding language, while salespeople might learn business development strategy of technologies like cloud or cybersecurity. To tailor curricula even further, AI-enabled learning experience platforms (LXPs) can adapt content to an individual's own pace and needs. One learner might thrive within a fast-paced curriculum that keeps her on her toes. Another might do better with a slower pace that allows him to chew on the subject matter. As learners progress, they gain *microcredentials*—certifications or badges for validating specific digital skills (for instance, "web scraping in Python") that can be acquired in a much shorter time than the traditional educational formats offered by universities. To offset the feeling of isolation that sometimes accompanies individualized learning, Westpac, one of Australia's biggest banks, also encourages community building among people who share similar areas of interest.

Continuous learning marks a new paradigm for education and career growth (see appendix for examples). This paradigm is inherently dynamic. It differs from the previous model that provided the stability of a fixed role and skill set for one's whole career. A common denominator of effective continuous learning programs is a blended approach that can be individualized for employee autonomy and flexibility. Capital One, the bank holding company, offers a blend of learning choices to its software engineering teams that include online courses, in-person workshops, boot camps, and trainings from outside experts. In addition to the tech curriculum offered through its own internal university, Capital One also partners with larger, distance-learning organizations.

For employees to feel comfortable reaching outside their wheelhouse and learning new skills for the rest of their professional lives, leaders must establish a culture of psychological safety that encourages exploration and the courage to fail. Ideally, leaders will model their own failures, as is done at Spotify. For example, the online travel and lodging agency

Booking.com has fostered an environment of continuous learning that allows employees to pursue completely different roles within the organization with the understanding that they will have become beginners and may not immediately be as proficient as they were in their previous role. Kim dos Santos, an employee who began in the human resources department, explains how his interest in design led him to take classes in user experience (UX) design offered by the company.[27] Despite having no previous background in UX before joining the company, he learned and progressed to such a degree that he was eventually hired internally as a UX designer.

While leadership and employee development have always been essential to organizational performance and stability, the rate of technological change inherent in the digital economy makes continuous learning a necessary component to achieve these goals. Support to develop leaders who can mentor less experienced employees and pathways for growth and mobility within the company are both crucial. For example, at AT&T, leaders provide emotional support, strategic advice, honest feedback, and of course, encouragement. The crowdsourcing business review platform Yelp, an early adopter of continuous learning, also encourages managers to mentor with the principle "leaders who teach." Horizontal learning and the exchange of new ideas and information across the company is fostered in several ways at Yelp. The engineering team regularly invites guest speakers for lunch—usually someone from within the company— enabling collaboration as well as stimulating growth. An informal, voluntary program introduces employees to someone within the company they haven't met in order to learn from one another or simply connect. Innovations that result from groups of engineers who participate in two-day hackathons are successful to the extent that team members learn from one another; they are also opportunities to meet new people.

Centralized support for people to learn and try new things is essential to nurture a culture that encourages continuous learning. Thoughtful attention to the learning environment and employee learning needs is as imperative to success as new knowledge and skill sets.

Fittingly, it's digitization itself that provides the technology for online, individualized, and autonomous learning that makes this possible.

GETTING TO 30 PERCENT

Transitioning and Preparing for Continuous Change

Digital transformation is when organizations redesign underlying systems and processes to align with today's data and digital technology, including artificial intelligence, machine learning, and the internet of things. Digital transformation is not a one and done; it's a state of perpetual transition; your task is not simply to adapt, but to *be adaptive*. Leaders can emphasize specific mindsets and strategies:

- Teams must become agile, autonomous, and collaborative. Communication must be fast and effective to keep up with the speed of digital transformation.

- Every member of the team must be able to identify how, why, when, and which digital tools align with strategic goals. Tech savvy is no longer strictly the realm of IT.

- Work backward: identify your strategic goals first, then find the right digital solution. Gain buy-in by showing team members how the solution achieves team goals. This is the work digitization process.

- Replace obstacles to learning new skills with boosts: hold training sessions, establish new targets, and recruit digital mindset influencers who can champion change.

- Use the adoption framework to turn frustration about digital change into inspiration. The framework is built on the following two questions team members must ask themselves: *Have I bought in?* and *Am I capable of learning?* To bring employees from "no" to "yes" on both questions, stress the importance of digital transformation for the organization, each employees' critical role in the process, and your confidence in their capacity to learn.

- For continuous learning to be sustainable, learners must be internally motivated and develop individual autonomy.

- For employees to feel comfortable learning new skills for the rest of their professional lives, leaders must establish a culture of psychological safety that encourages exploration and the courage to fail.

Upskill your team! The war for digital talent is fierce. Focus on upskilling talent within your ranks over hiring talent from the outside. Hard skills can be learned; institutional knowledge takes time to build. This new educational paradigm means employees and organizations must continually upskill to stay competitive.

Conclusion

It's Time!

Progress is impossible without change; and those who
cannot change their minds cannot change anything.

—George Bernard Shaw

Today, there is no business unaffected by digital transformation and no
type of work that isn't being changed, even if subtly, by digital tools.[1]
We've shown you why that's the case throughout this book. We've also
shown you why technical skills and deep interest in new technology are
not enough to thrive in the digital economy. And we've shown that we
can't wait for someone else to deal with our digital transformation goals.

Those who will thrive in the age of data, algorithms, and AI recognize that it's becoming less and less possible to be successful without a
digital mindset.

Your Digital Mindset Shift

Each chapter in this book has helped you to reach that all-important
30 percent level of digital competence in several areas that will help you
to think and act in new ways. You've learned how AI and machine learning algorithms work, how to interact with an intelligent technological
teammate, how to establish your digital presence, how data are classified
and created into data sets, what different kinds of statistical techniques

can and cannot tell you about those data, how security failures happen, how blockchain creates opportunities for new transactions, how you can conduct rapid experiments and fight the bureaucracy that aims to stifle them, and how to build a culture that embraces digital change and promotes continuous learning.

You've learned many new skills. But as we said at the outset, having the skills to work with digital technologies is not the same thing as having a digital mindset. Remember, developing a new mindset means that you build from your new skills to see the world in a new way and to change your behavior. Your digital mindset comes when you change how you approach collaboration, computation, and change.

In reshaping your *approach to collaboration*, you've learned how AI-enabled technologies are trained to recognize text and images and classify them in certain ways so that eventually they can recognize, classify, and make predictions about data on their own. When you think about collaborating with AI-enabled machines, you can now understand how they are reaching their conclusions, even if you can't see inside the black box to know exactly why they are reaching those conclusions. Armed with that knowledge, now you can ask how they were trained and with what data to assess particular biases the AI might possess. It will also help you to determine what level of trust you will have in AI-enabled machine recommendations, just like elite military teams do.

You know it's better to treat AI like machines, not people. It's easy to fall into the trap of treating AI technologies as though they are human, but as the lessons learned from using the scheduling chatbot Amy show, forgetting to treat technology like technology can pose major problems.

You've also learned how to maintain a digital presence effectively. One of the biggest shifts in people-to-people collaboration in the digital age is that relationships of all types (personal, work, romantic) might be predominantly digitally mediated.[2] Ironically, the digital tools that allow people to work together across time and space create a new problem: psychological separation. This separation causes us to overcommunicate as a way to close that gap—posting more and more pictures on social media or deluging our colleagues with messages on Slack. But doing this has the opposite of the intended effect. Herbert Simon won the Nobel Prize in economics for describing how when confronted with more information than they can process, people attend selectively to a small subset of that information that appears relevant to them and they ignore the rest.[3] In the digital age, the vicious cycle that ensues is that the more people communicate to be noticed, the more other people tune them out.

You're now equipped with the tools to collaborate more effectively with machines and people in the digital age. In addition to treating AI like machines, not people, you also know how to cultivate your digital presence to break through the information clutter that makes it difficult for you to reach others.

If you're like many readers of this book, you might not have had a systematic *approach to computation* before you started reading. But you did the hard work to embrace the challenge and now you understand how actions, text, photos, and other pieces of data are computed in ways that turn them into "things we know"—not to mention how the various analytic techniques run on those data turn them from "things we know" into "things we should do." And you recognize that building a strong foundation in statistical reasoning is key to being an astute consumer of analytics in the digital age.

These skills in analytics and statistics pay big dividends. You can more effectively understand, keep track of, and make use of the massive troves of data that are being collected all the time. As you're now aware, each time you send an email, text a friend or coworker, visit a web page, type in a search term, like someone's post, comment on a picture, give someone a badge, endorse someone's skills, make a meeting on your calendar, chat on a videoconferencing application, check in at a location, or—the list could go on and on . . . and on—you are leaving digital exhaust. Digital exhaust is the by-product of your activities on digital tools. That exhaust tells vendors, companies, your employer, law enforcement, or anyone else who has access to it whom you interact with and what you say and do. From those data, analysts are increasingly using advanced statistical models to make predictions about relatively benign things like what kinds of lotion you will want to buy and what color car you will want to drive to much more consequential things like whether you will quit your job or commit a crime.

Can you have confidence in these predictions? How do you incorporate them into decision-making? Should you? These are the kinds of questions you are now able to ask and answer with your new approach to computation. The specific skills that you've developed in statistical reasoning will help you to know if those data amassed from varied sources of digital exhaust were indeed representative and whether the conclusions derived from their analysis are valid. You've also learned through examples like that of UrbanSim how to think about presenting data in ways that are more persuasive to your audience. If you didn't have a specific way of approaching computation before, you do now, and this new approach will help you to be a smart consumer and producer of data-based insights.

As you've been exposed to cases from companies across numerous industries, you've come to recognize that the digital technologies you use don't ever act the same way twice—they perform new, learned computations on data sources that are themselves constantly changing. And because digital technologies are constantly changing, the uses to which they can be put change too. That means that organizations and the people in them are in a constant state of change.

We've covered how an *approach to change* that treats security as an evolving process is necessary for thriving in the digital age. We've also shown how the rapid set of changes characterizing the digital economy means that it's hard to predict exactly what kinds of organizational forms work best or what product designs are going to be the most successful. With a digital mindset you can appreciate how experimentation helps you to prepare for and react to changes in the best way possible. And you've got the skills to approach change in a new way.

Most importantly, your digital mindset has helped you recognize that the formal and informal structures that define our working lives are in continuous transition. You can appreciate how the speed with which we respond to the influx of available data is a critical driver for a successful digital organization. For some organizations, the most suitable structure will be agile teams that can be fluidly formed and easily disbanded once a target is met.

To facilitate continuous change, your digital mindset will help you recognize how crucial it is to spend time working on the implementation of digital tools to make sure they're used in ways that align with your major goals. You also now have a good understanding of how to determine the best way to train employees at scale. What is clear is that digital training must be a continuous process. Employees have to continuously develop their skills in the digital age and so do their bosses. This process of never-ending learning differs from simply acquiring a new skill for one's job each year; the jobs themselves are constantly changing, and employees must be able to move along with these changes in order to stay productively employable. Your digital mindset allows you to approach change not as something to achieve and then forget, but as a constant process requiring planning, intervention, and a lot of care.

Your Superpower

You have really ramped up your skills even if you didn't realize it as you were going along. And now, by doing the difficult work of learning the skills that have enabled you to shift your approaches to collaboration, computation, and change, you're able to see, think, and act in more nuanced and agile ways in this era of rapid change.

Your digital mindset is something of a superpower. You can now unlock opportunities you may never have imagined. This power is so much more than knowing how to code and how to do data analytics. You will no longer be shy about diving into conversations about technical topics, and you have a technical language that creates entirely new possibilities.

Perhaps the most important thing about your digital mindset is that it means you don't have to worry about finding your place in the digital future. You'll be helping to blaze pathways into that future that create value for you and those around you. Maybe you won't go to Kenya to plant potatoes, but we've seen time and again how a digital mindset not only sets up people for success where they are but also gives them new places to go.

Appendix

Continuous Learning Case Examples

These continuous learning case examples provide additional details about the learning principles pursued by the companies mentioned in chapter 7. These seven programs illustrate continuous learning models that testify to the serious investment that companies are making to support, encourage, and, in some cases, require upskilling and increasing digital proficiency. Some companies develop in-house curriculum and learning centers, others partner with outside organizations, and still others best support employee growth with a combination of the two. We consider these approaches to be best in class.

Capital One

Capital One, the American bank holding company, makes technology central to its business strategy by developing its software, employing innovative teams of software engineering talent, and reimagining traditional IT operating models. The company has built its own internal university, Tech College, that offers a comprehensive technology curriculum accessible to all employees. The college has the following key features:

- *Built by engineers, for engineers.* Capital One engineers design the curriculum to ensure the content is relevant and useful.

- *Breadth and depth.* The curriculum addresses twelve key disciplines that include software engineering, mobile, machine learning/AI, cloud computing, cybersecurity, and data.

- *Blended learning.* Online courses, in-person workshops, boot camps, and trainings from partners who are well known in the field of distance learning (such as Udacity, General Assembly, and Coursera) provide employees with a blended experience.

- *Learning from leaders.* Tech experts teach and inspire colleagues to learn and explore the latest advancements and teach them how to use those developments to enhance customer experiences.

- *Learning for all.* All employees, regardless of their previous experience or role in the company, have access to the curriculum to encourage the cross-organizational technology fluency that opens lines of communication and promotes agility.

Spotify

The Swedish-based audio streaming provider credits its culture of continuous learning for the company's success in essentially inventing an industry sector (the streaming platform) that has transformed the music industry. They take a "blended learning" approach to course offerings, which allows employees to pick and choose the format that works best for them. Options include in-person or streamed classroom training, online learning, sharing communities, and assessment. Very brief learning sessions can be integrated into the workday whenever employees have a moment while others take longer to process. Their approach includes six key concepts:[1]

- *Vision and purpose.* Citing self-determination theory, company leaders articulate a clear company vision so that employees can align their personal goals accordingly.

- *Self-ownership.* Peer-to-peer decentralized implementation means that all Spotifiers take responsibility for their own learning with the expectation that they learn from and with each other.

- *Autonomy.* Rather than micromanaging, Spotify points teams to specific goals. A robust central learning and development group (the GreenHouse team) helps groups of employees then decide for themselves how to reach those goals.

- *Failure.* The company culture not only accepts failure, but embraces the learnings that come from failure as crucial to creating an environment where great things happen. Because failure is not easy for anyone to accept, leaders make it psychologically safe by modeling their own failures.

- *Learning to love chaos.* Forgoing the stability of a fully structured top-down approach to learning, Spotify trusts that empowering employees to choose their own paths will enable them to make the unexpected connections and find new ideas that lead to the kind of company growth that is crucial for competitiveness in the digital age: innovative, agile, adaptive.

- *Interaction.* Collaboration and innovation are encouraged by empowering employees to choose learning paths that allow for organic exchanges, as employees share interests, curiosities, ideas, and learning from one another in the process.

Yelp

Yelp, one of the leading platforms for crowdsourced reviews of businesses, made continuous learning a defining trait of its company culture years before it became the ubiquitous trend it is today. A 2017 profile, "Inside Learning: How Yelp Created a Successful Learning Culture," identifies the following practices that make up Yelp's continuous learning environment:[2]

- *Employee autonomy.* Instead of formalized and enforced training programs, Yelp employees are given the space to define their own learning curriculum. For example, the engineering team brings in a guest speaker of its own choosing for lunch every Friday. The guest is usually someone from within the company, thereby facilitating an organic and effective form of knowledge exchange across Yelp departments. On the sales team—the company's biggest department—there is a fully developed certification program for the purpose of growing entry-level salespeople. The program, which is tailored specifically for the sales team, provides motivation for new team members in the unit and gives them a clearly visible path of upward mobility.

- *Horizontal learning.* In addition to highly individualized learning methods for each department, Yelp also invests in company-wide learning initiatives. A program called Yelp Beans—also voluntary—provides the opportunity for employees to meet someone they don't know within the organization, and learn from them. The exchange might offer a new perspective on work projects, or just make employees feel more connected across the company.

- *Servant leadership.* Yelp's guiding principle of leadership is "leaders who teach": leaders are not just managers but mentors who invest in the growth of their team members as employees and individuals. The company also brings in leaders from outside the organization—"Yelp Extended Faculty"—to give teaching sessions. Guest teachers have included mentors from Stanford and Berkeley, and insiders across different industries.

- *Gamification.* The company has a strong tradition of hackathons, sessions that last two days, in which engineers divide into groups and come up with an idea to work on together. The experience always leads to new and innovative solutions; but just as importantly, it gives the opportunity for team members to meet new people, exchange knowledge, and learn from one another in an organic way.

- *Stretch roles.* Yelp keeps its job roles open-ended so that its hires are able to learn to wear multiple hats at once. This approach is challenging for employees at first, but it grows people much faster and invests them more deeply in the company mission.

AT&T

AT&T invests $220 million each year in internal training programs, which offer almost 20 million hours of training a year and over $30 million annually in tuition assistance. As a result of this investment, at least 140,000 employees have been actively engaged in acquiring skills for new roles. The following three characteristics define the company's continuous learning culture:

- *Horizontal mobility.* By learning new skills, employees are encouraged to explore career opportunities internally with roles in other departments.

- *Servant leadership.* Leaders who serve as mentors provide emotional support, strategic advice, and honest feedback as well as encouragement to risk new growth and learning opportunities.

- *Upward mobility.* Employees are able to select new learning pathways in consultation with company forecasts of future job roles, categories, and competencies that are the most likely areas of growth and risk.

Westpac

One of Australia's biggest banks has taken a platform-based approach with a training program rolled out to all employees. This is a social learning environment where curated content is distributed and employees cocreate and share their own learning material. People have been encouraged to build communities around the areas they are interested in and focus on those tasks that will be particularly valuable in the future. Furthermore, Westpac has partnered with an Australian education tech startup called Go1 to provide an even more specialized continuous learning platform for its employees.[3] Go1 added a level of expertise that Westpac was unable to achieve within its own industry skill set. The platform, called Broker Academy, has two key dimensions:

- *Employee autonomy.* The platform is accessible on any computer or mobile device, and curriculum covers everything from compliance to business strategy, leadership, and well-being. Employees can thus take ownership over their own learning experience, choosing what they want to learn at whatever times fit best into their schedule.

- *Curated content.* The curriculum is refined through data from focus groups for each subject in order to ensure that the knowledge being offered is relevant and applicable.

Booking.com

The online travel and lodging agency operates under the following principles in building an environment of continuous learning:

- *Horizontal mobility.* Employees have opportunities to transition into completely different departments and roles through guided training.

- *Psychological safety.* The company culture makes it safe for employees to try new things even if uncertain of the end result by giving them the freedom to accept the accompanying inevitable failure.

- *Vertical mobility.* The company also strives to retain its employees by guiding their growth toward leadership roles. The company's goal is to provide those who want to pursue leadership roles the opportunity to do so, instead of letting them move on somewhere else in their search.

Philips

The health technology company is a leader in consumer health, home care, diagnostic imaging, image-guided therapy, patient monitoring, and health informatics. The company's values include employee autonomy, exploration, and informal on-the-job learning, values that are reflected in the characteristics of the Philips learning program:[4]

- *AI solutions.* Philips's continuous learning efforts are a key feature of the company's digital transformation journey. As the organization has transitioned from its identity as a supplier of health products into a provider of digital health services, AI has helped upskill its huge workforce.[5] Their challenge is how to support the acceleration of those changes. Like Westpac, Philips turned to an outside source for expertise. Cornerstone, which provides cloud-based learning and human resources software, has provided the infrastructure for Philips's continuous learning environment.

- *Individualization.* The AI-powered technology adapts to learners' specific needs and pace, so that each individual is able to learn under the specific conditions most suitable for success in each case. One learner might thrive within a fast-paced curriculum that keeps her on her toes. Another might do better with a slower pace that allows him to chew on the subject matter.

- *Socialization.* Employees can also share their "playlists" of tailored lessons with colleagues, much like the sharing of music playlists on streaming services like Spotify. For example, a sales expert in the company can contribute to a training program by creating a playlist that includes a video, a short e-learning course, several questions and answers, and some real-life situations. The social media function of the platform also facilitates connection between new employees and more experienced members who can serve as mentors. The platform thus works as a more organic, bottom-up approach to peer-mentor relationships than formal matching programs.

- *Mentorship.* Coupled with the technology platform is an intentional cultural shift that emphasizes leaders as teachers above all else. Leaders adopt the role of developing team members' futures—not just managing their work tasks. Leaders are also directed to share their expertise, knowledge, and passions for specific subjects in training sessions.

- *Tracking progress.* As the organization collects the data on employee usage of the platform, it can measure the correlation between continuous learning and high performance within the company. When they have sufficient data, they can track whether relationships exist between high-performance salespeople and how much training they do and whether creating playlists and learning nuggets means employees are learning in expected or unexpected ways.

GLOSSARY

30 Percent Rule: One of the foundational principles of this book. Grounded in research on developing proficiency in a foreign language, this rule states that, instead of needing to gain mastery over every digital skill, you only need to develop 30 percent fluency in a handful of technical topics to cultivate a digital mindset. Those topics are the focus of this book.

algorithm: A set of instructions for how to do a series of steps to accomplish a specific goal. This set of instructions takes what it receives (the input) and transforms it into something else entirely: the output. Computational algorithms—those that instruct computers—can work together to help perform any number of complex tasks. There are five core features of algorithms:

- *An algorithm is an unambiguous description* that makes clear what has to be implemented. In a computational algorithm, a step such as "Choose a large number" is vague: What is large? Is it 1 million, 1 trillion, or 100? Does the number have to be different each time, or can the same number be used on every run? Better is to describe the step as "Choose a number larger than 10 but smaller than 20."

- *An algorithm expects a defined set of inputs.* For example, it might require two numbers where both numbers are greater than zero. Or it might require a word, or a list of zero or more numbers.

- *An algorithm produces a defined set of outputs.* It might output the larger of the two numbers, an all-uppercase version of a word, or pictures from a set with the color blue in them.

- *An algorithm is guaranteed to terminate and produce a result,* always stopping after a finite time. If an algorithm could potentially run forever, it wouldn't be very useful because you might never get an answer.

- *Most algorithms are guaranteed to produce the correct result.* It's rarely useful if an algorithm returns the largest number 99 percent of the time, but 1 percent of the time the algorithm fails and returns the smallest number instead.

artificial intelligence (AI): Any machine that exhibits qualities associated with human intelligence.

back-end system: Structures such as servers, mainframes, and other systems that offer data services. Users don't see back-end systems because they support applications behind the scenes.

behavioral visibility: The amount of insight someone can gain into your behaviors and patterns from the data you produce, particularly through online activity.

blockchain: An array of distributed ledger technologies that promise to be a foundational technology, like the internet. Blockchain technologies facilitate highly secure, fast, private, peer-to-peer transactions without the use of a third party.

central tendency: Where values of a data set most commonly land.

code (source code): The actual inputs that make up an algorithm to instruct a computer how to execute an operation.

coding: How we actually get a computer to follow the instructions of algorithms. By using certain programming languages, each optimized for certain kinds of work, we can put together a script of instructions for the computer to execute. Coding is an essential skill for data scientists, engineers, and others who work in technical, data-heavy programming spaces, but it can also be used to create websites, design artwork, and more.

computer vision: Converting digital images and video into binary data readable by a computer, which can then perform analyses based on the data.

confidence interval: A plausible range of values for a given summary statistic (such as the mean) in the overall population, based on the features of the sample data set. The most commonly used confidence interval is 95 percent because this number represents a comfortable balance between precision and reliability.

conversational user interface: A means for interacting with AI on human terms, whether through writing or talking (for example, Siri).

cryptocurrency (for example, Bitcoin): Any type of digital currency run on a blockchain. Not affiliated with any bank or national currency, cryptocurrencies facilitate direct peer-to-peer transactions, threatening to disrupt more traditional financial systems.

data cleaning: Converting data into formats that can be digested by AI models.

descriptive statistics: The process of analyzing data with measurements that summarize overarching characteristics in terms of a single value.

digital: Refers to the interplay of data and technology. Data refer to any information that can be used for reference, analysis, or computation. Data can be numbers, or images and text that are turned into numbers that can be processed, stored, and transformed through technology (computing).

digital exhaust: The pieces of metadata created by an individual's online activity that constitute their digital footprint and together can form a picture of their behaviors and habits.

digital footprint: The collection of data (for example, digital exhaust) that together can represent an individual's behaviors and habits. The higher one's behavioral visibility, the more digital exhaust that can be collected, and thus the clearer the digital footprint that can be analyzed.

digital mindset: A set of attitudes and behaviors that enable people and organizations to see new possibilities and chart a path for the future using data, algorithms, AI, and machine learning.

digital presence: The extent to which a person is active and prominent in a technology-mediated remote environment, making contributions that are understood and recognized by team members through active and clear communication across digital tools.

digital transformation: Organizations redesigning their underlying processes and competencies to become more adaptive using data and digital technology, from artificial intelligence and machine learning to the internet of things.

dispersion: Descriptive statistics that analyze how data are spread out.

facticity: The extent to which something (e.g., data) can be considered absolutely true and accurate.

front-end system: All of the technologies and data sources of a technology stack that you, your employees, and your customers will interact with (e.g., user interface on an app).

hypothesis testing: A process for comparing two summary statistics in a data set. The test starts with what's called a "null hypothesis," most often a conservative position that assumes the status quo (e.g., "there is no difference between the two parameters being compared"), and then proposes an alternative hypothesis (e.g., "there is in fact a difference"). If there is enough statistical evidence to support the alternative hypothesis, the null hypothesis is rejected in favor of the alternative. However, if there is not enough statistical evidence, the null hypothesis remains.

inferential statistics: The process of using data from a sample to test hypotheses and make estimates of an overall population (in other words, making statements about the probability of summary statistics from a data set being reflective of the overall population).

machine learning: The ability of computer algorithms to automatically identify patterns through data analysis, and continuously refine their statistical techniques of prediction and inference by generating new rules without step-by-step instructions from human programmers. The more data that these algorithms process, the more they learn.

mean: A measurement of central tendency wherein each value of the data is added together and then divided by the number of values.

median: A measurement of central tendency represented by the value that falls at the midpoint in the range of data.

metaknowledge: Knowledge about "who knows what" and "who knows who."

middleware: The software linkages between the front end and the back end, enabling communication between database and data.

mode: A measurement of central tendency represented by the most common value in the range of data.

mutual knowledge problem: The lack of shared contextual understanding in a remote context.

natural language processing: Converting human language into vectors, or binary code that is readable by computers.

neural networks: A machine learning model to automatically classify features from data that's trained by using examples and selected approaches to emulate human neural networks.

predictive statistics: Using statistical models to predict outcomes.

Privacy by Design (PbD): A framework for product design developed by Dr. Ann Cavoukian that consists of seven key principles to proactively prioritize privacy rather than treat it as a regulatory afterthought.

programming language: Terms used to enable a specified set of commands and instructions that coders use to create algorithms.

p-value: The probability of observing the parameters of a data set under the assumption that the null hypothesis is true. A smaller p-value means there is stronger evidence in favor of the alternative hypothesis.

range: A measurement of dispersion represented by the difference between the highest and lowest values in a data set.

regression model: A method for analyzing the relationship between two or more variables or factors.

reinforcement learning: An advanced phase of machine learning in which the algorithm automatically refines its rules of categorization as it processes increasing amounts of data.

SaaS: Software as a Service, referring particularly to a business model in which software is licensed on a subscription basis and hosted centrally by the licensing company.

script: A document made up of multiple lines of code, typically designed to construct an algorithm.

significance level: The designated threshold that marks the maximum limit that a p-value can be before it is too high to reject the null hypothesis in favor of the alternative. A common significance level is 0.05: if the p-value is below 0.05, then the null hypothesis is rejected in favor of the alternative. If the p-value is above 0.05, then the alternative is rejected in favor of the null.

smart contracts: An application of blockchain, these contracts can automatically and immediately execute their terms without the need for a third-party mediator. Smart contracts are already changing how royalty payments, leases, wills, deeds, and more are processed.

standard deviation: A measure of how spread out the data are from the mean.

supervised learning: A primary phase of machine learning in which a programmer trains an algorithm to classify data into binary categories.

technical debt: The need for organizations to budget time and resources to continually update existing or old infrastructure due to the rate at which technologies, processes, and capabilities change in the digital ecosystem.

technology stack: All the hardware and software systems needed to develop and run a single application.

transitional state: Fixed periods of time in which an organization moves from a familiar set of structures, processes, and accompanying cultural norms into a completely new repertoire.

type I error: In hypothesis testing, the rejection of the null hypothesis when it is actually true.

type II error: In hypothesis testing, the failure to reject the null hypothesis when the alternative is true.

unsupervised learning: A more advanced phase of machine learning in which the algorithm automatically sorts data into the binary categories on its own.

variance: A measurement of dispersion represented by an estimate of the distance of each value from the mean.

vectors: Strings of numbers readable by computers.

NOTES

Introduction

1. Ethiopia has the second highest GDP in East Africa behind Kenya according to the World Economic Outlook Database (2019), but it ranks in the lowest quartile of the 2020 Human Development Index (ranked 173 out of 189 countries). See the June 23, 2021, *New York Times* article on the country's most recent food crisis, "Famine Hits 350,000 in Ethiopia, Worst Hit Country in a Decade."

2. Sara's digital journey toward becoming a successful CEO challenges the status quo in more ways than one—across all industries, the percentage of business leaders who are Black women is still very small. Take, for example, the CEOs of the businesses on the 2021 *Fortune* 500 list: forty-one are women (8.2 percent), and two of those women are Black (less than 1 percent of the five hundred CEOs).

3. P. Weill, T. Apel, S. L. Woerner, and J. S. Banner, "It Pays to Have a Digitally Savvy Board," *MIT Sloan Management Review* 60, no. 3 (2019): 41–45.

4. There are so many examples of companies not just encouraging employees to develop digital competencies but requiring them to do so. Later in the book, we'll give examples of how some big tech companies like Google, Amazon, and Atos approach this issue. Jonathan Vanian's "How Amazon Is Tackling the A.I. Talent Crunch," *Fortune*, June 1, 2021, describes Amazon's approach in detail: https://fortune.com/2021/06/01/how-amazon-is-tackling-the-a-i-talent-crunch/. But non-technical companies are making digital skills a requirement, too. J. P. Morgan recently began to require that all new staff take coding lessons. (See https://www.ft.com/content/4c17d6ce-c8b2-11e8-ba8f-ee390057b8c9.) Examples like this are becoming too numerous to list.

5. Quoted from Chambers keynote at Cisco Live 2015. An edited version of the transcript of his entire speech can be found here: https://www.mckinsey.com/industries/technology-media-and-telecommunications/our-insights/ciscos-john-chambers-on-the-digital-era.

6. Many recent surveys show data supporting this claim. A recent PWC report (https://www.pwc.com/gx/en/issues/upskilling/everyone-digital-world.html) discussing surveys of tech execs and their employees summarized their findings in this way:

> It's a new world that needs new skills. To many, that is an exciting prospect because it speaks to progress. Most of the CEOs and leaders we talk to agree in principle. But they also tell us that they are not ready. The sheer speed, scope and impact of technological change are challenging their businesses—and society at large—in fundamental ways. At the World Economic Forum in Davos, where we met with more than 150 business leaders last January, just about every conversation ended with the same question: how are we going to prepare our people?"

7. For a detailed discussion of the many ways in which technologies like phones generate new data through novel forms of computation see Youngjin Yoo, Ola Henfridsson, and Kalle Lyytinen, "The New Organizing Logic of Digital Innovation: An Agenda for Information Systems Research," *Information Systems Research* 21, no. 4 (2010): 724–735.

8. C. S. Dweck, *Mindset: The New Psychology of Success* (New York: Random House, 2008).

9. We suggest that the approach that J. P. Morgan took (see note 4 above) is narrowly focused on skills rather than on helping employees to develop a broader digital mindset that helps them orient to the world in new ways. Our research shows that skills are important, but not at the expense or in lieu of a mindset change.

10. D. Crystal, *English as a Global Language*, 2nd ed. (Cambridge University Press, 2003); T. Neeley, Tsedal, "Global Business Speaks English: Why You Need a Language Strategy Now," *Harvard Business Review*, May 2012, 116–124.

11. Over the past decade we have published many studies of digital transformation and technology use at work through which we have developed and tested these ideas. Some of those studies (conducted with many talented coauthors) include: P. M. Leonardi, D. Woo, and W. C. Barley, "Why Should I Trust Your Model? How to Successfully Enroll Digital Models for Innovation," *Innovation: Organization & Management* (February 2021); T. Neeley, *Remote Work Revolution: Succeeding from Anywhere* (New York: HarperCollins, 2021); P. M. Leonardi, W. C. Barley, and D. Woo, "On the Making of Crystal Balls: Five Lessons About Simulation Modeling and the Organization of Work," *Information & Organization* 31 (2021); P. M. Leonardi, "COVID-19 and the New Technologies of Organizing: Digital Exhaust, Digital Footprints, and Artificial Intelligence in the Wake of Remote Work," *Journal of Management Studies* 51 (2021), 247–251; P. M. Leonardi and J. W. Treem, "Behavioral Visibility: A New Paradigm for Organization Studies in the Age of Digitization, Digitalization, and Datafication," *Organization Studies* 41, no. 12 (2020): 1601–1625; T. B. Neeley and B. S. Reiche, "How Global Leaders Gain Power through Downward Deference and Reduction of Social Distance," *Academy of Management Journal* (2020); P. M. Leonardi, D. E. Bailey, and C. S. Pierce, "The Co-Evolution of Objects and Boundaries Over Time: Materiality, Affordances, and Boundary Salience," *Information Systems Research* 30, no. 2 (2019): 665–686; B. S. Reiche and T. B. Neeley, "Head, Heart, or Hands: How Do Employees Respond to a Radical Global Language Change over Time?" *Organization Science* 30, no. 6 (2019): 1252–1269; I. C. Cristea and P. M. Leonardi, "Get Noticed and Die Trying: Signals, Sacrifice, and the Production of Face Time in Distributed Work," *Organization Science* 30, no. 3 (2019): 552–572; P. M. Leonardi, "Social Media and the Development of Shared Cognition: The Roles of Network Expansion, Content Integration, and Triggered Recalling," *Organization Science* 29, no. 4 (2018): 547–568; T. B. Neeley and P. M. Leonardi, "Enacting Knowledge Strategy through Social Media: Passable Trust and the Paradox of Non-Work Interactions," *Strategic Management Journal* 39, no. 3 (2018): 922–946; T. Neeley, *The Language of Global Success* (Princeton, NJ: Princeton University Press, 2017); P. M. Leonardi and D. E. Bailey, "Recognizing and Selling Good Ideas: Network Articulation and the Making of an Offshore Innovation Hub," *Academy of Management Discoveries* 3, no. 2 (2017): 116–144; P. M. Leonardi, "The Social Media Revolution: Sharing and Learning in the Age of Leaky Knowledge," *Information and Organization* 27, no. 1 (2017): 47–59; T. B. Neeley and T. L. Dumas, "Unearned Status Gain: Evidence from a Global Language Mandate," *Academy of Management Journal* 59, no. 1 (2016): 14–43; T. Neeley, "Global Teams That Work," *Harvard Business Review*, October 2015, 74–81; P. M. Leonardi, "Ambient Awareness and Knowledge Acquisition: Using Social Media to Learn 'Who Knows What' and 'Who Knows Whom,'" *MIS Quarterly* 39, no. 4 (2015): 747–762; P. M. Leonardi, "Materializing Strategy: The Blurry Line Between Strategy Formulation and Strategy Implementation," *British Journal of Management* 26 (2015): 17–21; P. J. Hinds, T. B. Neeley, and C. D. Cramton, "Language as a Lightning Rod: Power Contests, Emotion Regulation, and Subgroup Dynamics in Global Teams," *Journal of International Business Studies* 45, no. 5 (2014): 536–561; P. M. Leonardi, "Social Media, Knowledge Sharing, and Innovation: Toward a

Theory of Communication Visibility," *Information Systems Research* 25, no. 4 (2014): 796–816; T. B. Neeley, "Language Matters: Status Loss and Achieved Status Distinctions in Global Organizations," *Organization Science* 24, no. 2 (2013): 476–497; P. M. Leonardi and C. Rodriguez-Lluesma, "Occupational Stereotypes, Perceived Status Differences, and Intercultural Communication in Global Organizations," *Communication Monographs* 80, no. 4 (2013): 478–502; P. M. Leonardi, "When Does Technology Use Enable Network Change in Organizations? A Comparative Study of Feature Use and Shared Affordances," *MIS Quarterly* 37, no. 3 (2013): 749–775; D. E. Bailey, P. M. Leonardi, and S. R. Barley, "The Lure of the Virtual," *Organization Science* 23, no. 5 (2012): 1485–1504; W. C. Barley, P. M. Leonardi, and D. E. Bailey, "Engineering Objects for Collaboration: Strategies of Ambiguity and Clarity at Knowledge Boundaries," *Human Communication Research* 38, no. 3 (2012): 280–308; M. Mortensen and T. B. Neeley, "Reflected Knowledge and Trust in Global Collaboration," *Management Science* 58, no. 12 (2012): 2207–2224; P. M. Leonardi and J. W. Treem, "Knowledge Management Technology as a Stage for Strategic Self-Presentation: Implications for Knowledge Sharing in Organizations," *Information and Organization* 22, no. 1 (2012): 37–59; P. M. Leonardi, T. B. Neeley, and E. M. Gerber, "How Managers Use Multiple Media: Discrepant Events, Power, and Timing in Redundant Communication," *Organization Science* 23, no. 1 (2012): 98–117; P. M. Leonardi, "Innovation Blindness: Culture, Frames, and Cross-Boundary Problem Construction in the Development of New Technology Concepts," *Organization Science* 22, no. 2 (2011): 347–369; D. E. Bailey, P. M. Leonardi, and J. Chong, "Minding the Gaps: Technology Interdependence and Coordination in Knowledge Work," *Organization Science* 21, no. 3 (2010): 713–730; P. M. Leonardi, J. W. Treem, and M. H. Jackson, "The Connectivity Paradox: Using Technology to Both Decrease and Increase Perceptions of Distance in Distributed Work Arrangements," *Journal of Applied Communication Research* 38, no. 1 (2010): 85–105.

12. Such anonymity is customary when presenting data in academic research. Because we did many of these studies before we knew we were going to write this book, we didn't always ask people for permission to use their real names or the names of their organizations. Where we could track them down, we did ask them. In other cases, we preserve the anonymity we promised them by using pseudonyms.

13. Tacit knowledge is like "feel." The canonical example of tacit knowledge is riding a bike: you can feel how to do it, but it's difficulty to write a set of rules for how. For an excellent treatise on tacit knowledge and its many forms see H. Collins, *Tacit and Explicit Knowledge* (Chicago: University of Chicago Press, 2010).

14. Thanks to Ian Buckley, "What Is Coding and How Does It Work?" MUO, June 3, 2021 (https://www.makeuseof.com/tag/what-is-coding/) for providing the example of Python code that we use here.

15. If you're interested to learn more about different language paradigms, or simply learn what various languages are good for, check out Robert Diana's useful list, "The Big List of 256 Programming Languages," DZone, May 16, 2013: https://dzone.com/articles/big-list-256-programming.

Chapter 1

1. For anthropological studies of how algorithms have changed trading see D. MacKenzie, *An Engine, Not a Camera: How Financial Models Shape Markets* (Cambridge, MA: MIT Press, 2008); D. Beunza and D. Stark, "Tools of the Trade: The Socio-Technology of Arbitrage in a Wall Street Trading Room," *Industrial and Corporate Change* 13, no. 2 (2004): 369–400; D. Beunza, *Taking the Floor* (Princeton, NJ: Princeton University Press, 2019).

2. For a deeper discussion of the difference between tools and platforms and how they make a difference for the kind of communication we can have in the workplace, see P. Leonardi, "Picking the Right Approach to Digital Collaboration," *MIT Sloan Management Review* 62, no. 2 (2021): 1–7.

3. There are, of course, important differences in the kind of technology underlying chatbots and advanced conversational agents. Much of the difference has to do with the type of learning algorithm upon which they are based. In Russell and Norvig's widely cited typology (S. Russell and P. Norvig, *Artificial Intelligence: A Modern Approach* [New York Pearson, 2002]), chatbots can range from being simple reflex agents, which act only on the basis of the current precept and ignore the rest of the precept history, to learning agents that can operate in unknown environments by learning from past performance and applying that learning when it takes in new precepts and decides on actions.

4. See, for example, research on the "Computers as Social Actors" (CASA) paradigm, including C. Nass, J. Steuer, and E. R. Tauber, "Computers Are Social Actors," in *Proceedings of the SIGCHI Conference on Human Factors in Computing Systems* (April 1994), 72–78; B. Reeves and C. Nass, *The Media Equation: How People Treat Computers, Television, and New Media Like Real People* (Cambridge: Cambridge University Press, 1996); L. Gong, "How Social Is Social Responses to Computers? The Function of the Degree of Anthropomorphism in Computer Representations," *Computers in Human Behavior* 24, no. 4 (2008): 1494–1509; S. S. Sundar, "Loyalty to Computer Terminals: Is It Anthropomorphism or Consistency?" *Behaviour & Information Technology* 23, no. 2 (2004): 107–118.

5. See J. McCarthy, M. L. Minsky, N. Rochester, and C. E. Shannon, "A Proposal for the Dartmouth Summer Research Project on Artificial Intelligence," *AI Magazine* 27, no. 4 (August 31, 1955): 12–15.

6. N. Bostrom, "How Long Before Superintelligence?" *International Journal of Futures Studies* 2 (1998).

7. For a classic and thorough text on the different functions of AI and their links to human cognition, see S. Russell and P. Norvig, *Artificial Intelligence: A Modern Approach* (New York: Pearson, 2002). For debates about how AI and human cognition are likely to be similar or diverge, see H. Dreyfus, S. E. Dreyfus, and T. Athanasiou, *Mind over Machine* (New York: Simon and Schuster, 2000); H. A. Simon, *The Sciences of the Artificial* (Cambridge, MA: MIT Press, 2019).

8. We borrow and build on this great list by Tim Urban, which is published at https://waitbutwhy.com/2015/01/artificial-intelligence-revolution-1.html. We present only a summary of the great ideas Urban uses; this link provides more detailed examples.

9. There are many recent examples of how AI is changing various industries. We've picked a few good summary articles here. For finance, see D. Belanche, L. V. Casaló, and C. Flavián, "Artificial Intelligence in FinTech: Understanding Robo-Advisors Adoption among Customers," *Industrial Management & Data Systems* 199, no. 7 (2019): 1411–1430; and for an early deep discussion see R. R. Trippi and E. Turban, eds., *Neural Networks in Finance and Investing: Using Artificial Intelligence to Improve Real World Performance* (New York: McGraw-Hill, 1992). For insurance see S. Hall, "How Artificial Intelligence Is Changing the Insurance Industry," *The Center for Insurance Policy & Research* 22 (2017): 1–8. And for medicine see P. Szolovits, ed., *Artificial Intelligence in Medicine* (New York: Routledge, 2019).

10. For a great article in which she breaks down this example see https://marilynika.medium.com/an-intro-to-ai-ml-and-deep-learning-ffd2f2fbf1e.

11. And this computing power is growing quickly. Research Lab OpenAI found that the amount of computing power used to train the largest AI models has doubled every 3.4 months since 2012—tracking Moore's law. This means that resources used today are doubling at a rate seven times faster than before. See https://www.technologyreview.com/2019/11/11/132004/the-computing-power-needed-to-train-ai-is-now-rising-seven-times-faster-than-ever-before/.

12. For a much more detailed discussion than is presented here, see Robins's full description: www.intel.com/content/www/us/en/artificial-intelligence/posts/difference-between-ai-machine-learning-deep-learning.html.

13. A. Djouadi and E. Bouktache, "A Fast Algorithm for the Nearest-Neighbor Classifier," *IEEE Transactions on Pattern Analysis and Machine Intelligence* 19, no. 3 (1997): 277–282; S. Suresh, K. Dong, and H. J. Kim, "A Sequential Learning Algorithm for

Self-Adaptive Resource Allocation Network Classifier," *Neurocomputing* 73, nos. 16–18 (2010): 3012–3019.

14. As we'll discuss later, this accuracy assumes appropriate training data. For a great discussion of how bias seeps into computer vision and facial recognition software see J. Lunter, "Beating the Bias in Facial Recognition Technology," *Biometric Technology Today* 2020, no. 9 (2020): 5–7.

15. To learn more about computer vision and its applications, see these two great resources: R. Szeliski, *Computer Vision: Algorithms and Applications* (Berlin: Springer Science & Business Media, 2010); and C. Szegedy, V. Vanhoucke, S. Ioffe, J. Shlens, and Z. Wojna, "Rethinking the Inception Architecture for Computer Vision," in *Proceedings of the IEEE Conference on Computer Vision and Pattern Recognition* (2016), 2818–2826. The first citation provides an overview aimed at a broader audience (though it is somewhat technical). The second provides a state of the art review of the technical innovations in computer vision.

16. For an excellent primer on NLP and a discussion of its benefits and drawbacks, see G. G. Chowdhury, "Natural Language Processing," *Annual Review of Information Science and Technology* 37, no. 1 (2003): 51–89.

17. For a great discussion by Yelp software engineer C. Wei-Hong, see https://engineeringblog.yelp.com/2015/10/how-we-use-deep-learning-to-classify-business-photos-at-yelp.html.

18. If you are interested in a deeper comparison of what these different approaches to learning can and cannot do, see R. Sathya and A. Abraham, "Comparison of Supervised and Unsupervised Learning Algorithms for Pattern Classification," *International Journal of Advanced Research in Artificial Intelligence* 2, no. 2 (2013): 34–38; and B. Mahesh, "Machine Learning Algorithms—A Review," *International Journal of Science and Research (IJSR)* 9 (2020): 381–386.

19. J. G. Nam, S. Park, E. J. Hwang, J. H. Lee, K. N. Jin, K. Y. Lim, and C. M. Park, "Development and Validation of Deep Learning–Based Automatic Detection Algorithm for Malignant Pulmonary Nodules on Chest Radiographs," *Radiology* 290, no. 1 (2019): 218–228.

20. Y. Liu, T. Kohlberger, M. Norouzi, G. E. Dahl, J. L. Smith, A. Mohtashamian, and M. C. Stumpe, "Artificial Intelligence–Based Breast Cancer Nodal Metastasis Detection: Insights into the Black Box for Pathologists," *Archives of Pathology & Laboratory Medicine* 143, no. 7 (2019): 859–868.

21. A very recent study by Sarah Leibowitz and colleagues describes the major changes that radiologists had to make to their work as they determined whether to incorporate AI judgment into this practice. This is a great example of how some radiologists can develop a digital mindset, while others cannot. See S. Leibowitz, N. Levina, and H. Lishivitz-Asad, "To Incorporate or Not to Incorporate AI for Critical Judgments: How Professionals Deal with Opacity When Using AI for Medical Diagnosis," *Organization Science* (forthcoming).

22. The statistics around data production are truly mind-numbing. For a regularly updated list of what the world's current data landscape looks like, see https://techjury.net/blog/big-data-statistics/#gref.

23. For a great discussion of IBM's latest moves in this area see https://www.wraltechwire.com/2021/07/06/quantum-computing-wars-ibm-honeywell-make-major-moves-as-competition-intensifies/.

24. For an early discussion that lays the groundwork and provides an accessible overview of conversational user interfaces see M. F. McTear, "Spoken Dialogue Technology: Enabling the Conversational User Interface," *ACM Computing Surveys (CSUR)* 34, no. 1 (2002): 90–169. For a more contemporary discussion of current issues and applications see P. Lauren and P. Watta, "A Conversational User Interface for Stock Analysis," in *2019 IEEE International Conference on Big Data (Big Data)* (December 2019): 5298–5305; S. Holmes, A. Moorhead, R. Bond, H. Zheng, V. Coates, and M. McTear, "Usability Testing of a Healthcare Chatbot: Can We Use Conventional Methods to Assess Conversational

User Interfaces?" in *Proceedings of the 31st European Conference on Cognitive Ergonomics* (September 2019): 207–214.

25. For an interesting discussion of Julie's evolution, see https://content.verint.com /LP=5353.

26. C. Nass and Y. Moon, "Machines and Mindlessness: Social Responses to Computers," *Journal of Social Issues* 56, no. 1 (2000): 81–103; C. Nass, B. J. Fogg, and Y. Moon, "Can Computers Be Teammates?" *International Journal of Human-Computer Studies* 45, no. 6 (1996): 669–678; C. Nass, Y. Moon, B. J. Fogg, B. Reeves, and D. C. Dryer, "Can Computer Personalities Be Human Personalities?" *International Journal of Human-Computer Studies* 43, no. 2 (1995): 223–239.

27. See also a great study by Kim and Sundar that discusses how inattention is related to anthropomorphism and the consequences that arise from it: Y. Kim and S. S. Sundar, "Anthropomorphism of Computers: Is It Mindful or Mindless?" *Computers in Human Behavior* 28, no. 1 (2012): 241–250.

28. Trust is, of course, a complicated construct. We like the definition offered by an interdisciplinary team of management researchers: "Trust is a psychological state comprising the intention to accept vulnerability based upon positive expectations of the intentions or behavior of another" (395): D. M. Rousseau, S. B. Sitkin, R. S. Burt, and C. Camerer, "Not So Different After All: A Cross-Discipline View of Trust," *Academy of Management Review* 23, no. 3 (1998): 393–404.

29. J. M. Logg, J. A. Minson, and D. A. Moore, "Algorithm Appreciation: People Prefer Algorithmic to Human Judgment," *Organizational Behavior and Human Decision Processes* 151: 90–103.

30. D. T. Newman, N. J. Fast, and D. J. Harmon, "When Eliminating Bias Isn't Fair: Algorithmic Reductionism and Procedural Justice in Human Resource Decisions," *Organizational Behavior and Human Decision Processes* 160 (2020): 149–167.

31. The research also suggests that these points apply to people's judgment of algorithmic or AI-based work monitoring. A recent study found that human-free tracking feels less judgmental and will, therefore, allow for a greater subjective sense of autonomy. The results of five experiments conducted by the authors supported these predictions, revealing that participants were more likely to accept technology-operated than human-operated tracking, an effect driven by reduced concerns about potential negative judgment, which, in turn, increased subjective sense of autonomy—and these results varied by the kinds of behaviors people believed were being tracked. See R. Raveendhran and N. J. Fast, "Humans Judge, Algorithms Nudge: The Psychology of Behavior Tracking Acceptance," *Organizational Behavior and Human Decision Processes* 164 (2021): 11–26.

32. E. Glikson and A. W. Woolley, "Human Trust in Artificial Intelligence: Review of Empirical Research," *Academy of Management Annals* 14, no. 2 (2020): 627–660.

33. M. J. Barnes, J. Y. Chen, and S. Hill, *Humans and Autonomy: Implications of Shared Decision-Making for Military Operations* (Aberdeen Proving Ground, MD: US Army Research Laboratory, 2017); A. R. Selkowitz, S. G. Lakhmani, and J. Y. Chen, "Using Agent Transparency to Support Situation Awareness of the Autonomous Squad Member," *Cognitive Systems Research* 46 (2017): 13–25.

34. This is not quite as simple as it sounds. There have been numerous discussions in the fields of informatics and science and technology studies that debate about the antecedents of "transparency" versus "opacity." For two good introductions to this discussion see J. Burrell, "How the Machine 'Thinks': Understanding Opacity in Machine Learning Algorithms," *Big Data & Society* 3, no. 1 (2016): 2053951715622512; P. Dourish, "Algorithms and Their Others: Algorithmic Culture in Context," *Big Data & Society* 3, no. 2 (2016): 2053951716665128.

35. Although most researchers and scientists agree that transparency is important in AI-based tools, the degree to which AI algorithms should be transparent or how they could be transparent is hotly debated. For some good summaries of these debates from very different perspectives see A. Rai, "Explainable AI: From Black Box to Glass Box,"

Journal of the Academy of Marketing Science 48, no. 1 (2020): 137–141; D. Castelvecchi, "Can We Open the Black Box of AI?" *Nature News* 538, no. 7623 (2016): 20; A. Adadi and M. Berrada, "Peeking Inside the Black-Box: A Survey on Explainable Artificial Intelligence (XAI)," *IEEE Access* 6 (2018): 52138–52160.

Chapter 2

1. C. D. Cramton, "The Mutual Knowledge Problem and Its Consequences for Dispersed Collaboration," *Organization Science* 12, no. 3 (2001): 346–371.

2. E. M. Eisenberg, "Ambiguity as Strategy in Organizational Communication," *Communication Monographs* 51, no. 3 (1984): 227–242; E. M. Eisenberg, *Strategic Ambiguities: Essays on Communication, Organization, and Identity* (Thousand Oaks, CA: Sage, 2006).

3. In a recent study, we found that individuals who worked remotely were much more likely to receive higher quality projects and better promotions when they caught the attention of those working at headquarters through ambiguous communication. Doing so allowed them to rise to the top of the information deluge that onsite managers experienced. See I. C. Cristea and P. M. Leonardi, "Get Noticed and Die Trying: Signals, Sacrifice, and the Production of Face Time in Distributed Work," *Organization Science* 30, no. 3 (2019): 552–572.

4. For good reviews of this research see S. Kumar, Y. Tan, and L. Wei, "When to Play Your Advertisement? Optimal Insertion Policy of Behavioral Advertisement," *Information Systems Research* 31, no. 2 (2020): 589–606; Y. Li, K. W. Wan, X. Yan, and C. Xu, "Real Time Advertisement Insertion in Baseball Video Based on Advertisement Effect," in *Proceedings of the 13th Annual ACM International Conference on Multimedia* (November 2005): 343–346.

5. See this *New York Times* story on the subject: https://bits.blogs.nytimes.com/2011/12/19/back-at-work-and-catching-up-on-online-shopping/.

6. For a review of this trend see P. M. Leonardi, "COVID-19 and the New Technologies of Organizing: Digital Exhaust, Digital Footprints, and Artificial Intelligence in the Wake of Remote Work," *Journal of Management Studies* (2020).

7. "How AI Demands Organizational Change," MIT Panel, January 4, 2021.

8. Tsedal B. Neeley and Paul M. Leonardi, "Enacting Knowledge Strategy through Social Media: Passable Trust and the Paradox of Nonwork Interactions," *Strategic Management Journal* 39, no. 3 (2018): 922–946.

9. "Metaknowledge Is Knowledge of 'Who Knows What' and 'Who Knows Whom'" in Y. Ren and L. Argote, "Transactive Memory Systems 1985–2010: An Integrated Framework of Key Dimensions, Antecedents, and Consequences," *Academy of Management Annals* 5, no. 1 (2011): 189–229. Research shows that when an individual's metaknowledge is distinguished by both correctness (he or she can correctly identify what and whom a coworker knows) and breadth (he or she can make such a correct identification not just of a few coworkers, but of many coworkers), metaknowledge is often linked to team performance on routine tasks; (Y. Ren, K. M. Carley, and L. Argote, "The Contingent Effects of Transactive Memory: When Is It More Beneficial to Know What Others Know?" *Management Science* 52, no. 5 [2006]: 671–682); people's ability to recombine existing ideas into new innovations (A. Majchrzak, L. P. Cooper, and O. E. Neece, "Knowledge Reuse for Innovation," *Management Science* 50, no. 2 [2004]: 174–188); reduction in work duplication across the organization (P. Jackson and J. Klobas, "Building Knowledge in Projects: A Practical Application of Social Constructivism to Information Systems Development," *International Journal of Project Management* 26, no. 4 [2008]: 329–337); and many more positive benefits.

10. This kind of borrowing is one of the key ways that innovation (especially in product and process) happens. Some researchers call it "brokering," but the main idea is that ideas generated in one place and time can be useful in different contexts. Thus recombination is key. See A. B. Hargadon, "Brokering Knowledge: Linking Learning and

Innovation," *Research in Organizational Behavior* 24 (2002): 41–85; R. S. Burt, "Structural Holes and Good Ideas," *American Journal of Sociology* 110, no. 2 (2004): 349–399.

11. We've discussed this point in more detail elsewhere. For a discussion about how important (but how hard it can be) to switch from reactive to proactive learning via social tools, see P. M. Leonardi, "Social Media, Knowledge Sharing, and Innovation: Toward a Theory of Communication Visibility," *Information Systems Research* 25, no. 4 (2014): 796–816.

12. C. Thompson, "Brave New World of Digital Intimacy," *New York Times Magazine*, September 5, 2008, 7.

13. This is what Pew Research says on this subject: https://www.pewresearch.org /internet/2016/11/11/social-media-update-2016/.

14. This insight builds on a long line of research about the importance of "informal" social relationships at work. In addition to the kind of lubrication for knowledge sharing we discuss here, there is ample evidence that people rely on informal relations and "friends" to find meaning in their work and to increase their productivity. And friendship correlates strongly with retention. See J. R. Lincoln and J. Miller, "Work and Friendship Ties in Organizations: A Comparative Analysis of Relation Networks," *Administrative Science Quarterly* 24, no. 2 (1979): 181–199; G. A. Ballinger, R. Cross, and B. C. Holtom, "The Right Friends in the Right Places: Understanding Network Structure as a Predictor of Voluntary Turnover," *Journal of Applied Psychology* 101, no. 4 (2016): 535.

15. For a specific analysis of the benefits of non-work interaction on work-related project effectiveness, see P. M. Leonardi and S. R. Meyer, "Social Media as Social Lubricant: How Ambient Awareness Eases Knowledge Transfer," *American Behavioral Scientist* 59, no. 1 (2015): 10–34; and T. B. Neeley and P. M. Leonardi, "Enacting Knowledge Strategy through Social Media: Passable Trust and the Paradox of Nonwork Interactions," *Strategic Management Journal* 39, no. 3 (2018): 922–946.

16. Hinds and Bailey offer a great research-based account of this problem: P. J. Hinds and D. E. Bailey, "Out of Sight, Out of Sync: Understanding Conflict in Distributed Teams," *Organization Science* 14, no. 6 (2003): 615–632.

Chapter 3

1. M. Lewis, "The No-Stats All-Star," *New York Times*, February 13, 2009.

2. Daniel Kahneman won the Nobel Prize in economics for this work with Amos Tversky in which they showed that people in general (not just high school students) are notoriously bad at dealing with probabilities—so bad in fact that it can skew their decision-making in profound ways. See, for example, Daniel Kahneman and Amos Tversky, "Prospect Theory: An Analysis of Decision under Risk," *Econometrica* 47, no. 2 (1979): 263–292.

3. For an excellent discussion of the production of data as a social object, see C. Alaimo and J. Kallinikos, "Managing by Data: Algorithmic Categories and Organizing," *Organization Studies* (2020): 0170840620934062.

4. But, of course, it couldn't stay that way for long. JoAnn Yates documents the rise of categorization and the role it played in control in her excellent historical analysis: J. Yates, *Control through Communication: The Rise of System in American Management* (Baltimore: Johns Hopkins University Press, 1993).

5. RFID is an important data-producing technology. For an accessible overview of what it is, see R. Want, "An Introduction to RFID Technology," *IEEE Pervasive Computing* 5, no. 1 (2006): 25–33.

6. And for a definitive account of its uses, see K. Finkenzeller, *RFID Handbook: Fundamentals and Applications in Contactless Smart Cards, Radio Frequency Identification and Near-Field Communication* (Hoboken, NJ: Wiley, 2010).

7. To learn more about this unfortunate story, see https://www.nytimes.com/2006 /02/15/us/a-onehouse-400-million-bubble-goes-pop.html.

8. For a detailed example of the proliferation of sensors in basketball, see https://techcrunch.com/2017/03/17/watch-sensors-track-a-full-court-basketball-game-in-real-time/.

9. So much has been written on the consequences of black-box technologies, but for a couple of great examples to expand your thinking in several different areas, see F. Pasquale, *The Black Box Society* (Cambridge, MA: Harvard University Press, 2015); D. Castelvecchi, "Can We Open the Black Box of AI?" *Nature News* 538, no. 7623 (2016): 20; P. Cortez and M. J. Embrechts, "Opening Black Box Data Mining Models Using Sensitivity Analysis," in *2011 IEEE Symposium on Computational Intelligence and Data Mining (CIDM)* (April 2011): 341–348.

10. G. C. Bowker and S. L. Star, *Sorting Things Out: Classification and Its Consequences* (Cambridge, MA: MIT Press, 2000).

11. The *New York Times* addresses the issue: https://www.nytimes.com/2008/11/23/magazine/23Netflix-t.html.

12. For more details on this story, see https://www.wired.com/insights/2014/03/potholes-big-data-crowdsourcing-way-better-government/.

13. J. Buolamwini and T. Gebru, "Gender Shades: Intersectional Accuracy Disparities in Commercial Gender Classification," in *Conference on Fairness, Accountability and Transparency, PMLR* (January 2018): 77–91.

14. For an overview of Brayne's studies, see S. Brayne, "Big Data Surveillance: The Case of Policing," *American Sociological Review* 82, no. 5 (2017): 977–1008; S. Brayne, *Predict and Surveil: Data, Discretion, and the Future of Policing* (New York: Oxford University Press, 2020); S. Brayne, "The Criminal Law and Law Enforcement Implications of Big Data," *Annual Review of Law and Social Science* 14 (2018): 293–308.

15. To read more about LASER's legal problems and its implementation by the LAPD, see https://www.latimes.com/local/lanow/la-me-laser-lapd-crime-data-program-20190412-story.html#:~:text=LASER%2C%20or%20%E2%80%9CLos%20Angeles',certain%20crimes%20in%20an%20area.

16. For full details, see K. Lum and W. Isaac, "To Predict and Serve?" *Significance* 13, no. 5 (2016): 14–19.

17. If you're interested in algorithms and bias, you must read Cathy O'Neil's cleverly and appropriately titled book: *Weapons of Math Destruction: How Big Data Increases Inequality and Threatens Democracy* (New York: Crown, 2016). O'Neil discusses how opacity and scale (and, of course, the use of proxies) make it more likely that bias will enter into the construction of algorithms that affect our lives in so many ways.

18. To learn more about Wadell's work and his simulation modeling for urban planning, see P. Waddell, "UrbanSim: Modeling Urban Development for Land Use, Transportation, and Environmental Planning," *Journal of the American Planning Association* 68, no. 3 (2002): 297–314; P. Waddell and G. F. Ulfarsson, "Introduction to Urban Simulation: Design and Development of Operational Models," in *Handbook of Transport Geography and Spatial Systems* (Newark, NJ: Emerald Group Publishing, 2004).

19. For a comprehensive overview of construal levels, see Y. Trope, N. Liberman, and C. Wakslak, "Construal Levels and Psychological Distance: Effects on Representation, Prediction, Evaluation, and Behavior," *Journal of Consumer Psychology* 17, no. 2 (2007): 83–95.

20. C. J. Wakslak, Y. Trope, N. Liberman, and R. Alony, "Seeing the Forest When Entry Is Unlikely: Probability and the Mental Representation of Events," *Journal of Experimental Psychology* 135, no. 4 (2006): 641–653.

21. Another example of this problem comes from a study we did of ten major product development organizations. In each organization we found that engineers would bring hundreds of slides to a decision-making meeting to try to persuade high-level managers of important design changes. We found the managers' propensity to be swayed by an argument was inversely correlated to the technical specificity of the presentation and, more on point, to the amount of evidence presented. Managers were most convinced when

the data were presented as a story with clear consequences. Engineers who could adopt that mode of data presentation and persuasion were nearly ten times as effective at pushing through a design change, especially late in the product development process.

22. B. M. Wiesenfeld, J. N. Reyt, J. Brockner, and Y. Trope, "Construal Level Theory in Organizational Research," *Annual Review of Organizational Psychology and Organizational Behavior* 4 (2017): 367–400.

Chapter 4

1. There has been nearly a century's worth of debate about the exact provenance of this quote. As usual, Quote Investigator provides a thorough investigation (complete with verified scans of documents) that discusses how this quote originated and how it has been adapted over time: https://quoteinvestigator.com/2014/01/15/stats-drunk/#note-7989-2.

2. This blog discusses Spotify's metrics: https://musicindustryblog.wordpress.com/tag/spotify-metrics/.

3. "Spotify's premium average revenue per user (ARPU) worldwide from 2015 to 2020" in Statista, retrieved March 09, 2020, from https://www.statista.com/statistics/813789/spotify-premium-arpu/. See also David Trainer, "It Sounds Like Spotify Is in Trouble," Forbes.com, October 13, 2020, https://www.forbes.com/sites/greatspeculations/2020/10/13/it-sounds-like-spotify-is-in-trouble/?sh=60b8bc2c813b.

4. N. Loose, et al., "eCommerce: Amazon.com (USA) Customers, Brand Report: Statista Global Consumer Survey," ecommerceDB, Statista, November 2019.

5. J. Harter, "Employee Engagement Is on the Rise in the U.S.," Gallup, August 26, 2018, retrieved March 8, 2020, https://news.gallup.com/poll/241649/employee-engagement-rise.aspx.

6. Geico.com Coverage Calculator, accessed March 10, 2020, https://www.geico.com/coverage-calculator/.

7. R. L. Miller and A. D. Stafford, *Economic Education for Consumers* (Mason, OH: Cengage, 2009), 475.

8. J. Dubé and P. Rossi, *Handbook of the Economics of Marketing*, vol. 1, Handbooks in Economics (Amsterdam: Elsevier Science & Technology 2019).

9. M. Jancer, "Too Hot or Cold? The Embr Wave Is Your Personal Thermostat," retrieved March 11, 2020, https://www.wired.com/story/embr-wave-personal-thermostat-wearable/.

10. F. Caudillo, S. Houben, and J. Noor, "Mapping the Value of Diversification," *McKinsey on Finance* 55 (2015): 10–12.

11. A/B testing is really just a popular name for controlled experiments. The important thing to remember about any controlled experiment is that the design sets the researchers up to isolate a change and be able to make a correlational or causal connection between that one change and the outcomes of interest.

12. N. P. N. Patel and Amazon, "3 A/B Testing Examples That You Should Steal [Case Studies]," retrieved March 21, 2019, https://www.crazyegg.com/blog/ab-testing-examples/.

13. R. White, "7 Incredible Examples of A/B Tests by Real Businesses," retrieved January 16, 2020, https://blog.hubspot.com/marketing/a-b-testing-experiments-examples.

14. L. Gonick and W. Smith, *The Cartoon Guide to Statistics* (New York: HarperCollins, 1993).

15. A regression is a method that analyzes the relationship between two or more variables. The method consists of fitting a straight line between data points of variables plotted on an X-Y axis, where the line represents the average change in the "response variable" (Y) based on the change in the "explanatory variable" (X).

16. V. Hunt, D. Layton, and S. Prince, "Diversity Matters," *McKinsey & Company* 1, no. 1 (2015): 1.

17. Ibid.

18. Ibid.

Chapter 5

1. For more on Shamoon, see https://en.wikipedia.org/wiki/Shamoon#:~:text =Shamoon%20was%20designed%20to%20erase,time%20on%20Wednesday%2C%20 August%2015; and https://money.cnn.com/2015/08/05/technology/aramco-hack/.

2. For a vivid illustration of such evolution, with specific examples from the mobile software industry, see B. D. Eaton, S. M. Elauf-Calderwood, C. Sorensen, and Y. Yoo, "Structural Narrative Analysis as a Means to Unfold the Paradox of Control and Generativity That Lies within Mobile Platforms," *Proceedings of the 10th International Conference on Mobile Business* (2011): 68–73.

3. For more on the Twitter bug, see https://www.zdnet.com/article/twitter-bug-shared -location-data-for-some-ios-users/#:~:text=In%20December%202018%2C%20Twit- ter%20said,non%2Dfollowers%20and%20search%20engines.

4. For a comprehensive review of the concept of technical debt and the various ways it can impact product development generally, and security specifically, see Z. Li, P. Avgeriou, and P. Liang, "A Systematic Mapping Study on Technical Debt and Its Management," *Journal of Systems and Software* 101 (2015): 193–220.

5. K. Beck, M. Beedle, A. Van Bennekum, A. Cockburn, W. Cunningham, M. Fowler, and D. Thomas, "Manifesto for Agile Software Development," Agile Alliance, http://agile manifesto.org/.

6. For more details about AppFolio and Eric Hawkin's effective approach to managing software development teams, see T. Neeley, P. Leonardi, and M. Morris, "Eric Hawkins Leading Agile Teams@ Digitally-Born AppFolio (A)," Case 9-419-066 (Boston: Harvard Business School, June 2019).

7. For an interesting "confessional" about refactoring from software developers, see D. Silva, N. Tsantalis, and M. T. Valente, "Why We Refactor? Confessions of Github Contributors," in *Proceedings of the 2016 24th ACM Sigsoft International Symposium on Foundations of Software Engineering* (November 2016): 858–870.

8. For more on the severity of the hacking, see https://www.nytimes.com/2018/03/15 /technology/saudi-arabia-hacks-cyberattacks.html.

9. Astute technology leaders like Jan Chong of fintech company Tally tell us that trying to convince C-level executives about the importance of making proactive changes to stay ahead of security concerns is one of the most difficult parts of the job. "Nobody wants to spend money on something that isn't broken" says Chong. But it's exactly that kind of thinking that leaves a company and its products vulnerable to security breaches.

10. For an excellent inside, behind-the-scenes account of what happened at Cambridge Analytica, see https://www.theguardian.com/news/2018/mar/17/data-war-whistleblower -christopher-wylie-faceook-nix-bannon-trump.

11. For a description of the unprecedented ruling, see https://www.ftc.gov/news-events /press-releases/2019/07/ftc-imposes-5-billion-penalty-sweeping-new-privacy-restric tions.

12. The size of data leaks of consumer information keeps growing. As of the writing of this book, the latest in a series of data leaks occurred at the carrier T-Mobile, exposing the data of more than 1 million users. For a regularly updated list of the world's largest data breaches, see https://spanning.com/resources/industry-research/largest-data -breaches-us-history/.

13. J. S. Brown and P. Duguid, *The Social Life of Information: Updated, with a New Preface* (Boston: Harvard Business Review Press, 2017).

14. This phenomenon is what researchers of social networking sites call "networked privacy." See A. E. Marwick and D. Boyd, "Networked Privacy: How Teenagers Negotiate Context in Social Media," *New Media & Society* 16, no. 7 (2014): 1051–1067; L. Palen and P. Dourish, "Unpacking 'Privacy' for a Networked World," in *Proceedings of the SIGCHI Conference on Human Factors in Computing Systems* (April 2003): 129–136.

15. For a detailed discussion of this process, see P. M. Leonardi and J. W. Treem, "Behavioral Visibility: A New Paradigm for Organization Studies in the Age of Digitization, Digitalization, and Datafication," *Organization Studies* 41, no. 12 (2020): 1601–1625.

16. T. Gillespie, "The Relevance of Algorithms," in T. Gillespie, P. J. Boczkowski, and K. A. Foot, *Media Technologies: Essays on Communication, Materiality, and Society* (Cambridge, MA: MIT Press, 2014): 167–194.

17. Bernard Woo and Bart Willemsen, "Hype Cycle for Privacy, 2020," *Gartner Research*, https://www.gartner.com/document/3987903?toggle=1.

18. List pulled directly from brochure presented by Deloitte and Ryerson University, "Privacy by Design: Setting a New Standard for Privacy Certification," co-written by the privacy expert who developed PbD, Dr. Ann Cavoukian: https://www2.deloitte.com/content/dam/Deloitte/ca/Documents/risk/ca-en-ers-privacy-by-design-brochure.PDF.

19. D. Mulligan and J. King, "Bridging the Gap between Privacy and Design," *University of Pennsylvania Journal of Constitutional Law* 14, no. 4 (2012), https://papers.ssrn.com/sol3/papers.cfm?abstract_id=2070401.

20. For a full interview about this topic, see https://www.itsinternational.com/its6/feature/here-ai-has-place-privacy-design.

21. For more on diamonds and blockchain, see https://www.babson.edu/academics/executive-education/babson-insight/technology-and-operations/diamonds-and-the-blockchain/#.

22. For more on the diamond industry, see A. Baker and T. Shikapa, "Blood Diamonds," *Time*, September 7, 2015, https://time.com/blood-diamonds/.

23. For an interesting overview of Everledger's business model, see https://venturebeat.com/2019/09/24/everledger-raises-20-million-to-track-assets-with-blockchain-tech/.

24. "The Growing List of Applications and Use Cases of Blockchain Technology in Business and Life," *Insider Intelligence*, March 2, 2020, https://www.businessinsider.com/blockchain-technology-applications-use-cases.

25. "What is Medrec?" MedRec, https://medrec.media.mit.edu/.

26. "IBM Food Trust," https://www.ibm.com/products/food-trust.

27. B. Dimitrov, "How Walmart and Others are Riding a Blockchain Wave to Supply Chain Paradise," *Forbes*, December 5, 2019, https://www.forbes.com/sites/biserdimitrov/2019/12/05/how-walmart-and-others-are-riding-a-blockchain-wave-to-supply-chain-paradise/?sh=70196faa7791.

28. M. Iansiti and K. R. Lakhani, "The Truth About Blockchain," *Harvard Business Review*, January–February 2017, 9–10.

29. I. Heap, "Smart Contracts for the Music Industry," *Medium*, March 15, 2018, https://medium.com/humanizing-the-singularity/smart-contracts-for-the-music-industry-3e641f87cc7; T. Felin and K. R. Lakhani, "What Problems Will You Solve with Blockchain?" *MIT Sloan Management Review* 60, no. 1 (Fall 2018): 32–38.

30. K. Lakhani, "How Does Blockchain Work?" hbr.org, September 20, 2017, https://hbr.org/video/5582134272001/whiteboard-session-how-does-blockchain-work.

31. M. Iansiti and K. R. Lakhani, "The Truth About Blockchain."

32. Ibid.

33. "Stellar-Based Lightyear Acquires Chain, Forms New Entity," Stellar, https://bitcoinmagazine.com/business/stellar-based-lightyear-acquires-chain-forms-new-entity.

34. J. Aki, "IBM Introduces 'World Wire' Payment System on Stellar Network," *Bitcoin Magazine*, September 5, 2018, https://bitcoinmagazine.com/articles/ibm-introduces-world-wire-payment-system-stellar-network.

35. "The Fintech 2.0 Paper: Rebooting Financial Services," Oliver Wyman, Anthemis Group, and Santander Innoventures, https://www.oliverwyman.com/our-expertise/insights/2015/jun/the-fintech-2-0-paper.html.

36. This phenomenon is often referred to as the "critical mass effect." For a discussion of this effect in the context of interactive media, see M. L. Markus, "Toward a

'Critical Mass' Theory of Interactive Media: Universal Access, Interdependence and Diffusion," *Communication Research* 14, no. 5 (1987): 491–511.

37. T. Felin and K. R. Lakhani. "What Problems Will You Solve With Blockchain?"

Chapter 6

1. For a poignant discussion of the widely known secret that crash test dummies are designed for men (the dummies of women are just scaled down versions of male dummies without any changes for female anatomy), see the wonderful recent article: M. Kuhn and H. Schank, "10,000 Women Die in Car Crashes Each Year Because of Bad Design," *Fast Company*, August 26, 2021, https://www.fastcompany.com/90669431/10000 -women-die-in-car-crashes-each-year-because-of-bad-design.

2. For excellent accounts of early experiments, including those of Thomas Edison at his Menlo Park laboratory, see A. Hargadon, *How Breakthroughs Happen: The Surprising Truth about How Companies Innovate* (Boston: Harvard Business School Press, 2003).

3. J. McCormick, B. Hopkins, and T. Schadler, "The Insights-Driven Business," Forrester Research, July 2016.

4. S. H. Thomke, *Experimentation Matters: Unlocking the Potential of New Technologies for Innovation* (Boston: Harvard Business School Press, 2003).

5. T. R. Eisenmann, M. Pao, and L. Barley, "Dropbox: 'It Just Works,'" case 9-811-065 (Boston: Harvard Business School, January 19, 2011).

6. M. Bertoncello, "How L'Oréal, a Century-Old Company, Uses Experimentation to Succeed in the Digital Age," https://www.thinkwithgoogle.com/intl/en-cee/future-of-market ing/digital-transformation/how-lor%C3%A9al-century-old-company-uses-experimenta tion-succeed-digital-age/.

7. P. M. Madsen and V. Desai, "Failing to Learn? The Effects of Failure and Success on Organizational Learning in the Global Orbital Launch Vehicle Industry," *Academy of Management Journal* 53, no. 3 (2010): 451–476.

8. Amy Edmondson and colleagues provide compelling examples for why it is so hard for most people and companies to learn from failure, but why it's so essential that they learn to do so: A. C. Edmondson, "Strategies for Learning from Failure," *Harvard Business Review*, April 2011, 48–55; A. L. Tucker and A. C. Edmondson, "Why Hospitals Don't Learn from Failures: Organizational and Psychological Dynamics That Inhibit System Change," *California Management Review* 45, no. 2 (2003): 55–72; M. D. Cannon and A. C. Edmondson, "Failing to Learn and Learning to Fail (Intelligently): How Great Organizations Put Failure to Work to Innovate and Improve," *Long Range Planning* 38, no. 3 (2005): 299–319.

9. D. Coppola, "E-Commerce Worldwide—Statistics and Facts," Statista, September 17, 2021, https://www.statista.com/topics/871/online-shopping/.

10. See "Number of Global Social Network Users 2017–2025," https://www.statista.com /statistics/278414/number-of-worldwide-social-network-users/, January 8, 2021.

11. See S. Kemp, "Digital 2020: Global Digital Overview," Datareportal, January 30, 2020, https://datareportal.com/reports/digital-2020-global-digital-overview.

12. For data see P. M. Leonardi, "Ambient Awareness and Knowledge Acquisition," *MIS Quarterly* 39, no. 4 (2015): 747–762.

13. For a discussion of how such predictions can be made as well as their implications for privacy see P. Leonardi and N. Contractor, "Better People Analytics," *Harvard Business Review*, November–December 2018, 70–81.

14. For lengthy discussion of how major tech companies are doing this, you must read S. Zuboff, *The Age of Surveillance Capitalism: The Fight for a Human Future at the New Frontier of Power* (New York: PublicAffairs, 2019).

15. See the *New York Times* piece here: https://www.nytimes.com/interactive/2021/02 /08/opinion/stimulus-checks-economy.html.

16. See Zuboff, *The Age of Surveillance Capitalism*.

17. For a great discussion of this trend, see S. H. Thomke, *Experimentation Works: The Surprising Power of Business Experiments* (Boston: Harvard Business Review Press, 2020).

18. H. J. Wilson and K. Desouza, "8 Ways to Democratize Experimentation," hbr.org, April 18, 2011, https://hbr.org/2011/04/8-ways-to-democratize-experime.html.

19. One big reason is that knowledge generated in another part of the company often suffers from the "not-invented-here syndrome." For a discussion of how this syndrome arises and how to combat it, generally, see the great work by M. Hansen, *Collaboration: How Leaders Avoid the Traps, Build Common Ground, and Reap Big Results* (Boston: Harvard Business Press, 2009).

20. As the leaders of IDEO, one of the world's most successful design firms, note in their various books about the company's innovation process, recognizing that most attempts will fail is one of the most important things innovators can do. See T. Kelley and D. Kelley, *Creative Confidence: Unleashing the Creative Potential within Us All* (New York: Currency, 2013); T. Brown, "Design Thinking," *Harvard Business Review*, June 2008, 84.

21. Amy Edmondson has written extensively on this topic. For her most foundational work see A. Edmondson, "Psychological Safety and Learning Behavior in Work Teams," *Administrative Science Quarterly* 44, no. 2 (1999): 350–383; and for a more accessible translation see A. C. Edmondson, *The Fearless Organization: Creating Psychological Safety in the Workplace for Learning, Innovation, and Growth* (Hoboken, NJ: Wiley, 2018).

22. A. C. Edmondson, R. M. Bohmer, and G. P. Pisano, "Disrupted Routines: Team Learning and New Technology Implementation in Hospitals," *Administrative Science Quarterly* 46, no. 4 (2001): 685–716.

23. For a detailed review of Project Aristotle see C. Duhigg, "What Google Learned from Its Quest to Build the Perfect Team," *New York Times Magazine*, February, 2016.

Chapter 7

1. T. Neeley, J. T. Keller, and J. Barnett, "From Globalization to Dual Digital Transformation: CEO Thierry Breton Leading Atos into 'Digital Shockwaves' (A)," case 9-419-027 (Boston: Harvard Business School, June 2019).

2. Barbara Czarniawska and Carmelo Mazza, "Consulting as a Liminal Space," *Human Relations* 56, no. 3 (2003): 267–290.

3. E. L. Wagner, S. Newell, and W. Kay, "Enterprise Systems Projects: The Role of Liminal Space in Enterprise Systems Implementation," *Journal of Information Technology* 27, no. 4 (2012): 259–269.

4. K. E. Weick and R. E. Quinn, "Organizational Change and Development," *Annual Review of Psychology* 50, no. 1 (1999): 361–386.

5. In the digital world, the basics of change as outlined in Kotter's famous model (that just about every business school student ever has read) still hold. But the context in such models of change assumes that once a change happens, it's over. In the digital era, change is like an M.C. Escher drawing—one change bleeds seamlessly into the next. This means that not only our vocabulary but our conceptualization of what change is and how it happens needs to—change. J. P. Kotter, *Leading Change* (Boston: Harvard Business Review Press, 2012).

6. N. Furr, J. Gaarlandt, and A. Shipilov, "Don't Put a Digital Expert in Charge of Your Digital Transformation," hbr.org, https://hbr.org/2019/08/dont-put-a-digital-expert-in-charge-of-your-digital-transformation.

7. W. R. Kerr, F. Gabrieli, and E. Moloney, "Transformation at ING (A): Agile," case 9-818-077 (Boston: Harvard Business School, January 2018, revised May 2018).

8. T. Neeley, *Remote Work Revolution: Succeeding from Anywhere* (New York: Harper-Collins, 2021).

9. M. Iansiti, K. Lakhani, H. Mayer, and K. Herman, "Moderna (A)," Case N9-621-032 (Boston: Harvard Business School, September 2020).

10. Of course, big pharma is not the only industry in which work is siloed. The smart book *The Silo Effect* by Gillian Tett describes the rise and proliferation of structural siloing in the modern corporation. See G. Tett, *The Silo Effect: The Peril of Expertise and the Promise of Breaking Down Barriers* (New York: Simon & Schuster, 2015).

11. J. A. Chatman and S. E. Cha, "Leading by Leveraging Culture," *California Management Review* 45, no. 4 (2003).

12. R. M. Kanter, B. Stein, and T. D. Jick, *The Challenge of Organizational Change: How Companies Experience It and Leaders Guide It* (New York: Free Press, 1992), 492–495.

13. T. Neeley, "Global Business Speaks English: Why You Need a Language Strategy Now," *Harvard Business Review,* May 2012, 116–124.

14. T. Neeley, J. T. Keller, and J. Barnett, "From Globalization to Dual Digital Transformation: CEO Thierry Breton Leading Atos into 'Digital Shockwaves' (A)," case 9-419-027 (Boston: Harvard Business School, June 2019).

15. G. C. Kane, D. Palmer, A. N. Phillips, D. Kiron, and N. Buckley, "Achieving Digital Maturity," *MIT Sloan Management Review* 59, no. 1 (2017).

16. T. Neeley and J. T. Keller, "From Globalization to Dual Digital Transformation: CEO Thierry Breton Leading Atos into 'Digital Shockwaves' (B)," case supplement 419-046 (Boston: Harvard Business School, April 2019).

17. For an analysis of this Englishnization process and its parallels to digital transformation see T. Neeley, *The Language of Global Success* (Princeton, NJ: Princeton University Press, 2017).

18. We borrow some of the material in this section from Paul Leonardi's "You're Going Digital—Now What?" *MIT Sloan Management Review* (Winter 2020), which we use with permission of the publisher.

19. D. Leonard-Barton and I. Deschamps, "Managerial Influence in the Implementation of New Technology," *Management Science* 34, no. 10 (1988): 1252–1265; W. Lewis, R. Agarwal, and V. Sambamurthy, "Sources of Influence on Beliefs about Information Technology Use: An Empirical Study of Knowledge Workers," *MIS Quarterly* 27, no. 4 (2003): 657–678.

20. A huge program of research on technology acceptance has focused on this issue, showing convincingly that people ask themselves if a new technology is useful and if it is easy to use. If people can't answer these questions in the affirmative, they are likely to reject a new technology even if they are asked specifically to use it. For a dizzying review of such studies see V. Venkatesh, M. G. Morris, G. B. Davis, and F. D. Davis, "User Acceptance of Information Technology: Toward a Unified View," *MIS Quarterly* (2003): 425–478.

21. For a very clear example of this rhetoric versus reality in the area of total quality management see M. J. Zbaracki, "The Rhetoric and Reality of Total Quality Management," *Administrative Science Quarterly* (1998): 602–636.

22. A seminal article that described how users can appropriate the features of new technologies in many different ways (despite being told to use them in one consistent way) is G. DeSanctis and M. S. Poole, "Capturing the Complexity in Advanced Technology Use: Adaptive Structuration Theory," *Organization Science* 5, no. 2 (1994): 121–147.

23. For a detailed analysis of these social network changes, see P. M. Leonardi, "When Does Technology Use Enable Network Change in Organizations? A Comparative Study of Feature Use and Shared Affordances," *MIS Quarterly* (2013): 749–775.

24. G. C. Kane, A. N. Phillips, J. R. Copulsky, and G. R. Andrus, *The Technology Fallacy: How People Are the Real Key to Digital Transformation* (Cambridge, MA: MIT Press, 2019); J. Battilana and T. Casciaro, "Change Agents, Networks, and Institutions: A Contingency Theory of Organizational Change," *Academy of Management Journal* 55, no. 2 (2012): 381–398.

25. For an overview of the science of social networks and why they work the way they do see P. R. Monge, N. S. Contractor, P. S. Contractor, R. Peter, and S. Noshir, *Theories of Communication Networks* (New York: Oxford University Press, 2003). For a more

accessible approach to using social networks for organizational analysis see R. Cross, J. Liedtka, and L. Weiss, "A Practical Guide to Social Networks," *Harvard Business Review*, March 2005, 124–132.

26. A. Palmer, "Lifelong Learning Is Becoming an Economic Imperative," *The Economist*, January 14 2017, 12.

27. For more on Kim dos Santos and Booking.com, see https://www.themuse.com /advice/keep-learning-at-work-why-this-company-prioritizes-personal-development.

Conclusion

1. The epigraph is from *Everybody's Political What's What?* by George Bernard Shaw (1944), 330.

2. In 2021 digital technologies such as Facebook, Instagram, and Twitter connected people with friends, family members, colleagues, and often simple acquaintances. A study shows that more than 60 percent of people's social interactions now occur on such mediated platforms. At work, tools such as Slack, Yammer, and Workpl@ce (by Facebook) connect employees who work in different cities, states, and countries. But these digital technologies don't just connect people who live and work in different geographic areas; they also are becoming the increasing platforms of choice for people who live and work in close physical proximity. A study we conducted at a major imaging device company showed that even employees who worked in the same office building (separated by no more than 120 linear feet from each other) did 85 percent of their communication through digital tools. As a consequence, these employees rarely stopped by each other's desks and even began to conduct most of their meetings through digital tools like Zoom and Microsoft Teams. As one employee remarked, "I feel very separated from my colleagues."

3. H. A. Simon, *Models of Bounded Rationality: Empirically Grounded Economic Reason*, vol. 3 (Cambridge, MA: MIT Press, 1997).

Appendix

1. The company's instruments for faster learning are described in this Spotify HR blog: https://hrblog.spotify.com/2018/02/25/six-instruments-for-faster-learning/.

2. See "Inside Learning: How Yelp Created a Successful Learning Culture," Always Learning Blog, September 1, 2017, https://www.continu.co/blog/yelp-successful-learning -culture.

3. See M. Gladden, "How Westpac Group Is Re-Imagining the Delivery of Learning," Go1, July 13, 2020, https://www.go1.com/customer-story/how-westpac-group-is-re -imagining-the-delivery-of-learning.

4. See "20 Companies Where You'll Keep Learning Every Day," The Muse, https:// www.themuse.com/advice/20-companies-that-value-learning.

5. See B. Goodwin, "Philips Looks to Artificial Intelligence to Train Its Workforce," ComputerWeekly.com, October 29, 2018, https://www.computerweekly.com/news/2524 51426/Philips-looks-to-artificial-intelligence-to-train-its-workforce.

INDEX

ACKNOWLEDGMENTS

Our own journeys toward a digital mindset began in the early 2000s when we enrolled in Stanford University's Management Science and Engineering PhD program. Neither one of us had an engineering background, though both of us had worked in or with high-tech companies and were convinced that technology would be core to the future of work. The experience of working alongside engineers while learning new methodologies and ways of thinking charted the course for the next decades of our work that helped us build and refine our conceptualization of a digital mindset. We will be forever grateful to Steve Barley, Bob Sutton, Diane Bailey, and Pam Hinds at Stanford's Center for Work, Technology, and Organization for helping us start down this path and for always providing encouragement and insights along the way.

We are lucky to have been surrounded by so many inspiring colleagues who have also shaped our thinking about the concepts in this book. Tsedal has learned tremendously about digital work from many conversations with intellectual partners including James Barnett, Iav Bojinov, Vittorio Colao, Marco Iansiti, Marily Nika, Michael Norris, Jin Paik, Hanspeter Pfister, Jeff Polzer, and Sebastian Reiche. A special thanks to Amy Bernstein, Tsedal's nephew Emmanuel Mengistab, and Karim Lakhani who have provided precious support and insights from the very start.

Paul's work has benefited from colleagues at Northwestern University, including Noshir Contractor, Barbara O'Keefe, Pablo Boczkowski, Eszter Hargittai, Darren Gergle, Brian Uzzi, Willie Ocasio, Klaus Weber,

Jim Spillane, Jeannette Colyvas, and Elizabeth Gerber. At UC Santa Barbara, Kyle Lewis, Matt Beane, Jessica Santana, Dave Seibold, Gary Hansen, Cynthia Stohl, Michael Stohl, Ron Rice, Linda Putnam, and Jennifer Gibbs have provided valuable insights that have found their way into many of the ideas and examples in this book. Finally, Paul extends an enormous thank you to his PhD students, past and present, including Jeff Treem, Will Barley, Casey Pierce, Samantha Keppler, Lindsay Young, DJ Woo, Camille Endacott, and Virginia Leavell, whose research on their quests to build their own digital mindsets constantly inspires him.

On a more personal note, we are both grateful to our loving families for their unwavering support. Tsedal has been blessed to have parents who always encouraged her to pursue purposeful work. A very special thank you to Lawrence, Gabe, and Daniel for encouraging and inspiring her to remain curious. Paul's parents have always encouraged him to explore new areas and try new things. Rodda, Amelia, Norah, and Eliza are constant sources of inspiration and hope. Their laughter, love, and good deeds fill his life with joy.

We are also very grateful to Karen Propp for her outstanding editorial support. We also extend special thanks to JT Keller, Patrick Sanguineti, and Fed Chavez, who have contributed tremendously to the research and development of this book. We are thankful to our editor, Scott Berinato, at Harvard Business Review Press who was a steady hand throughout our many revisions. His guidance on how to best communicate our content in an accessible way was invaluable.

Finally, we thank the thousands of people who work in the organizations we've done research in, consulted for, advised, and taught—some of whom were on the cutting edge of technological innovation and others who were struggling to move fully into the digital era. There are too many of you to thank individually for your wisdom and kindness. But if you see yourself or your company in this book by real name, pseudonym, or allusion, please know that we are grateful for everything you taught us. We hope that this book will help you and others to continue on your journey into the digital future confident that you have the ability to see, think, and act in new ways.

ABOUT THE AUTHORS

PAUL LEONARDI is an award-winning researcher, professor, and consultant who focuses on helping organizations become more innovative and creating change that improves the work lives of leaders, managers, and team members. As a leading expert in digital transformation, remote work, and social networks, his goal is to prepare organizations and their employees to succeed in the rapid transition into the new era of data-intensive and technology-supported work.

Paul has published more than 100 articles on these topics in top research-oriented journals, as well as numerous managerial-oriented articles based on his original research in magazines such as *Harvard Business Review* and *MIT Sloan Management Review*. This work has been covered by media outlets such as the *New York Times*, the *Wall Street Journal*, *Financial Times*, *Fortune*, and *Fast Company*. Paul has published four research-focused books on digital transformation.

Over the past two decades, he has consulted with for-profit and non-profit organizations about how to improve communication between departments, how to use social technologies to enhance internal knowledge sharing, how to structure global product development operations, and how to manage the human aspects of new technology implementation. He is also a regular keynote speaker for corporate trainings and user conferences on these and other topics related to innovation and change.

Paul has won more than thirty awards for his research and teaching, including multiple outstanding article awards from professional associations such as the Academy of Management, Strategic Management Society, and the National Communication Association. In 2021 he was elected a fellow of the International Communication Association, where he also received the Fredric Jablin Award for lifetime contributions to the study of organizational communication. He has also won major awards for his teaching to undergraduate and graduate students for his courses on digital transformation, managing innovation, and the future of work.

At the University of California Santa Barbara, he holds the Duca Family Endowed Chair in Technology Management and serves as director of the PhD program in Organization Studies in the College of Engineering. Previously, he served as the founding director of the Master of Technology Management (MTM) program, a professional management program for technical leaders, which he launched in 2014 and ran until 2019.

Before joining UCSB, Paul worked at Northwestern University, where he was jointly appointed across the School of Communication, the McCormick School of Engineering, and the Kellogg School of Management. He received his PhD in management science and engineering from Stanford University.

TSEDAL NEELEY is an award-winning scholar and teacher as the Naylor Fitzhugh Professor of Business Administration and Senior Associate Dean of Faculty Development and Research Strategy at Harvard Business School. Recognized as one of the 100 People Transforming Business by *Business Insider*, Tsedal focuses on helping leaders scale their organizations by developing and implementing global and digital strategies. She regularly advises top leaders worldwide who are embarking on virtual work and large-scale change that involves global expansion, digital transformation, and becoming more agile.

Her bestselling book, *Remote Work Revolution: Succeeding from Anywhere*, provides remote workers and leaders with the best practices necessary to perform at the highest levels in their organizations. Her award-winning book, *The Language of Global Success*, chronicles the behind-the-scenes globalization process of a company over the course of five years. Her "Managing a Global Team" is one of the most extensively used cases worldwide on the subject of virtual work. She holds a patent for her widely adopted software simulation, *Global Collaboration: Tip of the Iceberg.*

Prior to her academic career, Tsedal spent ten years working for companies like Lucent Technologies and the Forum Corporation in various roles, including strategies for global customer experience, performance software management systems, sales force/sales management development, and business flow analysis for telecommunication infrastructures.

She currently serves on the board of directors of Brightcove, Brown Capital Management, Harvard Business Publishing, and The Partnership, Inc. She also serves on Rakuten's People & Culture Lab advisory board.

Tsedal received her PhD from Stanford University in management science and engineering, specializing in work, technology, and organizations. Tsedal was named to the Thinkers50 list for making lasting contributions to management, was honored as a Stanford Distinguished Alumnus Scholar, and was a Stanford University School of Engineering Lieberman award recipient for excellence in teaching and research.